Suffering in Paul

Suffering in Paul

Perspectives and Implications

EDITED BY
Siu Fung Wu

FOREWORD BY
Michael Gorman

PICKWICK *Publications* · Eugene, Oregon

SUFFERING IN PAUL
Perspectives and Implications

Copyright © 2019 Wipf and Stock Publishers. All rights reserved. Except for brief quotations in critical publications or reviews, no part of this book may be reproduced in any manner without prior written permission from the publisher. Write: Permissions, Wipf and Stock Publishers, 199 W. 8th Ave., Suite 3, Eugene, OR 97401.

Pickwick Publications
An Imprint of Wipf and Stock Publishers
199 W. 8th Ave., Suite 3
Eugene, OR 97401

www.wipfandstock.com

PAPERBACK ISBN: 978-1-5326-1177-3
HARDCOVER ISBN: 978-1-5326-1179-7
EBOOK ISBN: 978-1-5326-1178-0

Cataloguing-in-Publication data:

Names: Wu, Siu Fung, editor.

Title: Suffering in Paul : perspectives and implications / edited by Siu Fung Wu.

Description: Eugene, OR : Pickwick Publications, 2019 | Includes bibliographical references and index.

Identifiers: ISBN 978-1-5326-1177-3 (paperback) | ISBN 978-1-5326-1179-7 (hardcover) | ISBN 978-1-5326-1178-0 (ebook)

Subjects: LCSH: Suffering—Biblical teaching. | Bible. Epistles of Paul—Criticism, interpretation, etc.

Classification: LCC BS680.S854 S8 2019 (print) | LCC BS680.S854 (ebook)

Manufactured in the U.S.A.

Scripture quotations marked ESV are taken from The ESV® Bible (The Holy Bible, English Standard Version®), copyright © 2001 by Crossway, a publishing ministry of Good News Publishers. Used by permission. All rights reserved.

Scripture quotations marked NIV are taken from the Holy Bible, New International Version®, NIV®. Copyright © 1973, 1978, 1984, 2011 by Biblica, Inc.™ Used by permission of Zondervan. All rights reserved worldwide. www.zondervan.com The "NIV" and "New International Version" are trademarks registered in the United States Patent and Trademark Office by Biblica, Inc.™

Scripture quotations marked NRSV are from the New Revised Standard Version Bible, copyright 1989, Division of Christian Education of the National Council of the Churches of Christ in the United States of America. Used by permission. All rights reserved.

*I dedicate this book to all those
who suffer in this world of chaos and pain.*

Contents

Foreword by Michael J. Gorman | ix
Acknowledgments | xiii
Contributors | xv
Abbreviations | xviii

Chapter 1: Introduction | 1
—Siu Fung Wu

PART 1: ESSAYS

Chapter 2: Suffering in Romans 1–8 in Light
of Paul's Key Scriptural Intertexts | 7
—Roy E. Ciampa

Chapter 3: The Sufferings of Paul in Romans 9–11:
Paul's Vicarious Intercession and His Prophetic Identity | 29
—Xiaxia E. Xue

Chapter 4: "The Weapons of Righteousness":
Righteousness and Suffering in 2 Corinthians | 51
—David I. Starling

Chapter 5: Suffering, Salvation,
and Solidarity in 2 Corinthians 1:3–11 | 64
—Sean F. Winter

Chapter 6: Participating in Christ's Suffering
and Being Conformed to the Image of the Son | 82
—Siu Fung Wu

Chapter 7: Suffering and Glory in Philippians | 106
—Haley Goranson Jacob

Chapter 8: "The Fellowship of Christ's Sufferings" (Phil 3:10): Politics,
Sufferings, and Social Identity Formation in Philippians | 127
—Kar Yong Lim

Chapter 9: Semantics of Suffering: Thematic Meaning of the Language
of Suffering in Romans and 2 Corinthians | 152
—Sunny Chen

PART 2: RESPONSES

Chapter 10: Making Sense of Christian Suffering:
Contextual implications for Christians Today | 179
—Sanyu Iralu

Chapter 11: Hopeful and Unsettled: Reckoning with Suffering | 187
—Timothy G. Gombis

Chapter 12: Power in Weakness: Conclusion and Reflection | 194
—Siu Fung Wu

Author Index | 203
Index of Ancient Sources | 208

Foreword

Michael J. Gorman

THERE ARE TWO MARKS of the Christian church that are undisputable across time, yet they are far too often neglected by both lay people and scholars. First, the Christian church is a *global* body. Second, the Christian church is a *suffering* body. Moreover, one could quite easily argue that these two characteristics derive in no small way from the experience and theology of the apostle Paul. Accordingly, a third mark of the Christian church is its *Pauline* character—that is, its indebtedness to the apostle Paul.

All three of these marks of the church come together in this remarkable volume of essays. Written by scholars from across the globe, they testify to the universality, not only of the Christian church, but also of Christian theological scholarship. The authors represent three continents and five countries. Furthermore, they bear witness to the centrality of suffering in the Pauline correspondence, and to its centrality also in both human experience generally and Christian experience in particular.

One of the highly significant features of this volume (helpfully summarized in the responses by Timothy Gombis and Siu Fung Wu) is its attention to social location and concrete experience, including that of Christ (e.g., Sean Winter's essay), Paul (e.g., Xiaxia Xue's chapter), the writers of the scriptural texts Paul cites (e.g., Roy Ciampa's contribution), the audiences to which his letters are addressed (e.g., the essays by David Starling and Kar Yong Lim), the authors of these essays themselves, the churches and cultures within which the contributors live and write (e.g.. Sanyu Iralu's contribution), the persecuted church globally, and the (potential) readers of this book. Of course, these are not mutually exclusive concerns; the essays generally attend to multiple social locations and experiences of suffering. Siu Fung Wu, for instance, considers the situations of Paul, several Pauline churches, and his own varied social locations in which suffering has been (or has not been) the norm.

Social location, the essays instruct us, affects people's experience of suffering, their understanding of it, and their empathy (or lack thereof) toward the suffering of others. One result of this attention to social location is the integrated character of the scholarship on display in this book. The authors do not ask us to choose between the political and the theological, or between the practical and the spiritual. Nor do they allow us to leave behind careful linguistic analysis of the vocabulary of suffering (see especially Sunny Chen's chapter).

Another significant aspect of this book is the way in which the essays both build on previous scholarship and move it forward. The work of Ann Jervis and the recent work of the editor, Siu Fung Wu, are important for this book. There are, however, fewer "classic treatments" of the theme of suffering, including persecution, in Paul than one might expect. The scholars assembled here, especially those early in their academic vocation, may very well change that situation as they continue their own work.

Still another important contribution of this book is the way it shows that for Paul, and for those who read Paul as Scripture, persecution and other forms of suffering are actually normal for Christian believers. Furthermore, such suffering, properly understood, can be a grace that is an essential part of participation in Christ and of transformation into his image. (Moreover, paradoxically, suffering may also even be a demonstration of glory—so Haley Goranson Jacob's essay). Indeed, the theological theme that unites the various chapters of this volume is the central Pauline motif of participation. The editor therefore reminds us that, in Christ, true power is found in weakness.

There is still one thing to say about this set of essays. Not only is the Pauline scholarship rich and global, and not only is the topic critical, but—just as importantly—the global scholars who have contributed to this book know their subject deeply. These are not theoretical academic exercises. They are produced with sensitivity to situations of real suffering, often experienced firsthand in the authors' own social locations; they are written by people who see addressing such suffering, whether through concrete action or through scholarship (and frequently both), as a form of ministry—perhaps even a form of participation and solidarity.

It is rare in the field of biblical studies to see all of these dimensions of scholarship brought together in one volume. For this reason—actually, for *these* reasons—I strongly commend this book, its editor, and its contributors to all.

Michael J. Gorman holds the Raymond E. Brown Chair in Biblical Studies and Theology at St. Mary's Seminary & University in Baltimore, Maryland, USA.

Acknowledgments

I thank Professor Michael Gorman for writing the Foreword and for the inspiration of his academic publications. I also thank Dr. Chris Spinks, the editor at Pickwick, for his support and advice. I am very grateful to Professor Michael Gorman, Professor Timothy Gombis, Dr. George Wieland, Professor Keith Dyer, Dr. Armen Gakavian, and Professor Sean Winter for reviewing several essays. I appreciate their valuable comments. My thanks also go to other readers who gave helpful feedback. They are Tim Cross, Caleb Wu, Matthew Julius, and especially David Fenn and Beryl Turner. The keen-eyed observations of David and Beryl are invaluable, for which I am deeply grateful. I thank the faculty and staff of Whitley College, especially Academic Dean, Rev Dr Anne Mallaby, for their welcome and support over the years. My heartfelt thanks go to Professor Keith Dyer and Professor Mark Brett, whose advice and friendship I value greatly. I am also thankful to Sung Sung Lian Hrang, who allowed me to use her testimony as an example in my chapter to illustrate how God's glory may be reflected in our suffering. I need to thank my wife, Catherine, and my son, Caleb, for their unswerving support during the course of this project. I want to specially thank them for patiently listening to my many and frequent remarks and stories on suffering in Paul. I thank God for the Spirit's guidance and empowerment throughout this project, and I thank Jesus, who suffered and died for us. Finally, this book is dedicated to all those who suffer in this world of chaos and pain. May the love of the crucified Christ and risen Lord bring them peace, joy, and hope.

Siu Fung Wu
January 2019

Contributors

Sunny Chen is an Honorary Postdoctoral Associate at the University of Divinity, Australia, and Adjunct Lecturer at Pilgrim Theological College. He received his ThM at Dallas Theological Seminary and a PhD from the University of Divinity. Sunny has published in the *Journal of Greco-Roman Christianity and Judaism*, and his monograph, *Paul's Anthropological Terms in the Light of Discourse Analysis*, will be published by SIL International. Sunny is the Chaplaincy Coordinator at The University of Melbourne, and he is a member of a local church that welcomes and cares for refugees.

Roy E. Ciampa is the S. Louis and Ann W. Armstrong Professor of Religion and Chair of the Religion Department at Samford University in Birmingham, AL. He holds an MDiv from Denver Seminary and a PhD from the University of Aberdeen, UK. His publications include *The Presence and Function of Scripture in Galatians 1 and 2* (Mohr Siebeck, 1998) and (with Brian Rosner) *The First Letter to the Corinthians* in the Pillar New Testament Commentary Series (2010). Roy is an ordained Baptist minister and previously served as a Professor of New Testament and Chair of the Division of Biblical Studies at Gordon-Conwell Theological Seminary.

Timothy G. Gombis is Professor of New Testament at Grand Rapids Theological Seminary. He received his PhD from the University of St. Andrews, UK. He has written *The Drama of Ephesians: Participating in the Triumph of God* (IVP Academic, 2010), and is writing the Mark volume in the Story of God Bible Commentary Series. He volunteers at a local charity that helps homeless families get into sustainable housing.

Sanyu Iralu is Principal of Shalom Bible Seminary, Kohima, Nagaland, India. He holds a ThM from Regent College, Vancouver, Canada, and a PhD from SAIACS, Bangalore, India. He wrote "Colossians and Philemon" for the one-volume South Asia Bible Commentary (Open Doors/Langham, 2015), and is currently working on *1 and 2 Peter, Jude* for the India Commentary on the New Testament Series. Sanyu is an ordained minister with the Baptist Church in Nagaland. Sanyu regularly visits hospitals, prisons, and orphanages with his students as part of their ministry training.

Haley Goranson Jacob is Assistant Professor of Theology at Whitworth University in Spokane, WA. She holds an MANT and an MATH from Gordon-Conwell Theological Seminary and a PhD from the University of St Andrews, UK. Haley is the author of *Conformed to the Image of His Son* (IVP Academic, 2018). Her heart for the persecuted church stems from her various experiences in Eastern Europe and Central Asia.

Kar Yong Lim is Lecturer in New Testament Studies at Seminari Theoloji Malaysia, Seremban. He is also the Director of Postgraduate Studies and the Director of the Centre for Bible Engagement at the seminary. He received his PhD from the University of Wales, UK. His publications include *"The Sufferings of Christ are Abundant in Us"* (T & T Clark, 2009) and *Metaphors and Social Identity Formation in Paul's Letters to the Corinthians* (Pickwick, 2017). Kar Yong served as a minister with the Anglican Diocese of West Malaysia. He volunteers as a member of the Board of Trustees of World Vision Malaysia, a child-focused humanitarian organization dedicated to overcoming poverty and injustice.

David I. Starling teaches at Morling College, where he serves as the head of the Bible and Theology department. He received his PhD from the University of Sydney, Australia. His publications include *Hermeneutics as Apprenticeship* (Baker, 2016) and *UnCorinthian Leadership* (Cascade, 2014). David was previously a Baptist pastor in the inner-western suburbs of Sydney, and is a member of the Baptist World Alliance's Doctrine and Christian Unity Commission.

Sean F. Winter is Head of Pilgrim Theological College in Melbourne and Associate Professor within the University of Divinity, Australia. He received his DPhil from the University of Oxford, UK. Sean has taught

New Testament at the Universities of Bristol, Oxford, and Birmingham. He was lecturer in New Testament at Northern Baptist College, Manchester (2000–2008) and within the United Faculty of Theology, Melbourne (2009–2014). He is the author of several articles on the interpretation of Paul's letters, and the biblical interpretation of Dietrich Bonhoeffer.

Siu Fung Wu is Lecturer in New Testament Studies at Whitley College and Honorary Research Associate at University of Divinity, Australia. He received his MPhil from Trinity College, University of Bristol, UK, and PhD from the University of Divinity. He was a factory worker, software developer, before becoming a pastor in an inner-city church. He then worked in aid and development. He is the author of *Suffering in Romans* (Pickwick, 2015) and several articles on Pauline studies.

Xiaxia E. Xue is Assistant Professor of New Testament at China Graduate School of Theology (CGST), Hong Kong. She holds an MCS and a ThM from CGST, and received her PhD from McMaster Divinity College, Canada. Xiaxia has written *Paul's Viewpoint on God, Israel, and the Gentiles in Romans 9—11* (Langham, 2015), and is a volunteer pastor in Tai Po Baptist Church. She is a supporter of two organisations in Hong Kong that serve the disadvantaged and people living with a disability.

Abbreviations

AB	Anchor Bible
ANTC	Abingdon New Testament Commentary
BCOT	Baker Commentary on the Old Testament
BDAG	Walter Bauer, Frederick W. Danker, W. F. Arndt, and F. W. Gingrich. *A Greek-English Lexicon of the New Testament and Other Early Christian Literature*. 3rd ed. Chicago: University of Chicago Press, 2000.
BDF	Friedrich Blass and Albert Debrunner. *A Greek Grammar of the New Testament* and *Other Early Christian Literature*. Translated and revised by Robert W. Funk. Chicago: University of Chicago Press, 1961.
BECNT	Baker Exegetical Commentary on the New Testament
BNTC	Black's New Testament Commentary
BHT	Beiträge zur historischen Theologie
BLG	Biblical Languages: Greek
BT	*The Bible Translator*
BTB	*Biblical Theology Bulletin*
BZNW	Beihefte zur Zeitschrift für die neutestamentliche Wissenschaft
CBET	Contributions to Biblical Exegesis and Theology
CBQ	*Catholic Biblical Quarterly*
EGGNT	Exegetical Guide to the Greek New Testament
FAT	Forschungen zum Alten Testament

HBT	*Horizons in Biblical Theology*
ICC	International Critical Commentary
JBL	*Journal of Biblical Literature*
JGRChJ	*Journal of Greco-Roman Christianity and Judaism*
JR	*The Journal of Religion*
JSPL	*Journal for the Study of Paul and his Letters*
JSNT	*Journal for the Study of the New Testament*
JSNTSup	Journal for the Study of the New Testament: Supplement Series
JSOT	*Journal for the Study of the Old Testament*
JSOTSup	Journal for the Study of the Old Testament: Supplement Series
JTI	*Journal of Theological Interpretation*
KEK	Kritisch-exegetischer Kommentar über das Neue Testament
LNTS	Library of New Testament Studies
LSJ	Henry George Liddell, Robert Scott, and Henry Stuart Jones. *A Greek-English Lexicon*. 9th ed. Oxford: Clarendon, 1996.
LWF	Lutheran World Federation
Louw & Nida	Louw, J. P., E. A. Nida, R. B. Smith, and K. A. Munson, eds., *Greek-English Lexicon of the New Testament: Based on Semantic Domains*. 2nd ed. 2 vols. New York: United Bible Societies, 1988, 1989.
LXX	The Septuagint
MT	Masoretic Text
NCBC	New Cambridge Bible Commentary
NCC	New Covenant Commentary
NIB	New Interpreter's Bible
NIBC	New International Biblical Commentary

NICNT	New International Commentary on the New Testament
NICOT	New International Commentary on the Old Testament
NIGTC	New International Greek Testament Commentary
NovT	*Novum Testamentum*
NovTSup	Supplements to Novum Testamentum
NT	New Testament
NTL	New Testament Library
NTS	*New Testament Studies*
OG	Old Greek
OT	Old Testament
PKNT	Papyrologische Kommentare zum Neuen Testament
PNTC	Pillar New Testament Commentaries
RevExp	*Review & Expositor*
SBL	Studies in Biblical Literature
SBLDS	Society of Biblical Literature Dissertation Series
SGBC	The Story of God Bible Commentary
SIL	Summer Institute of Linguistics
SNTSMS	Society for New Testament Studies Monograph Series
SP	Sacra Pagina
SJT	*Scottish Journal of Theology*
THNTC	Two Horizons New Testament Commentary
TLG	*Thesaurus Linguae Graecae*
TMSJ	*The Master's Seminary Journal*
TDNT	*Theological Dictionary of the New Testament.* 10 vols. Edited by Gerhard Kittel and Gerhard Friedrich. Translated by Geoffrey W. Bromiley. Grand Rapids: Eerdmans, 1964–76.
WBC	Word Biblical Commentary

WUNT	Wissenschaftliche Untersuchungen zum Neuen Testament
ZNW	*Zeitschrift für die Neutestamentliche Wissenschaft und die Kunde der Älteren Kirche*

1

Introduction

Siu Fung Wu

SUFFERING IS AN IMPORTANT theme in Paul's letters and there are many implications for the church. Pauline scholars are very aware of this. For example, Scott Hafemann says, "Paul's suffering is not an addendum to his preaching. Nor is it merely a consequence of it. Rather, it is constitutive of it."[1] When speaking of Paul's view of power and weakness, Gordon Fee says that the "present suffering is a mark of discipleship, whose model is our crucified Lord."[2] And in his book, *Suffering and Hope*, J. Christiaan Beker says that the church is called to redemptive suffering.

> Suffering because of human injustice and idolatry evokes Paul's *prophetic* response. The church is here called to redemptive suffering, that is, to resist human idolatry and injustice and to suffer redemptively in the world *against* the world *for* the world.[3]

The vocation of the church to participate in Christ's suffering is well summarized by L. Ann Jervis in her superb book, *At the Heart of the Gospel: Suffering in the Earliest Christian Message*.

> At the heart of the gospel is "the word of the cross" (1 Cor 1:18). The cross's presence at the center of his good news means that Paul does not shy away from either the existence or the

---

1. Hafemann, "Role of Suffering," 184.
2. Fee, *Paul, the Spirit*, 145.
3. Beker, *Suffering and Hope*, 103. Emphasis original.

experience of suffering. He sees clearly that the good news he preaches and lives does not promise its converts transformation into super-humans capable of transcending or avoiding the troubles of human existence, *and* that it obligates them to share in God's redeeming project—which is to take on an increase of suffering.[4]

We are called to action, to be "with Christ" in engagement on the side of God's justice, and to accept the inevitable sufferings that go along with such engagement. By virtue of suffering "with Christ" we are called to face the darkness, to face down what destroys, to reshape what is so that it comes to be dominated not by suffering but by God's glory.... We, of course, do not do this on our own steam. Suffering "with Christ" is to suffer with the Messiah, not to be the Messiah.... For, we suffer not on our own but *with* the one whose sufferings drew him inexorably into God's luminous life.[5]

Given the fact that such insightful studies are already available, the purpose of this book is not to rehash what has been done or to present a comprehensive study on suffering in Paul. Rather, the primary goal of the project is to make fresh contributions to the topic. While monographs on suffering in Paul do appear from time to time, the relatively small number of major studies does not, in my view, do justice to such a significant theme in the Pauline corpus.[6] It is hoped that the essays in this volume will arouse greater interest among scholars, and provide researchers and educators with a resource on the topic.

Apart from making a contribution to scholarship, the purpose of this book is also to explore the implications of Paul's view of suffering for the global church today. Our social location and cultural backgrounds do influence how we understand suffering. It is, therefore, gratifying that our authors come from a diverse background. They are based in five countries across three continents. Eight authors have written on specific

---

4. Jervis, *At the Heart of the Gospel*, 129. Emphasis original.
5. Jervis, *At the Heart of the Gospel*, 137. Emphasis original.
6. Significant works on suffering in Paul since 2015 include: Clark, *Completing Christ's Afflictions*; Crisler, *Reading Romans as Lament*; Davey, "Sight in the Tempest"; Dunne, "Persecution in Galatians"; Dunne, "Suffering and Covenantal Hope"; Free, "Suffering in Paul"; Starling, "For Your Sake"; Wu, *Suffering in Romans*. I have included in this list three monographs, two unpublished doctoral dissertations, and three journal articles. Apart from Free's article, all of these affirm the significance of suffering in Paul's letters. I will briefly interact with Free in my chapter.

Pauline texts and themes by focusing on Romans, 2 Corinthians, and Philippians,[7] and most of them concluded their essays with brief comments on the implications of their findings for the followers of Jesus. Three contributors responded to the eight articles from their own cultural and social contexts—as a North American, a South Asian, and an Asian-Australian.

It is not a common practice for editors to point out the shortcomings of their books. But I do need to comment on the range of authors in this volume. I regret that only two of the contributors are women. I spent six months looking for female Pauline scholars who might be interested in the topic. But often they were already committed to other projects and hence could not write for this book. I also regret that there are no contributors from outside Asia, Australia, and North America. There are no Indigenous authors either. These deficiencies are due to the small size of my network and hence the limited capacity to find more female contributors and scholars from different cultural backgrounds.

The essays are ordered according to their different focuses, themes, and approaches. Roy Ciampa, Xiaxia Xue, and David Starling discuss suffering in Paul by focusing on several selected texts and intertexts. Their studies on Romans and "the weapons of righteousness" in 2 Corinthians bring unique contributions to our subject. Sean Winter, Haley Goranson Jacob, and I pay special attention to the notion of participation in Christ and the relationship between suffering and glory. The analyses in these essays reveal the cross-shaped Christ-centered character of suffering and the paradoxical coexistence of suffering and glory. Kar Yong Lim and Sunny Chen provide further insights into suffering in Paul by employing their expertise in social identity theory and discourse analysis. According to their studies, suffering is key to Christian identity formation, and the thematic meaning of the terms θλῖψις and στενοχωρία emphasizes corporate solidarity and ecclesial relationships. Finally, Sanyu Iralu, Timothy Gombis, and I respond to the essays through our different cultural and social lenses. These responses serve to enrich our understanding of suffering by opening our eyes to each other's perspectives. My chapter will also function as a conclusion for the book.[8]

---

7. These are the letters in the undisputed Pauline corpus that refer to affliction most substantially. Unfortunately, 1 Thessalonians is not included because no authors offered to write on it.

8. The following authors in this book use the UBS5/NA28 edition of the Greek New Testament: Sunny Chen, Kar Yong Lim, David Starling, and Sean Winter. These

I am grateful for the participation of the contributors. Their insights have been a blessing to me personally. May this book be beneficial to all who read it.

Bibliography

Beker, J. Christiaan. *Suffering and Hope*. Grand Rapids, MI: Eerdmans, 1994.
Clark, Bruce T. *Completing Christ's Afflictions: Christ, Paul, and the Reconciliation of All Things*. WUNT 2.383. Tübingen: Mohr Siebeck, 2015.
Crisler, Channing L. *Reading Romans as Lament: Paul's Use of Old Testament Lament in His Most Famous Letter*. Eugene, OR: Pickwick, 2016.
Davey, Wesley Thomas. "Sight in the Tempest: Suffering as Participation with Christ in the Pauline Corpus." PhD diss., Southern Baptist Theological Seminary, 2016.
Dunne, John Anthony. "Persecution in Galatians: Identity, Destiny, and the Use of Isaiah." PhD diss., University of St Andrews, 2015.
———. "Suffering and Covenantal Hope in Galatians: A Critique of the 'Apocalyptic Reading' and Its Proponents." *SJT* 68 (2015) 1–14.
Fee, Gordon D. *Paul, the Spirit, and the People of God*. Peabody, MA: Hendrickson, 1996.
Free, Marian. "Suffering in Paul: A Case for Exaggeration." *St. Mark's Review* 239 (2017) 75–92.
Hafemann, Scott. "The Role of Suffering in the Mission of Paul." In *The Mission of the Early Church to Jews and Gentiles*, edited by Jostein Ådna and Hans Kvalbein, 165–84. WUNT 1.127. Tübingen: Mohr Siebeck, 2000.
Jervis, L. Ann. *At the Heart of the Gospel: Suffering in the Earliest Christian Message*. Grand Rapids, MI: Eerdmans, 2007.
Starling, David. "For Your Sake We Are Being Killed All Day Long": Romans 8:36 and the Hermeneutics of Unexplained Suffering." *Themelios* 42.1 (2017) 112–21.
Wu, Siu Fung. *Suffering in Romans*. Eugene, OR: Pickwick, 2015.

---

authors use the UBS4/NA27: Roy Ciampa, Haley Goranson Jacob, Xiaxia Xue, and Siu Fung Wu.

PART 1: ESSAYS

2

Suffering in Romans 1–8 in Light of Paul's Key Scriptural Intertexts

Roy E. Ciampa

Introduction

THIS ESSAY WILL EXAMINE the relationship between some of Paul's key scriptural intertexts in Romans 1–8 and the topic of suffering. It will pay particular attention to the way Paul frames references to suffering in Romans 1–4 and how they relate to his more explicit references to suffering in Romans 5–8.[1] It will be argued that Paul's argument in Romans 5–8 speaks to the issues raised in the original contexts of the scriptural intertexts cited in Romans 1–4 in ways readers may not have anticipated at the end of Romans 4. The intertexts we will pay closest attention to include Hab 2:4 (Rom 1:16–17), the scriptural catena in Rom 3:10–18, the discussion of Abraham and Sarah in Rom 4:16–21, and, finally, Paul's quotation from Ps 44:22 in Rom 8:36.[2] Along the way we will argue that

---

1. Key words for suffering appear primarily in the fifth and eighth chapters of Romans. For example, the word θλῖψις (which BDAG defines and glosses as "trouble that inflicts distress, oppression, affliction, tribulation; or inward experience of distress, affliction, trouble") appears in Rom 2:9; 5:3; 8:35; 12:12. The word πάθημα appears in Rom 7:5 (where is it understood in the sense, "an inward experience of an affective nature, feeling, interest " [BDAG], rather than as "that which is suffered or endured, suffering, misfortune") and 8:18. The word συμπάσχω (BDAG: "to have the same thing happen to one, suffer with, also suffer the same thing as") appears only in Rom 8:17.

2. Of course, there are many other scriptural intertexts in play in these chapters, but space limitations will require focusing on those that are most explicit.

in some places (especially in chapter 3) Paul seems to read "against the grain" of his intertexts (ignoring the concerns and perspectives of their authors), while in other places he is reading "with the grain" of those intertexts, reflecting their authors' concerns. We will also briefly reflect on our own opportunities to read with or against the "grain" of Paul's textual strategy as it orients our perceptions of suffering in the redemptive plan of God.

Suffering in Romans 1–4 and in Paul's Key Intertexts

Suffering and Habakkuk 2:4

Paul's key intertext on becoming righteous by faith, Hab 2:4, is cited in Rom 1:17 as follows: ὁ δὲ δίκαιος ἐκ πίστεως ζήσεται. Arguably, Paul frames the citation (v. 17b) as an explanation of how God's righteousness is revealed through faith (v. 17a)—in other words (see the γάρ at the start of v. 17), it explains how the gospel "is the power of God for salvation to everyone who has faith" (v. 16).[3] While, arguably, Paul uses this text primarily to introduce and underwrite his understanding of the relationship between faith and righteousness (the meaning of each of these terms being disputable), it seems relevant to remind ourselves that Hab 2:4 fits within a larger context that is not concerned with the question of how God can find it possible to forgive and be reconciled with sinful people, but with the question of what God will do to intervene when violence and injustice are thriving even among the people of God.[4]

Habakkuk cries out:

> O LORD, how long shall I cry for help, and you will not listen? Or cry to you "Violence!" and you will not save? Why do you make me see wrongdoing and look at trouble? Destruction and violence are before me; strife and contention arise. (Hab 1:2–3)

Those references to violence, wrongdoing, trouble, and destruction remind us that Habakkuk's concern was not focused on the problem of guilt as it was the problem of suffering perpetrated on some people

---

3. Unless otherwise indicated, scriptural citations are from the NRSV. English translations of the LXX/OG follow NETS, unless otherwise noted. Citations from the LXX/OG follow Rahlfs and Hanhart, *Septuaginta*.

4. For a careful analysis of the possible place of the context of Hab 2:4 and of Paul's other OT intertexts in Rom 1–3, see Ochsenmeier, *Mal, souffrance et justice de Dieu*. On Habakkuk as background to Romans, see especially pp. 81–84.

by others. It is not just about people perpetrating these things, but that people are *experiencing* violence, wrongdoing, trouble, and destruction—that is, various kinds of traumatic suffering—and it seems to Habakkuk that that should not be so. In the Old Greek of Hab 1:2, Habakkuk cries out ἀδικούμενος (wrongdoing/injustice) and wants to know why God does not save (βοήσομαι πρὸς σὲ ἀδικούμενος καὶ οὐ σώσεις).[5] Paul is also concerned about the need for God to save, but on first look he seems more concerned with the forgiveness *of* the perpetrator. The gospel is the power of God for salvation (εἰς σωτηρίαν; Rom 1:16). Habakkuk, on the other hand, was more concerned about salvation *from* the perpetrator.

Suffering and the Catena of Rom 3:10–18

If we jump forward to the chain of citations in Romans 3, we can find a similar pattern.[6] In fact, while Hab 1:3 (in the OG), asks God why he made him "look at wretchedness (ταλαιπωρία) and impiety," in Rom 3:16 Paul quotes from the complaint in the OG of Isa 59:7 where the same word (ταλαιπωρία) is used: "their feet run to evil, swift to shed blood, and their reasonings are reasonings of fools; destruction and wretchedness (ταλαιπωρία) are in their ways." But again, Paul frames the discussion as one where the scriptural texts establish the guilt of all humanity (including even the Jews).[7] The series of OT quotations runs from Rom 3:10 to 3:18. On both sides he frames the quotations in such a way that they are expected to speak to human culpability. In 3:9–10 we read, "we have already charged that all, both Jews and Greeks, are under sin [ὑφ' ἁμαρτίαν], as it is written . . ." The καθὼς γέγραπται with which 3:10 begins shows that subjection to the power of sin is what will be established.[8] Then, as Paul concludes his catena of citations, he says, "Now we know that whatever the law says, it speaks to those who are under the law, so that every mouth may be silenced, and the whole world may be

5. Ochsenmeier, *Mal, souffrance et justice de Dieu*, 81.

6. For a concise list of elements in Rom 1–3 that relate to the presence of evil or suffering, see, Ochsenmeier, *Mal, souffrance et justice de Dieu*, 245.

7. On the importance of the framing of citations, see Kujanpää, "From Eloquence to Evading Responsibility," 185–202. On Paul's way of framing this catena, see Hays, *Echoes of Scripture*, 50.

8. To be "under sin" (ὑφ' ἁμαρτίαν) may suggest suffering in the sense of slavery to sin's power, though it is unclear whether the expression would suggest any empathy rather than condemnation on Paul's part.

held accountable to God" (3:19). The texts he had just quoted were to be understood as part of the law and served to silence every mouth before God's judgment.

The fact that the texts do not effectively serve Paul's argument as well as some others has been noted by many scholars and has contributed to the view that the catena was not actually formulated by Paul for this present argument. In their view it was either a catena formulated by someone else and which was familiar to Paul and the Romans[9] or that it had been formulated by Paul himself at some earlier point and was being reemployed here, despite the imperfect fit in his argument.[10]

Erwin Ochsenmeier, however, argues that Paul may well have constructed the catena for this context, given the similar lexical and thematic patterns found in the contexts of the cited texts and those of Paul's larger argument in Romans, and that some Roman Christians could well have had the capacity to recognize the sources of the citations and the relevance of their contexts for Paul's argument.[11] His argument pushes for a maximalist understanding of the capabilities of Paul and his readers. The careful study of the contexts of the LXX/OG texts cited in the catena is a fruitful and valuable exercise that deserves careful engagement by all who study Romans.

Whether Paul wrote the catena himself at a prior point in time or for this occasion, or was employing it because it was something he thought it would be familiar to the Romans as it was to him, is perhaps not essential to the point I seek to make here. Paul endorses the contents of the catena even as he frames it in a particular way to advance his own argument.

On first sight his way of framing these texts, and the particular parts of the texts that have been excerpted by the original composer of this catena, seems to represent a kind of reading against the grain of the Psalms and the Isaianic text from which they are taken. That is, most of these texts, as found in their canonical contexts, are not making universalized statements about humanity in general, but are types of complaints about categories of people from whom the speakers would distinguish

---

9. This is the argument of, e.g., Reasoner, "'Promised Beforehand,'" 128–58.

10. This is the argument of Koch, *Die Schrift als Zeuge des Evangeliums*, 183–84. Koch's view is followed by Stanley, *Paul and the Language*, 88–89.

11. See Ochsenmeier, *Mal, souffrance et justice de Dieu*, 195–207. For another careful analysis concluding that Paul authored the catena, see Shum, *Paul's Use of Isaiah*, 181–84. Mark Seifrid's statement is overly simplistic: "The catena appears to be his own composition, since it has no parallels" (Seifrid, "Romans," 616).

themselves. They are complaining about the wicked.¹² As in the opening complaint of Habakkuk, they speak of the wickedness of those who fit the category of the "fool" (Ps 14:1), or those who are "boastful," "who speak lies," as well as "the bloodthirsty and deceitful" (Ps 5:5–7), and whose violence causes the psalmist to cry out to God (e.g., Ps 5:1–4).¹³ In Psalm 140 the psalmist cries out, "Deliver me, O LORD, from evildoers; protect me from those who are violent, who plan evil things in their minds and stir up wars continually" (Ps 140:1–2). Clearly it is not all people are categorized as "evildoers" and "violent" but those who fit that description bring great suffering to others, like the psalmist, and the latter cry out to God for protection from them (e.g., Ps 140:4). In Psalm 10 the wicked are distinguished from the poor that they persecute (Ps 10:2). It is the former who, like the fool of Psalms 14 and 53 claim "there is no God," who "murder the innocent," prey on "the helpless," and seek to "seize the poor and drag them off in their net" (Ps 10:8–9).

In Isaiah 59 there is a distinction between "you" (plural) and "we/us." On the one hand, "your hands are defiled with blood, and your fingers with iniquity; your lips have spoken lies, your tongue mutters wickedness" (Isa 59:3). Injustice is perpetrated by the "you" group and therefore "justice is far from us, and righteousness does not reach us. . . . We wait for justice, but there is none; for salvation, but it is far from us" (Isa 59:9–11). Similarly, in Psalm 36 it is the wicked who have "no fear of God before their eyes" (v. 1). They are to be distinguished from the psalmist, "those who know you," and "the upright of heart" (v. 10). The latter are crying out to the Lord for protection from the former (see vv. 10–12).

Those not theologically or culturally predisposed to respond favorably to Paul's interpretation of scripture (or his arguments in general) might well conclude that he has coopted the words of these complaints to use them in the service of an argument that largely ignores the concerns and hopes of those who composed them. An unsympathetic reader, aware that these texts represent the voices of people witnessing and/or experiencing great suffering and trauma, might suggest that Paul's choice to employ them in a theological argument about the universality of human

---

12. Cf. Keesmaat, "Psalms in Romans," 145–46.

13. Eccl 7:20 LXX may be cited in Rom 3:10 (οὐκ ἔστιν δίκαιος). In the near context the author distinguishes between righteous and wicked: "there are righteous people who perish in their righteousness, and there are wicked people who prolong their life in their evildoing" (Eccl 7:15–17, here v. 15).

guilt reflects a coopting to make a theological point that fails to demonstrate sensitivity to and solidarity with the suffering which provided the original context for those words. How far should one go in making abstract theological points that are divorced from the actual human suffering and complaints about that suffering that gave them birth?

What interests me is the strong impression that while the texts that are excerpted to create the catena of Rom 3:10–18 could have been very effectively exploited by Paul to develop his argument and bring out the implications regarding a theology of suffering, he shows no interest in doing so in Romans 1–3. He frames these texts in a way that distracts the reader from such a line of thought and focuses it on the narrower question of the universality of human guilt and culpability. What Ochsenmeier does in his careful study is to draw out of those intertexts all the things that Paul could have drawn out of them but did not. I am reminded of William Scott Green's complaint that Richard Hays had done the text's work for it.[14] Ochsenmeier does an excellent job of showing what can be done by way of integrating the themes from those intertexts into Paul's argument. But Paul's argument seems to move in a very different direction in this part of Romans. And it seems that the rhetorical function of the catena may depend in part on the reader not being overly distracted by the specific backgrounds to each of the individual texts from which the catena is composed, but on reading the catena as an integrated text that refers to the same group of sinners throughout, rather than acknowledging that the texts come from different contexts and refer to different sets of sinners who were antagonizing the (often different) speakers in each case.

A large part of the catena is built out of texts that refer to different body parts of the wicked who are being described.[15]

> All have turned aside, together they have become worthless; there is no one who shows kindness, there is not even one. *Their throats* (ὁ λάρυγξ αὐτῶν) are opened graves; they use *their tongues* (ταῖς γλώσσαις αὐτῶν) to deceive. The venom of vipers is under *their lips* (τὰ χείλη αὐτῶν). *Their mouths* (ὧν τὸ στόμα)

14. Green says, "If the texts under study are constructed to do precisely what the analytical method seeks to expose, then the method does the text's work for it. The language of analysis loses its critical force" ("Doing the Text's Work," 63).

15. As Longenecker points out, "The first five and the last statements in this catena of passages (vv. 10b–12 and v. 18) are held together by a sixfold repetition of the phrase "there is none" (οὐκ ἔστιν). In addition, there appears in the last six verses of the passage (vv. 13–18) a catalog of various parts of the human body ("throats," "tongues," "lips," "mouths," "feet," and "eyes")" (Longenecker, *Epistle to the Romans*, 357).

are full of cursing and bitterness. *Their feet* (οἱ πόδες αὐτῶν) are swift to shed blood; ruin and misery are in *their paths* (ταῖς ὁδοῖς αὐτῶν), and the way of peace they have not known. There is no fear of God before *their eyes* (τῶν ὀφθαλμῶν αὐτῶν). (Rom 3:12–18)[16]

Paul's use of pronouns suggests that the reader is to construct an image of one wicked group that has all of the offending body parts rather than various groups, each marked by just one or some of the body parts. In the case of the mouth and the eyes, he has changed what were singular pronouns in the OG to plurals so that all the references could seem to have the same referents.[17]

Paul describes one group of sinners marked by wicked throats, tongues, lips, mouths, feet, eyes, and paths. This is a discursive Frankenstein's monster, created out of the parts of various dead villains. Paul brings together texts that share in common references to body parts and cites those parts of the texts. Perhaps he is also very conscious of the other ways their contexts would speak to the issues he wants to develop, and he expects his readers to recognize that as well. But Paul does not cite these texts in such a way as to highlight their individual standing (as he does, e.g., when he uses *gezerah shawah* in Romans 4 to bring together Gen 15:6 and Ps 31:2 LXX; or as he does in Galatians 3 to bring together Hab 2:4 and Lev 18:5). Rather, he creates a new, single text, out of the various texts, and frames them in a way that does not seem intended to lead the reader to do the work Ochsenmeier has done (and which probably explains why it has taken so long for someone to do the kind of work Ochsenmeier has done).[18]

---

16. Emphasis added. NRSV quotation marks and verse numbers have been removed to better represent the sense of the Greek.

17. See Stanley, *Paul and the Language*, 93–94, 99.

18. A more moderate and feasible view is suggested by Steve Moyise: "Paul's interpretative comments in Romans 3:9, 19 steer the reader towards the conclusion that all need the gospel, but the old context adds a second voice that God has always been with the righteous and against the wicked. Our response to the catena, therefore, should not be to ignore the clash of contexts (Dodd, Barrett), or completely explain them (Dunn), but to allow them to interact with one another. The essence of the gospel does not lie in its replacement of the old covenant but in its interaction with it (3:31). Paul clearly saw the danger of losing this second voice in the threat of antinomianism (3:5f, 6:1). Somehow, he must persuade his readers that being 'justified by his grace' (3:23) does not mean that God no longer distinguishes between righteousness and wickedness (6:13) and the 'voice' of the catena is one of the ways that he achieves this. No one can read Rom 3:10–18 and conclude that God does not distinguish between

Has Paul's reading strategy actually resulted in the silencing of those voices calling out in pain for God to intervene and protect the righteous from the suffering perpetrated by their compatriots? While they may be rather muted in this particular part of Paul's argument, it seems they have not been completely silenced. The tendency has been to focus on the texts' role in establishing universal human culpability, perhaps in part because in the history of American and Western European scholarship biblical and theological research and exposition was carried out primarily by those with elite social status in the ivory towers of academia. But anyone who has experienced a lack of kindness (Rom 3:12), poisonous deception (v. 13), cursing, bitterness (v. 14), bloodshed, ruin, misery (vv. 15–16), and the impact of those who follow un-peaceful ways or who feel no moral accountability (vv. 17–18) is likely to recognize the pain and suffering evoked by these texts, unless they are filtered out by traditional hermeneutical lenses.[19]

Suffering Shame: Abraham and Sarah in Rom 4:16–21

One of the few places in Romans 1–4 where suffering is discussed in a way that perhaps reflects greater empathy for the one experiencing suffering is in the treatment of Abraham and Sarah's experience of dealing with Sarah's barrenness in Rom 4:16–21. Western readers, who might tend to think of suffering more narrowly in terms of physical pain, might be less likely to recognize this as a passage dealing with suffering. However, anyone familiar with the sense of shame and honor associated with barrenness or fertility in Paul's world (or anyone from any culture who has suffered from an inability to conceive despite a deep longing to have children) will recognize the shame and suffering that would be associated

---

righteousness and wickedness!" The idea that "the old context adds a second voice" fits well with post-structuralist understandings of intertextuality. The question is the extent to which early readers (or readers throughout history) would access the old contexts and hear those voices. Moyise, "Catena of Rom," 370.

19. It may be that in the ancient context the very mention of "sin" would evoke thoughts of suffering. But while some of that suffering would relate to suffering imposed or perpetrated on others (through evil and unjust acts), sin would also be associated with the suffering experienced by the person who sinned, through the suffering in their bones (e.g., Ps 38:3; Prov 14:30). And sins related to ritual impurity would have evoked a more indirect relationship between sin and suffering. These are issues worthy of further exploration, but outside of the focus here on the relationship between Paul's explicit scriptural intertexts and suffering perpetrated on others.

with their inability to have a child—one that had been longed for and promised according to the Genesis narrative, with much of Genesis 15–18 taken up with the theme, and the resolution of the problem with the birth of Isaac not being narrated until Genesis 21. This is all captured in Paul's portrayal of Abraham. Abraham, he says,

> did not weaken in faith when he considered his own body, which was already as good as dead (for he was about a hundred years old), or when he considered the barrenness of Sarah's womb. No distrust made him waver concerning the promise of God, but he grew strong in his faith as he gave glory to God, being fully convinced that God was able to do what he had promised. (Rom 4:19–21)

Paul stresses Abraham's perseverance in faith, but the emphasis on that perseverance highlights the extended period over which Abraham and Sarah struggled with this issue with the assumption that wavering, a lack of faith, might have been expected of a lesser man than Abraham given the long-term struggle that it was. Paul's references to the deathlike state of Abraham's body and to the hope of the resurrection in vv. 17–19 ("in the presence of the God in whom he believed, who gives life to the dead.... He did not weaken in faith when he considered his own body, which was already as good as dead"), hint that the fulfillment of Abraham's hope for a son through Sarah may point to the general Christian hope in the resurrection of the dead as the anticipated end of suffering for Paul's readers. That this passage comes at the end of Romans 4 may prove to be significant, as we turn to the way the issue of suffering is engaged in Romans 5–8.

Suffering in Romans 5–8: Paul Pivots from Culpability to Solution

While most texts in Romans 1–4 that relate to human suffering seem to be employed in ways that emphasize their ability to contribute to the themes of human guilt and culpability rather than in ways that draw attention to the processing or experience of suffering itself, chapters 5–8,[20] in con-

---

20. The theme of suffering in Rom 5–8 has been addressed much more thoroughly than it has elsewhere in Romans, and the treatment here will focus on the relation of the wider argument to Paul's scriptural intertexts. For fuller and more general treatments of suffering in these chapters, see, e.g., Wu, *Suffering in Romans*; Beker, "Suffering and Triumph"; Beker, *Suffering and Hope*; Fredrickson, "Paul, Hardships, and

trast, are framed by texts that do suggest the processing and experience of human suffering are central concerns in the apostle's thought in that section.[21] Someone reading the letter to the Romans for the first time might think, upon arriving at (what we call) chapter 5 and before realizing where the argument of the letter is going on a larger scale, that Paul has carried out a surprising pivot, as he shows he is actually concerned about the suffering sin causes and not simply the guilt that it establishes.

Paul's introduction to this section begins with a chain of thoughts that includes reference (twice in Rom 5:3) to the experience of θλίψεις, often translated "suffering(s)" (e.g., NRSV, NIV, NET), but also "tribulations" (e.g., KJV, ASV, NASB), "afflictions" (CSB, NAB), "problems and trials" (NLT), "problems"/"trouble" (CEB). The Greek word literally referred to "pressing/pressure" but came to be employed metaphorically as here, for "trouble that inflicts distress" (BDAG, emphasis removed).[22]

These references to suffering or tribulations follow Paul's affirmation that we have (or exhortation to have) peace with God and his assertion that "we boast in our hope of sharing the glory of God." These two themes, of peace with God and the hope of sharing the glory of God, point us to the expected end-point of God's redemptive plan, where God's *shalom* and glory are manifest throughout creation. That is the denouement to which Paul refers in Romans 8, where Paul brings the themes of suffering (there, τὰ παθήματα) and glory together again:

> 18 I consider that the sufferings of this present time are not worth comparing with the glory about to be revealed to us. 19 For the creation waits with eager longing for the revealing of the children of God; 20 for the creation was subjected to futility, not of its own will but by the will of the one who subjected it, in hope 21 that the creation itself will be set free from its bondage

---

Suffering"; Gieniusz, *Romans 8:18–30*; Starling, "'For Your Sake'"; Still, "Placing Pain in a Pauline Frame."

21. According to Longenecker, "Many of the themes of 5:1–11 are taken up again in 8:18–39, thereby setting up something of a rhetorical *inclusio* or type of 'ring composition'—especially the themes of 'hope' (in 5:2 and 8:20–25), of 'the glory of God revealed' (in 5:2 and 8:18–21), of 'boasting in sufferings' (in 5:3 and 8:35–37), and of 'the love of God expressed in the giving of Christ' (in 5:5 and 8:31–39)." Longenecker, *Romans*, 540. Cf. Ochsenmeier, *Mal, souffrance et justice de Dieu*, 39, 262, 264.

22. For a careful study of the theology of suffering in Romans from an audience-focused approach and with special attention to chapters 5 and 8, see especially, Wu, *Suffering in Romans*. Wu pays careful attention to the OT backgrounds to Paul's argument throughout.

to decay and will obtain the freedom of the glory of the children of God. (vv. 18–21)

Of course, looking beyond the references to suffering that bracket chapters 5–8 via the use of *inclusio*,[23] it can be seen that the contents of those chapters more directly address the concerns of Habakkuk and of the complaints found in the texts Paul cites in chapter 3. As Gieniusz points out, the reader should not "yield too easily to the temptation to subordinate the theme of suffering, as if it were only a dark background against which the other themes shine more brightly."[24] Rather, the theme is essential to the argument of chapters 5–8, as Paul moves far beyond the question of how God can forgive/justify such oppressive sinners to the question of how God is changing humanity to (re-)create human society in a reign of grace and life rather than sin, suffering, and death. He will stress how Christ undoes the reign of sin and death introduced by Adam which has resulted in the devastating harm and suffering about which Habakkuk and other OT voices cried out in complaint.

Romans 5–8 as Solution to Abraham and Sarah's (and Others') Suffering and Shame

Given the proximity of Paul's discussion of Abraham and Sarah's struggle with barrenness in the final part of chapter 4 to his discussion of the relationship between suffering, endurance, character, and hope (including its fulfillment) in Rom 5:3–5, one wonders if Paul still has Abraham's example in mind in the latter passage. Paul indicates that Abraham and Sarah suffered the shame of barrenness until Abraham was "about a hundred years old" (4:19) and that he "did not weaken in faith" even "when he considered his own body, which was already as good as dead." That suggests the suffering of Abraham and Sarah had produced endurance. The lack of distrust and the decision to give glory to God (both in v. 20) might be pointers to the character that the suffering and endurance had produced. In v. 18 Paul explicitly asserted that Abraham had been "hoping against hope." The same passage suggests God's granting Abraham the ability to father a son was a kind of resurrection of the dead, since his

---

23. Cf. Still, "Placing Pain in a Pauline Frame," 74–6; Wu, *Suffering in Romans*, 52–54. References to "hope" in 4:18 and in Rom 5 and 8 also serve as thematic and verbal links between these chapters, as do references to life, death, and body.

24. Gieniusz, *Romans 8:18–30*, 53.

body was "as good as dead" and yet Abraham trusted in God, "who gives life to the dead (v. 17) and the same righteousness that was reckoned to Abraham "will be reckoned to us who believe in him who raised Jesus our Lord from the dead" (v. 24). Of course, in Romans 8 (and elsewhere) it is the hope of the resurrection of the dead to which believers look forward as the ultimate vanquishing of suffering and death.

Ochsenmeier perceptively points out that the language of boasting in 5:2, 5 probably reflects an ironic antithesis to being (a)shamed. "The family of words in καυχ- is thus, in a certain sense, antonymous to what is sometimes denoted by the family of words in σχ-. While affliction can destabilize, disturb, the believer can boast in the ordeal. This is confirmed by the text of Paul: καυχώμεθα ἐπ ἐλπίδι τῆς δόξης; 5:2, ἡ δὲ ἐλπὶς οὐ καταισχύνει, 5:5."[25] Perhaps Paul would say that in Abraham's case, he was able to glory in his situation rather than be ashamed of/in it.[26] David Fredrickson points out that in contrast to philosophic approaches, "Paul explores the relationship between friendship and suffering" and understands that "hope is secure and can replace reason in the face of hardships" because "friendship with God means a mutual sharing of suffering and joy."[27] Thus Paul expounds on Christ's death for believers as a demonstration of God's love, and stresses the theme of reconciliation (καταλλάσσειν) in 5:9–11. In chapter 8, where Paul returns to the theme of Christian hope in the midst of suffering, the sharing of suffering and joy is no longer tied merely to friendship, but to the bonds of family, as the Spirit of God confirms believers are truly children of God (8:14–17, 19, 21), even as they await their adoption (v. 23) by the power of the Spirit who binds them and God together through Christ (vv. 23–27), to whose

---

25. Ochsenmeier, *Mal, souffrance et justice de Dieu*, 263. See also his wider discussion on these themes, 262–63. Cf. Wu, *Suffering in Romans*, 62. Translations of Ochsenmeier throughout this chapter are my own.

26. Fredrickson points out that "[s]ome philosophers regarded hope as a moral disease, because hope placed happiness in externals, over which no one has control. Pursuit of externals can only lead to shame (Seneca, *Epp.* 5.7; 13.13; 23.2; 24.1; 71.14; 99.5, 13; 101.4). Thus, by introducing hope as the product of character [and, following Ochsenmeir's observation, as something in which believers can glory and which would not put one to shame], Paul begins his critique of the philosophic view of suffering." Fredrickson, "Paul, Hardships, and Suffering," 186. Cf. Jewett, "Paul, Shame, and Honor," 562–63.

27. Fredrickson, "Paul, Hardships, and Suffering," 186.

image they will be conformed, "in order that he might be the firstborn within a large family" v. 29).[28]

Romans 5–8 and Freedom from Slavery to Sin

It turns out that chapters 5–8 as a whole unit, and not just the most obvious passages, 5:1–9 and 8:18–39, addresses precisely the concerns that were foremost on the hearts or minds of Habakkuk and those whose texts Paul cited in Rom 3:10–18. It is here that Paul explains both why people cause suffering in the world and what God has done, is doing, and will do to bring about the end of such suffering and the universal establishment of righteousness throughout creation. According to Paul, through Adam's sin he unleashed a reign of sin and death upon the world, one that God is undoing through Christ (Rom 5:12–14, 17, 21; 6:9, 12).[29] Thanks to the reign of sin and death people were slaves to sin, but now believers have been freed from that slavery by Christ.

As Ochsenmeier puts it, "one of the major effects of the work of Christ will be precisely to free people from slavery (3.24, 6.6, 8.2, etc.). It is only through the work of Christ that people will be able to accomplish good, which will have both personal and social consequences."[30] He summarizes well the implications of the stream of Paul's argument in Romans 5–8 for the issue of suffering as it concerned Habakkuk and those who contributed to the catena in Romans 3:

> One is no longer a slave of sin, as was the case under the law. The believer has been freed from sin (ἐλευθερόω, 6.18, 22, 7.24, 8.2). They can no longer remain in sin because they were put to death and raised with Christ (6.1–14). They can no longer obey their covetousness and deliver their members as weapons of injustice (ἀδικία, 6.13), they must walk in newness of life (6.9, 7.4–6), it is now possible for them to do good, a choice that was impossible before (7.18–19). Obedience to justice becomes possible (6.16f., cf. 12.1). Chapter 8 will explain the reason for this reversal, this possibility of living differently. By the Spirit, liberation from sin has taken place (7.24–25; 8.1–2), the tendencies of the Spirit make it impossible to walk as before (8.1–11). Those who are

---

28. Cf. Beker, "Suffering and Triumph," 110. Cf. also, the helpful discussion of this passage in Fredrickson, "Paul, Hardships, and Suffering," 187–90, his emphasis on the role of friendship (rather than familial standing) notwithstanding.

29. See Ciampa, "Genesis 1–3," 103–22.

30. Ochsenmeier, *Mal, souffrance et justice de Dieu*, 146.

led by the Spirit are sons of God, they walk in the Spirit, they can live differently.[31]

In Rom 8:4 Paul suggests that now "the just requirement of the law might be fulfilled in us, who walk not according to the flesh but according to the Spirit." Later, in Rom 13:8–10, he reveals at least one way in which this fulfillment of the just or righteous requirement of the law relates to the issue of suffering. It is the person who loves others who "has fulfilled the law". Why? "The commandments, 'You shall not commit adultery; You shall not murder; You shall not steal; You shall not covet'; and any other commandment, are summed up in this word, 'Love your neighbor as yourself.'" (v. 9). Paul's summary statement is a key to the implications for suffering perpetrated by people on each other: "Love *does no wrong to a neighbor*; therefore, love is the fulfilling of the law" (v. 10, emphasis added).

Ann Jervis's argument that Paul's "intense focus on [sin] is rooted not in moral distaste so much as in his profound concern for humanity's troubles"[32] is not one that can be clearly affirmed when looking strictly at Romans 1–4, but one that gains traction only after having thought through the larger argument of Romans 5–8.

Scholars often distinguish between various categories of suffering in Paul's argument.[33] In some cases these may be helpful distinctions for us to make, but as other scholars have pointed out, Paul himself does not seem to distinguish different types of suffering in Romans 8 but, rather, casts a wide net, intending to include, as Moo puts it, "the whole gamut of suffering, including things such as illness, bereavement, hunger, financial reverses, and death itself."[34] This is the direction in which the lists and rhetoric of vv. 35–39 point.

---

31. Ochsenmeier, *Mal, souffrance et justice de Dieu*, 268.

32. Jervis, *At the Heart of the Gospel*, 79.

33. Beker suggests, "Paul distinguishes between suffering at the hands of human injustice and suffering at the hands of the power of death" ("Suffering and Triumph," 108, cf. 109–11) and Jervis suggests a distinction between what it means to suffer "in Christ" and what it means to suffer "with Christ" (*At the Heart of the Gospel*, 97–98).

34. Moo, *Romans*, 511. See, also, e.g., Gieniusz, *Romans 8:18–30*, 110; Wu, *Suffering in Romans*, 119; Longenecker, *Romans*, 718.

Suffering in Rom 8:17–39 and Paul's Quotation from Ps 44:22

Paul brings this section of his letter to a climactic conclusion in 8:17–39. Since the focus of this essay is on how some of Paul's key scriptural intertexts inform his argument and how it relates to the topic of suffering, we will focus primarily on Paul's citation of Ps 44:22 in Rom 8:36 while also seeking to explain how Paul's overall argument impinges on our understanding of the role of that intertext in the argument.[35]

In Rom 8:15–39 Paul emphasizes the believers' (and even creation's) union with Christ, so that the pattern of his experience—suffering followed by glory—becomes the expected pattern for their existence as well. Christ is, of course, the Son of God, and Paul argues that believers are also "children of God" thanks to the Spirit who unites them (vv. 15–17). So believers are "joint heirs with Christ" with an important rider: "if, in fact, we suffer with him so that we may also be glorified with him." Suffering with Christ must precede glorification with him. That same pattern applies to creation, which Paul personifies as waiting "with eager longing for the revealing of the children of God" (v. 19). Creation's suffering is depicted in terms of its "groaning in labor pains" (v. 22), but that suffering will not be the end of the story, since "the creation itself will be set free from its bondage to decay and will obtain the freedom of the glory of the children of God" (v. 21). In fact, both believers and creation groan in this present time (vv. 22–23). But these sufferings are not evidence that we will not experience glory. In fact, they are nothing compared to "the glory about to be revealed to us" (v. 18).[36]

Paul makes several direct references to Christ's death (and thus direct or indirect references to Christ's suffering), as well as his resurrection in vv. 28–39: God "did not withhold his own Son, but gave him up for all of us" (v. 32); "It is Christ Jesus, who died, yes, who was raised, who is

---

35. For detailed discussions of Paul's use of Ps 44:22 in Rom 8:36, and varying interpretations, see, Starling, "'For Your Sake'"; and Stewart, "Cry of Victory."

36. Gieniusz has shown that when the expression οὐκ ἄξιος πρὸς (usually translated, "not worthy of being compared") is used in relation to two antithetically opposed things/people it indicates that one thing is not merely being compared to the other but, more forcefully, is "not able to oppose" the other (thus the subtitle of his work). In this case it would mean the suffering of believers does not contradict or disprove the fact that they are justified and will experience the glory promised by/in Christ. See Gieniusz, *Romans 8:18–30*, 90–100, and also the discussion in Wu, *Suffering in Romans*, 135–36.

at the right hand of God" (v. 34); "we are more than conquerors through him who loved us" (v. 37). In this context, Paul's assertion in v. 29 that God predestined believers "to be conformed to the image of his Son, in order that he might be the firstborn within a large family" also reinforces believers' identification with Christ in experiencing both suffering and resurrection/glory as part of what it means to be conformed to his image.

The climax of Paul's argument comes in the final five verses of the chapter, which are framed by references to God's/Christ's love, which also appear in its middle (vv. 35, 37, 39). In the midst of those references to God's love with the accompanying assurance of ultimate victory over all that might oppose Christ's followers,[37] we find Paul's citation from Psalm 44, "For your sake we are being killed all day long; we are accounted as sheep to be slaughtered" (Rom 8:36). "Even though they are like sheep being led to slaughter, the love of Christ will see them through. This theme of God's abiding love in Christ is at the center of the argument throughout 8:35–39."[38]

Paul's citation of Ps 44:22 in Rom 8:36 seems to portray the suffering of Christ-followers in terms reminiscent of the suffering laments.[39] Paul places Christians (including Paul's Gentile "readers"/converts) in the role of Israelites who had suffered at the hand of Gentile nations. In Paul's reading, Jewish and Gentile Christ-followers adopt the role of the righteous Israelite complaining about the suffering experienced at the hand of others. Jewett points in particular to the way, in v. 35, Paul refers to "us" as a key to the way he frames the list of hardships in v. 35 (hardship, distress, persecution, famine, nakedness, peril, sword) and the citation in v. 36. In his view, "[t]he 'us' [in, "Who will separate us"] is the first clue that the forms of adversity to be listed in this sentence have all been experienced by Paul and the Roman congregations."[40] That is, Paul "amplifies the theme of Christian suffering through the accumulation

---

37. As Wu suggests, "with the celebratory claim of super-victory the letter affirms the value of their co-suffering with Christ." Wu, *Suffering in Romans*, 195.

38. Wu, *Suffering in Romans*, 195. Cf. Still: "For Paul, the love of God, experienced through the Holy Spirit in the present and demonstrated through Christ's death in the past, will enable believers to be conquerors in the future over all things, even over suffering and its sinister effects." Still, "Placing Pain in a Pauline Frame," 84.

39. For a full discussion of the relationship between Romans the laments, see Crisler, *Reading Romans*.

40. Jewett, *Romans*, 543.

of outward forms of tribulation that Paul had experienced."[41] Similarly, Dunn suggests, "The parallel with 2 Cor 11:23-27 also makes clear that such a list is not a mere literary form but is a firsthand expression of Paul's own experience. Since he regarded his own experience as the outworking of the eschatological tension between the ages (of Adam and of Christ), he naturally saw his experience as typical for all his fellow believers."[42]

The suggestion that Paul's list of hardships in v. 35 in large part reflects his own personal experience, especially in the light of the noted parallel with 2 Cor 11:23-27, reminds us that Paul had had numerous experiences where he might well have turned to texts like Ps 44:22 in the midst of his own life-threatening sufferings. In that earlier letter he had recounted his experience of

> far greater labors, far more imprisonments, with countless floggings, and often near death. Five times I have received from the Jews the forty lashes minus one. Three times I was beaten with rods. Once I received a stoning. Three times I was shipwrecked; for a night and a day I was adrift at sea; on frequent journeys, in danger from rivers, danger from bandits, danger from my own people, danger from Gentiles, danger in the city, danger in the wilderness, danger at sea, danger from false brothers and sisters in toil and hardship, through many a sleepless night, hungry and thirsty, often without food, cold and naked. (2 Cor 11:23-27)

That he had "received from the Jews the forty lashes minus one" five times, and later mentions again that he experienced danger from his "own people" highlights the number of times he may have been tempted to pray (all or parts of) Psalm 44. The Psalm recounts how God had given victory to the Israelites in the nation's earliest days and had normally given them success in their encounters with their foes: "we push down our foes; through your name we tread down our assailants" (v. 5). But now (in the time of the speaker's experience) God had seemed to abandon his people and them "the taunt of our neighbors, the derision and scorn of those around us" (v. 13). They were now "a byword among the nations" [=Gentiles] (v. 14), and experience shame and disgrace in the face of their "taunters and revilers" (vv. 15-16). That would have been reasonable if they had been unfaithful to the Lord but, on the contrary, "we have not forgotten you, or been false to your covenant. Our heart has

---

41. Jewett, *Romans*, 36.
42. Dunn, *Romans*, 505.

not turned back, nor have our steps departed from your way" (vv. 17–18). It is in this state of faithful obedience that they "are being killed all day long, and accounted as sheep for the slaughter" (v. 22).[43] As Wu recognizes, "the scriptural citation places believers' experience in the category of righteous suffering."[44]

As Psalm 44 comes to a close, the psalmist cries out for God to "rise up" and "come to our help" (v. 26).[45] Paul guarantees that "we are more than conquerors through him who loved us" (Rom 8:37). Thus, "with the celebratory claim of super-victory" Paul "affirms the value of [believers'] co-suffering with Christ. In all this, God's abiding love is the basis of their assurance."[46]

The relationship between Paul's own experience of trials and suffering and its likely relationship to the list he provides in Rom 8:35 brings us back again to the question of the texts from which the catena in Rom 3:10–18 was constructed. Earlier we looked at those texts in light of the way Paul frames the catena and suggested his use of the catena to make his theological point about universal guilt seemed distant from the actual concerns of the texts themselves (in which the speakers cried out to God for an end to such suffering). It was pointed out that Paul actually addresses those concerns in the argument of chapters 5–8 where both human transformation and the transformation of creation are seen as the endpoints to which the redemptive narrative points. One would not be surprised if the complaints found in the texts from which the catena of Rom 3:10–18 is constructed, and the catena itself, would have resonated with Paul precisely as he was experiencing some of his trials. Since Paul framed the catena in a way that suggested it spoke especially of Jewish guilt (so that both Jews and Gentiles would be understood to be culpable), it would seem to fit well with his own experience of persecution at the hands of his Jewish compatriots. In those very contexts, as he was awaiting lash after lash (up to 39 times), as he was suffering accusations of unfaithfulness to God and as his own blood was being shed (cf. Rom

---

43. For discussion on some of the parallels between Ps 44 and Rom 8, as part of a strongly anti-imperial reading of the chapter, see Keesmaat, "Psalms in Romans," 150–51.

44. Wu, *Suffering in Romans*, 195.

45. Keesmaat, "Psalms in Romans," 151–52, suggests subtle allusions to Ps 110:1 (Christ is at the right hand of God, per Rom 8:34), and Ps 118:6 point to the psalmists' confidence that God would make them victorious in the end.

46. Wu, *Suffering in Romans*, 195.

3:12–17) did he recall those ancient complaints or (if it had been composed at such an early time) the catena itself? We can never know. Of course, his list of trials reminds us that he also "suffered . . . at the hands of the civic magistrates who represented Roman authority, being beaten on three occasions with the lictors' rods."[47] In any case, these connections remind us of a much greater possibility that those texts (or that catena) had actually played a role in his own experiences of suffering and that they were not merely tools employed in the production of a theological argument.

Implications for Today

Some stories only make sense when we get to the end. This is the case for the story of suffering in Paul's letter to the Romans. It does not make great sense if we stop at the end of chapter 4. But by the time the reader arrives at the end of chapter 8 it makes much better sense.[48] So also, in the life of the people of Israel, in the life of Paul and believers in his day, as well as in our lives today, suffering experienced at other points along the way can best be conceptualized only in light of the end of the story, in light of God's ultimate redemptive purposes. Paul's understanding of the metanarrative points to God's ultimate redemption of all believers and of all creation, in Christ, such that they share in his glory just as they will have shared in his suffering. In the words of Pastor S. M. Lockridge (informed by Paul's teaching), "It's Friday, but Sunday's coming," and on *that* Sunday, the glory experienced will destroy any shadow left by the sufferings that preceded it. It was a confidence that God had promised such an ultimate victory that led the psalmists to cry out to God in their complaints and their laments.

Thus, for the Christian, suffering is not associated with shame but with boasting/glory since we are reminded (by the Psalms of lament cited by Paul and also by the experience of the ancient Israelites, Jesus, and Paul) that the righteous suffer but only as a prelude to vindication and glory. As Still suggests, "Paul conjoined suffering and hope" since "in

---

47. Thrall, *Second Epistle to the Corinthians*, 738, on 2 Cor 11:25. Cf. Harris, *Second Epistle to the Corinthians*, 803.

48. Of course, there is much more material that is quite relevant to the issue of suffering in chapters 9–16, but our topical focus and limits of space have not permitted a survey of that material.

Paul's hands, suffering becomes something of a harbinger of hope" the end of which is "sharing the glory of God."[49]

We have also noted that biblical texts may have more resources to offer those who suffer than the uses to which they are put at any particular place in the canon. The texts from which the catena of Rom 3:10–18 is constructed have much more to offer those who suffer than what Paul does with them in that chapter. In other contexts as well we may find that our ability (and the ability of others) to wrestle with aspects of suffering in this world will sometimes be best facilitated by engaging in readings that are different from those pursued by a particular New Testament author. Christians may benefit from the interpretations of Old Testament texts provided by New Testament authors, but should not expect that those authors have done all of the possible work of the texts that they cite. There may always be more to be found than what has been excavated so far.

In the end, it seems clear that the salvation Paul has in mind and to which he refers in Rom 1:16 does not simply entail forgiveness and right standing with God but also includes deliverance from the suffering and pain alluded to in his key intertexts and addressed through the solution to which chapters 5–8 (especially 8:18–39) point.

Bibliography

Beker, J. Christiaan. *Suffering and Hope: The Biblical Vision and the Human Predicament*. Grand Rapids: Eerdmans, 1994.

———. "Suffering and Triumph in Paul's Letter to the Romans." *HBT* 7 (1985) 105–19.

Ciampa, Roy E. "Genesis 1–3 and Paul's Theology of Adam's Dominion in Romans 5–6." In *From Creation to New Creation: Essays on Biblical Theology and Exegesis*, edited by Daniel M. Gurtner and Benjamin L. Gladd, 103–22. Peabody, MA: Hendrickson, 2013.

Crisler, Channing L. *Reading Romans as Lament: Paul's Use of Old Testament Lament in His Most Famous Letter*. Eugene, OR: Pickwick, 2016.

Dunn, James D. G. *Romans 1–8*. WBC 38A. Dallas, TX: Word, 1998.

Fredrickson, David E. "Paul, Hardships, and Suffering." In *Paul in the Greco-Roman World*, edited by J. Paul Sampley, 172–97. Harrisburg: Trinity, 2003.

Gieniusz, Andrzej. *Romans 8:18–30: Suffering Does Not Thwart the Future Glory*. University of South Florida International Studies in Formative Christianity and Judaism 9. Atlanta, GA: Scholars, 1999.

Green, William Scott. "Doing the Text's Work for It: Richard Hays on Paul's Use of Scripture." In *Paul and the Scriptures of Israel*, edited by Craig A. Evans and James A. Sanders, 58–63. JSNTSup 83. Sheffield: JSOT Press, 1993.

---

49. Still, "Placing Pain in a Pauline Frame," 82.

Harris, Murray J. *The Second Epistle to the Corinthians: A Commentary on the Greek Text.* NIGNT. Grand Rapids, MI: Eerdmans, 2005.
Hays, Richard B. *Echoes of Scripture in the Letters of Paul.* New Haven: Yale University Press, 1989.
Jervis, L. Ann. *At the Heart of the Gospel: Suffering in the Earliest Christian Message.* Grand Rapids: Eerdmans, 2007.
Jewett, Robert. "Paul, Shame, and Honor." In *Paul in the Greco-Roman World,* edited by J. Paul Sampley, 551–74. Harrisburg: Trinity, 2003.
———. *Romans: A Commentary.* Hermeneia. Minneapolis, MN: Fortress, 2006.
Keesmaat, Sylvia C. "The Psalms in Romans and Galatians." In *The Psalms in the New Testament,* edited by Steve Moyise and M. J. J. Menken, 139–62. London: T & T Clark, 2004.
Koch, Dietrich-Alex. *Die Schrift als Zeuge des Evangeliums: Untersuchungen zur Verwendung und zum Verständnis der Schrift bei Paulus.* BHT 69. Tübingen: J. C. B. Mohr, 1986.
Kruse, Colin G. *Paul's letter to the Romans.* PNTC. Grand Rapids, MI: Eerdmans, 2012.
Kujanpää, Katja. "From Eloquence to Evading Responsibility: The Rhetorical Functions of Quotations in Paul's Argumentation." *JBL* 136 (2017) 185–202.
Longenecker, Richard N. *The Epistle to the Romans: A Commentary on the Greek Text.* NIGTC; Grand Rapids, MI: Eerdmans, 2016.
Moo, Douglas J. *The Epistle to the Romans.* NICNT. Grand Rapids, MI: Eerdmans, 1996.
Moyise, Steve. "The Catena of Rom. 3:10–18." *Expository Times* 106 (1995) 367–70.
Ochsenmeier, Erwin. *Mal, souffrance et justice de Dieu selon Romains 1–3: Étude exégétique et théologique.* BZNW 155. Berlin: de Gruyter, 2007.
Rahlfs, Alfred, and Robert Hanhart, eds. *Septuaginta.* Rev. ed. Stuttgart: Deutsche Bibelgesellschaft, 2006.
Reasoner, Mark. "'Promised Beforehand Through His Prophets in the Holy Scriptures': Composite Citations in Romans." In *Composite Citations in Antiquity: New Testament Uses,* edited by Sean A. Adams and Seth M. Ehorn. LNTS. London: T & T Clark, 128–58.
Seifrid, Mark A. "Romans." In the *Commentary on the New Testament Use of the Old Testament,* edited by G. K. Beale and D. A. Carson, 607–94. Grand Rapids, MI: Baker, 2007.
Shum, Shiu-Lun. *Paul's Use of Isaiah in Romans: A Comparative Study of Paul's Letter to the Romans and the Sibylline and Qumran Sectarian Texts.* WUNT 2.156. Tübingen: Mohr Siebeck, 2002.
Stanley, Christopher D. *Paul and the Language of Scripture: Citation Technique in the Pauline Epistles and Contemporary Literature.* SNTSMS 74. Cambridge: Cambridge University Press, 2008.
Starling, David. "'For Your Sake We Are Being Killed All Day Long': Romans 8:36 and the Hermeneutics of Unexplained Suffering." *Themelios* 42.1 (2017) 112–21.
Stewart, Tyler. "The Cry of Victory: A Cruciform Reading of Psalm 44:22 in Romans 8:36." *JSPL* 3.1 (2013) 25–46.
Still, Todd D. "Placing Pain in a Pauline Frame: Considering Suffering in Romans 5 and 8." In *Interpretation and the Claims of the Text: Resourcing New Testament Theology: Essays in Honor of Charles H. Talbert,* edited by Jason A. Whitlark, Bruce W. Longenecker, Lidija Novakovic, and Mikeal C. Parsons, 73–86. Waco: Baylor University Press, 2014.

Thrall, Margaret E. *A Critical and Exegetical Commentary on the Second Epistle to the Corinthians*. ICC. London: T & T Clark, 2004.
Wu, Siu Fung. *Suffering in Romans*. Eugene, OR: Pickwick, 2015.

3

The Sufferings of Paul in Romans 9–11

*Paul's Vicarious Intercession
and His Prophetic Identity*

XIAXIA E. XUE

Introduction

THERE IS NO DOUBT that Paul suffered a lot during his ministry. He lists a series of awful hardships that he endured in 2 Cor 11:23–29, including imprisonments, floggings, being stoned, danger from bandits, and other perils. There are many books and articles that discuss these tribulations,[1] and many Scriptures have been investigated.[2]

In addition, there are about four types of explanations of Paul's sufferings. First, both Paul and believers suffer from persecution of this world (1 Thess 1:6; Phil 1:27–30)—suffering which is abnormal and temporary.[3] Second, Paul associates his sufferings with Christ's own suf-

---

1. Lim, *Sufferings of Christ*; Pate, *Glory of Adam*; Smith, *Paul's Seven Explanations*; Pobee, *Persecution and Martyrdom*; Hafemann, *Suffering and Ministry*; Wu, *Suffering in Romans*; and Adewuya, "Sacrificial-Missiological Function." See also Tang, *Toward a Theology of Suffering*, 74–89.

2. The relevant Pauline passages include 2 Cor 6:1–10; 11:23–29; 1 Cor 4:11; 15:35–58; Rom 5:1–11; 6:1–11; 8:17–39; Phil 1:27–30; 2:5–11; 3:10–21; Col 1:15–29; 3:1–11; Gal 3:26–29; 4:26; 6:12–18; Eph 1:15–23; 3:13; 2 Thess 2:1–12; 1 Tim 2:1–15; 2 Tim 2:8–13. See also Pate, *Glory of Adam*; Smith, *Paul's Seven Explanations*.

3. Smith, *Paul's Seven Explanations*, 34–43.

fering (Rom 8:17; 2 Cor 1:5, 4:10; Phil 3:10);[4] that is, the suffering is participation in the suffering of Christ.[5] Third, Paul's suffering is viewed as martyrdom, both from Judaism's martyrological perspective[6] and from a Graeco-Roman perspective.[7] Finally, Paul's suffering is interpreted from the sacrificial-missiological perspective.[8] That is, Paul understands his sufferings "as part of his discipleship and apostolic vocation."[9] As helpful as these four types are, more is needed.

Among these interpretations of Paul's suffering, the martyr-like suffering of the prophets has not yet been noted. In fact, relatively little attention has been paid to examining Rom 9–11 for Paul's suffering. This essay will, therefore, attempt to fill these gaps in scholarship. It will argue that Paul suffers as a Mosaic prophet for the sake of persuading his kindred to believe in Jesus Christ, which, in turn, implies Paul's own "prophetic identity." The essay will first discuss the role of Romans 9–11 in its literary context, and then will focus on Paul's martyr-like suffering and his prophetic identity in the passage. Finally, an implication for today will be provided.

The Role of Romans 9–11 in Its Literary Context

Romans 9–11 was viewed to depart from the trajectory of justification by faith and Christ's inauguration of a new age presented in chapters 1–8. These chapters have, therefore, been considered as an addendum to Rom 1–8.[10] However, this view is rejected by most recent commentators, for they see them as a very significant part of, or the climax of, Paul's argument in the whole letter.[11] We agree that these three chapters play an

---

4. Smith, *Paul's Seven Explanations*, 174–83.
5. See also Wu, *Suffering in Romans*, 98–129.
6. Pobee, *Persecution and Martyrdom*.
7. Seeley, *Noble Death*.
8. Hafemann, *Suffering and Ministry*; Adewuya, "Sacrificial-Missiological Function," 88–98.
9. Adewuya, "Sacrificial-Missiological Function," 89.
10. Dodd treats it as an appendix: "It has been suggested that the three chapters were originally a separate treatise which Paul had by him, and which he used for his present purpose." Dodd, *Epistle of Paul to the Romans*, 148. See also Wakefield, "Romans 9–11," 66; Dunn, *Romans 9–16*, 519.
11. Hays, *Echoes of Scripture*, 63, indicates that they are not some excursus or appendix peripheral to the letter's theme, but are the heart of the matter. For Wright,

important role in understanding Paul's argumentation for God's salvific plan among the Israelites and the Gentiles. As Cranfield has rightly commented, "A closer study reveals the fact that there are very many features of chapters 1 to 8 which are not understood in full depth until they are seen in the light of chapters 9–11.... These chapters may be seen to be an integral part of the working out of the theme of the epistle."[12]

Romans 9–11, therefore, cannot be separated from chapters 1–8 and 12–16. Broadly speaking, the subjects in Romans 9–11 appear in the other parts of Romans as well. Firstly, Paul, as one of the key subjects of Romans 9–11, appears in the opening of Romans as an apostle to the Gentiles in 1:1–15 (cf. 10:15; 11:13). Secondly, the subject of faith-righteousness in 9:30—10:4 is the main issue discussed in Rom 3–4. Thirdly, Paul's mission to the Gentiles will finally achieve God's plan of salvation of Israel (11:13–14, 25–26), which connects the salvation of Israel and Gentiles together. This paves the way for 14:1—15:6, where Paul exhorts Jewish and Gentile believers to be united as the evidence and outworking of their salvation.

Now let us focus on the correlation between Romans 8 and 9–11. Romans 8 speaks of the Spirit's and Christ's intercession for God's children (8:26, 34). In Romans 9–11, Paul is the intercessor for Israel (e.g., Rom 9:1–5, 10:1).[13] In Rom 8:35–39, Paul emphasizes that nobody, nor anything in all creation, is able to separate Christians from the love of God. In Rom 9:3, Paul offers himself as a sacrifice for his Jewish kinsmen, for he is willing to be cut off from Christ for their sake. Moreover, Rom 8:16–18 identifies the children of God with Christ through co-suffering and co-glorification with Christ. In other words, believers participate in the suffering of Christ.[14] Indeed, as it will be argued, in Rom 9–11 Paul suffers for and intercedes for Israel as a persecuted prophet. He expresses his deep passion for Israel. His intercession and willingness to be cut off from Christ proceeds from his great love for them. Indeed, his suffering comes from his ministry for Christ and his role as an intercessory prophet for Israel.

Climax of the Covenant, 234, "Romans 9–11 functions as the climax of the theological argument." See also Wakefield, "Romans 9–11," 65.

12. Cranfield, *Romans*, 445.
13. Wiles, *Paul's Intercessory Prayers*, 255.
14. Smith, *Paul's Seven Explanations*, 177–78.

Paul's Martyr-Like Suffering and His Prophetic Identity in Romans 9–11

Romans 9–11 speaks of Paul's self-presentation as an intercessory prophet figure in the Mosaic tradition. Moses, the prototypical prophet for the people of Israel, underwent and endured sufferings. As YHWH's messenger, he was misunderstood and rejected by Israel (cf. Acts 7:17–44).[15] This suffering prophetic servant of God suffers for others and his suffering is viewed as voluntary sacrifice (see Exod 32:30–32), though not in the sense of atonement for others.[16] If Moses is prototypical of the suffering prophetic servant, then Isaiah and Elijah are in a similar prophetic tradition.[17] Paul follows this suffering prophetic tradition by presenting himself as a prophet afflicted for the sake of God's people. Paul's suffering is martyr-like sacrifice in the context of his missionary labors. He understands his suffering as part of his apostolic vocation—the suffering is intrinsic to his calling and missionary activities. "For Paul, living a self-giving life in participatory suffering with Christ is the model for ministry."[18]

Paul's self-reference of his identity is a prominent feature of these three chapters.[19] Most importantly, the understanding of his own identity forms a framework for his argument in Rom 9–11.[20] Paul's self-understanding as the suffering prophet can be inferred from the discourse pattern of these three chapters. At the beginning of each section (Rom 9:1–29; 9:30—10:21; 11:1–36) Paul designates his identity or his concerns for Israel (Rom 9:1–3, 10:1; 11:1–2) before he starts the argument. In addition, the overall discourse pattern in Romans 9–11 resembles that of prophetic discourse.[21] In the following, the related sections of Romans 9–11 will be examined and then the overall discourse pattern will be explained.

---

15. Tillar, "Eschatological Images of Prophet," 37.

16. *Contra* the view of Tillar. See Tillar, "Eschatological Images of Prophet," 37.

17. See 2 Kgs 17:7–23; 21:1–15; cf. Deut 31–32; O'Kane, "Isaiah," 29–51; and 1 Kgs 19:1–18; cf. Exod 19:9, 20; Childs, "On Reading the Elijah Narratives," 128–37; Vanlaningham, "Paul's Use of Elijah's Mt. Horeb Experience," 223–32.

18. Adewuya, "Sacrificial-Missiological Function," 89.

19. Windsor, Dunn and Holladay, *Paul and the Vocation of Israel*, 196.

20. Windsor, Dunn and Holladay, *Paul and the Vocation of Israel*, 196–97.

21. Xue, *Paul's Viewpoint*, x.

Paul Laments Over Israel (Rom 9:1-5)

Romans 9:1-29 focuses on God's faithfulness. Paul shows his strong concern for the Israelites and speaks of God's blessings to them at the beginning of the section (Rom 9:1-5). In Rom 9:1-3, Paul expresses his lament over Israel and solidarity with them, as he says, "I have great sorrow and unceasing anguish in my heart. For I could wish that I myself were accursed and cut off from Christ for the sake of my own people, my kindred according to the flesh." (9:2-3).[22] In his willingness to be accursed in place of Israel he characterizes himself as a Mosaic figure for Israel, for Moses said to YHWH that he was willing to be blotted out of the book for the sake of Israel (cf. Exod 32:30-32).

Through the use of the finite verbs λέγω and ψεύδομαι in Rom 9:1, Paul emphasizes his great sorrow in the ὅτι clause in the following verse. The double expression of λύπη (pain of mind or spirit, grief, sorrow, affliction) and ὀδύνη (mental pain, distress) intensifies the great grief that Paul suffers. The term ἀδιάλειπτος (unceasing, constant) increases this painful emotional intensity. Furthermore, the participle clause συμμαρτυρούσης μοι τῆς συνειδήσεώς μου ἐν πνεύματι ἁγίῳ (my conscience confirms it by the Holy Spirit) in verse 1 emphasizes this statement about Paul's painful suffering.[23]

This semantic chain of sorrow and anxiety is commonly found in Jewish prophetic laments. For example, Jeremiah laments over Jerusalem in Jer 4:19-21. He states, "I feel pain in my stomach, my stomach and the sense of my heart. My soul is torn, my heart cannot be silent, because my soul has heard the sound of the trumpet, the outcry of war." (ἣν κοιλίαν μου τὴν κοιλίαν μου ἀλγῶ καὶ τὰ αἰσθητήρια τῆς καρδίας μου μαιμάσσει ἡ ψυχή μου σπαράσσεται ἡ καρδία μου οὐ σιωπήσομαι ὅτι φωνὴν σάλπιγγος ἤκουσεν ἡ ψυχή μου κραυγὴν πολέμου.)[24] These verses express, in part, the prophet's anguish. A similar discourse pattern can be recognized in other prophetic laments, such as, Isa 35:10; 51:11; Jer 4:19; 14:17.[25] In light of the above, we may infer that Paul identifies himself with a prophet in his lament over Israel in Rom 9:1-2.[26]

---

22. Unless otherwise noted, all scriptural citations are from the NRSV.

23. See Xue, *Paul's Viewpoint*, 50-51, regarding these observations on Rom 9:1-2.

24. My translation. The LXX text is from Rahlfs and Hanhart, *Septuaginta*. In Jeremiah, the prophet suffered from pain over the destruction of Jerusalem.

25. Cf. Dunn, *Romans*, 524; and Xue, *Paul's Viewpoint*, 50.

26. Xue, *Paul's Viewpoint*, 50.

With a γὰρ in the beginning of verse 3, Paul now provides the reason for his grief and sorrow. The imperfect verb ηὐχόμην (pray) indicates the genuineness of Paul's desire.[27] The prepositional phrase ὑπὲρ τῶν ἀδελφῶν μου τῶν συγγενῶν μου (for the sake of my brothers, my kindred) expresses the vicarious nature of Paul's suffering. It demonstrates Paul's "passionate concern for and intensely felt commitment to the future good of his fellow Jews."[28] The rhetorical apex of his love for his kindred is found at the mention of his wish to be "accursed" and "cut off from Christ" for the sake of his fellow Jews.[29] The clause ἀνάθεμα εἶναι αὐτὸς ἐγὼ ἀπὸ τοῦ Χριστοῦ indicates his willingness to identify with Israel to the point of death. The phrase ἀπὸ τοῦ Χριστοῦ contrast sharply with 8:38–39, which states the love of God is experienced "in Christ."[30] For Paul, "in Christ" denotes one's identity of covenantal membership and it is the sum of eternal life and blessings (Rom 3:24; 6:11, 23; 8:1, 2, 39, etc.).[31] In other words, to be separated from Christ is a status of condemnation of being driven out of the covenant community. This is an ultimate sacrifice for the sake of his kindred.[32] The idea expressed here mirrors Moses' intercession for Israel after they committed the sin of worshipping the golden calf at Mount Sinai (cf. Exod 32:32). Moses, like Paul, is willing to be blotted out of the book for his people. We can infer that Paul has Moses' story in his mind, and that he attempts to set Moses as his example.[33]

A closer look at Moses in Exod 32–34 will help us to further understand Paul's martyr-like intercession for Israel. This section of Exodus finds Israel embroiling themselves in rebellion and idolatry with the golden calf.[34] The text depicts Israel as stiff-necked people several times (Exod 32:9; 33:3, 5; 34:9) and views their sin as a great sin of idolatry, which could blot them out of the book (32:30–33). Being blotted out from the book means being severed from their relationship with YHWH and his deliverance (cf. Dan 12:1–2). Moses' petition is a request to "stand

---

27. Dunn, *Romans*, 524.
28. Dunn, *Romans*, 524.
29. Xue, *Paul's Viewpoint*, 51.
30. Dunn, *Romans*, 525.
31. Abasciano, *Paul's Use of the Old Testament*, 97.
32. Abasciano, *Paul's Use of the Old Testament*, 98.
33. Moo, *Romans*, 558.
34. Abasciano, *Paul's Use of the Old Testament*, 101.

in the place of the guilty party and receive vicarious punishment."[35] He turns down YHWH's offer to establish himself as the seed of a new people (Exod 32:10) and determines to offer himself as a vicarious sacrifice for Israel (32:32). Paul parallels himself with Moses, for he sees his contemporaries' unbelief and rejection of Christ as being as severe as the ancient Israel's sin of idolatry. To remain in unbelief will lead to an eternal curse. Paul, as an apostle of Christ, identifies himself with Israel and is willing to take upon himself the doom of his kinsmen in order to bring them back into the sphere of Christ. As Dunn points out, "Paul echoes . . . the martyr aspiration that by sacrifice of oneself others, or indeed, as here, the nation as a whole, might be saved from God's wrath."[36]

In Exod 32:11–14, Moses resorts to the source of the heritage of Israel, the patriarchs (Abraham, Isaac, and Israel), in his intercession for Israel. Similarly, Paul's martyr-like intercession is followed by the statement of Israel's heritage and its origin in Rom 9:4–5. However, Paul intentionally adds the Messiah to the account of Israel's heritage. He places Christ within the sphere of Israel's heritage, which, in turn, serves to persuade the Jews to follow Jesus Christ—who is the Messiah they are waiting for.

In sum, Paul's unceasing grief is because of Israel's refusal to accept Jesus as the Messiah. His sorrow resembles a prophetic figure's heart-felt passion for God's people. By echoing Moses' prayer for Israel, Paul most likely wants to present himself as a Mosaic prophet, who is willing to sacrifice himself as a substitute for the condemnation of Israel.

Paul's Critique of Israel's Resistance of the Gospel and the Suffering Servant (Rom 9:30—10:21)

In the second section of Rom 9–11, which starts at 9:30 and ends at 10:21,[37] Paul criticizes Israel for their failure to attain God's righteousness. The voice of critique arrives at its apex with a citation from the book of Isaiah, "All day long I have held out my hands to a disobedient and contrary people." (Rom 10:21; citing Isa 65:2). However, Paul does not blame Israel for the sake of blaming, nor does he display a bias against his own kindred. The critique comes from his heartfelt concern for them. Therefore, in Rom 10:14–21, Paul implicitly employs the subject of the sacrifice of

---

35. Widmer, *Moses, God, and the Dynamics*, 132.
36. Dunn, *Romans*, 525.
37. See Xue, *Paul's Viewpoint*, 113–15, for the reasons of this delimitation.

the suffering servant through his use of Isaianic texts. By doing so, Paul attempts to emphasize the prophetic critique that is based on his willingness to sacrifice himself for the sake of the salvation of God's people.

Romans 9:30—10:4:
Paul's Critique of Israel Out of His Heartfelt Love for Them

By the juxtaposition of different types of righteousness (e.g., God's righteousness vs. Israel's own righteousness; faith-righteousness vs. work-righteousness) in Rom 9:30–33 and 10:2–4, Paul explicitly points out Israel's ignorance of, and failure to attain, God's righteousness.[38] God's righteousness is based on faith, for whoever believes in Jesus Christ as the Messiah is made righteous. It is not by means of works (their obedience to the law), for Christ is the goal (τέλος) of the law (Rom 10:4).[39] In other words, Israel has stumbled over the "stumbling stone"—Jesus Christ. Israel's failure is due to their ignorance of God's way of righteousness in Christ. That is, if you confess with your lips that Jesus is Lord and believe in your heart that God raised him from the dead, then you will be saved (10:9). For Paul, this message of salvation is from God, but Israel fails to realize it.

Between the two passages expressing contrasting pairs of righteousness language, Paul's personal intimate tone for Israel is expressed in Rom 10:1, "Brothers and sisters, my heart's desire and prayer to God for them is that they may be saved." Starting with the language of family, ἀδελφός, Paul interweaves the emotional and psychological terms (εὐδοκία τῆς ἐμῆς καρδίας) with expressions of religious intercession (δέησις πρὸς τὸν θεόν) to appeal for God's salvation for Israel. Paul's desire for the goodness of Israel can also be seen in the prepositional phrases ὑπὲρ αὐτῶν and εἰς σωτηρίαν. The word "ὑπέρ" with a genitive refers to "a marker of a participant who is benefited by an event or on whose behalf an event take place."[40] For instance, one person might die for the sake of (ὑπέρ) the nation. The phrase εἰς σωτηρίαν illustrates further Paul's inmost desire for Israel to experience the salvation available in the gospel. These heartfelt expressions can refer back to Paul's previous intercession for Israel in

---

38. Xue, *Paul's Viewpoint*, 122.

39. The meaning of τέλος in this verse, see the discussions in Xue, *Paul's Viewpoint*, 122–23 and n. 34.

40. Louw & Nida, 803.

Rom 9:1–3 when Paul portrays himself as a Mosaic figure interceding for Israel.[41] As Dunn perceives, Paul stands in the noble tradition of Israel—praying for his own people.[42] For instance, the prophet Jeremiah prays for remnant Israel to be rescued from the king of Babylon (Jer 42:2–4, 19–22); and Samuel prays for the salvation of Israel from the hand of the Philistines (1 Sam 7:5–11).[43] Therefore, Paul's heart suffers for his kinsmen, so that he admonishes them hoping to bring them to Jesus Christ. As Wagner observes, "If Paul sharply criticizes his fellow Jews, he does so not as an outsider slinging mud, but as a prophet, wounding that he may heal."[44]

Therefore, if Rom 9:1–5 presents Paul as a martyr-like Mosaic prophet, chapter 10 continues to place Paul in the prophetic tradition to pray for Israel. The prayers appear to be followed by a series of critiques of Israel's failure in submitting to God's righteousness (10:2–4, 18–21). It is worth noting that the critique proceeds from a prophetic heartfelt concern for the salvation of God's people.

Romans 10:14–21:
Israel's Resistance to the Gospel and the Suffering Servant

Starting with a series of questions, Paul criticizes Israel's unbelief and their disobedience to God in refusing the gospel of Jesus Christ that was proclaimed to them (Rom 10:14–21).[45] This passage continues Paul's indictment of Israel who failed to be subject to God's righteousness in vv. 2–3. Paul uses passages from the Hebrew prophets to illustrate the people's lack of response. Therefore, as Moo has rightly indicated, "the fault rests with Israel: she has been 'disobedient and obstinate.'"[46] In Rom 10:19–21, Paul marries the prophet Isaiah's voice with that of Moses to confirm the appropriateness of his critique of Israel's disobedience.[47] Paul

---

41. Xue, *Paul's Viewpoint*, 119.
42. Dunn, *Romans*, 586.
43. See also Xue, *Paul's Viewpoint*, 119n19.
44. Wagner, *Heralds of the Good News*, 178.
45. Xue, *Paul's Viewpoint*, 158–64. Note that the words "belief," "gospel," and "the words of Christ" correspond to οὐ ... ὑπηκοθσαν ... ἐποστεθσεν (not ... obey ... believe). Cf. Rom 10:15–18.
46. Moo, *Romans*, 663.
47. Xue, *Paul's Viewpoint*, 169.

probably considers both Moses, the model for any future prophet (Deut 18:15, 18), and Isaiah as key representatives of the prophetic role in the history of Israel and identifies himself with them.[48] As *Tg. Neophyti* (Deut 32:1) rightly says regarding the role of Moses and Isaiah in witnessing against Israel: "Two prophets arose to testify against Israel, Moses the prophet and Isaiah the prophet.... And the two of them because they feared the holy name, arose to testify against Israel."[49]

Since this passage is mainly composed of the Jewish scriptures, the meaning of the text cannot be explained clearly without examining them in their original context. The prominent texts come from Isaiah (52:7 [Rom 10:15], 53:1 [Rom 10:16], 65:1–2 [Rom 10:20–21]). Three things should be noted regarding these. First, the central theme of Isaiah, the prophetic book, relies on the metaphor that Israel is a light to the nations.[50] Second, the immediate literary context of Isa 52:7 is 52:1–12, which is about God's promise to restore the Holy City, Jerusalem. Finally, the immediate literary context of Isa 53:1 is 52:13—53:12, the famous fourth Suffering Servant Song.[51] If we read the oblique Jewish scriptures with the Pauline text, we can infer that (1) Paul intends to point out that Israel is supposed to deliver the gospel of Christ to the Gentiles as he, himself, is doing; and (2) God will bring the final salvation to Israel, but a suffering servant will come first, who will sacrifice himself, bear the sins of many, and make intercession for the transgressor (cf. Isa 53:1–12).

The historical background of Isa 52:1—53:12 relates to the exiles in the Babylonian captivity (Isa 52:11). In Isa 52:1–12, the Lord promises to restore the Holy City, Jerusalem. The opening verse instructs Zion-Jerusalem with the double imperative "awake, awake," which corresponds with the double imperative, "depart, depart," in the closing verses (vv. 11–12). Just as in the exodus from Egypt, where the Lord was present with Israel (Exod 13:22, 14:19), the new exodus from Babylon is assured of the Lord's presence and hence the safety of Israel.[52]

---

48. Xue, *Paul's Viewpoint*, 163.

49. See Wagner, *Heralds of the Good News*, 189n206. The translation of *Tg. Neophyti* here is taken from Wagner.

50. Clements, "Light to the Nations," 57–69.

51. Regarding the relationships between the fourth song and the previous three songs, see the suggestions made by Tang, *Servant as Messenger*, 127–29.

52. Tang, *Servant as Messenger*, 331.

After the assurance of the salvation of Jerusalem, the suffering servant is brought into view.[53] Isaiah 53:2-3 describes the suffering figure in a similar manner to a prophetic office. Childs has provided several Jeremiah texts to explain this similarity: "I sat alone, because your hand was upon me" (Jer 15:17). "I have become a laughingstock all day; everyone mocks me" (20:7). "Terror is on every side! Denounce him!" (20:10).[54] He explicitly says, "much like Jeremiah, the description of prophetic suffering depicts a calling, even an office, into which a servant of God has been summoned."[55] However, there is a sense of vicarious suffering in the subsequent texts (53:4-10). He was wounded "for our transgressions, crushed for our iniquities." (v. 5). He "was cut off from the land of the living, stricken for the transgression of my people." (v. 8). The vicarious suffering is depicted in Isaiah 53 at great length.[56]

In sum, the salvation of Jerusalem and her people is followed by a detailed description of a suffering servant, most probably in the manner of the description of prophetic suffering infused with a vicarious tone. This indicates that Paul's heartfelt desire for Israel's salvation in Rom 10:1 goes together with a figure's vicarious suffering for them through the use of the Isaianic texts in Rom 10:14-17.[57]

Paul Resembling a Persecuted Prophet (Rom 11:1-36)

Romans 11:1-2a: Paul Allies with Israel

After sharply criticizing Israel's rebellious refusal of God (Rom 10:21), Paul raised a question from Israel's side—whether God has rejected his people (11:1b). The answer to the question includes three parts. First is the direct and strong denial to the question (11:1c; μὴ γένοιτο); then Paul introduces his Jewish identity (11:1d-f); and third is a direct answer to the question but with indicative tone—God has not rejected his people whom he foreknew (2a).

---

53. It is ambiguous who the suffering servant is. The figure could be understood either in a collective sense or in the singular sense, or both. See Childs, *Isaiah*, 412; Friesen, *Isaiah*, 332-33.

54. Childs, *Isaiah*, 414. Translation of the Isaianic texts are Childs's.

55. Childs, *Isaiah*, 414.

56. Childs, *Isaiah*, 415; Whybray, *Thanksgiving for a Liberated Prophet*, 29.

57. As Childs has argued that "the vicarious role of the servant lies at the very heart of the prophetic message." Childs, *Isaiah*, 418 (cf. Friesen, *Isaiah*, 335).

It is worthwhile to note Paul's self-introduction in between the two direct denials of God's rejection of Israel. The reason for Paul's reference to his Jewish identity is probably to offer a case study for God's non-abandonment of Israel. Here is the logic: if God has rejected his people, then Paul as an Israelite, a descendant of Abraham has been rejected already.[58] As Paul intercedes for Israel anxiously in Rom 9:1–3 and 10:1, he allies himself with Israel by recounting his origin to the tribe of Benjamin. Therefore, the three parts of denial of God's rejection confirm that God's salvific plan toward Israel remains unchanged.

Romans 11:2b–4: The Story of Elijah

After affirming God's non-abandonment of Israel in verses 1–2a, the story of the prophet Elijah is introduced (11:2b–4). The scripture related to Elijah is from 1 Kgs 19:1–18. It is a story of king Ahab's attack on the prophet Elijah, Elijah's runaway, and his encounter with YHWH. After Ahab slaughtered the prophets and Jezebel threatened Elijah with the same fate (vv. 1–2), Elijah fled to Beer-sheba and then into the wilderness, where he lamented over his fate and then encountered YHWH (vv. 3–18). Romans 11:3–4 employs elements of the dialogue, when Elijah accused Israel by listing their sins: killing the prophets, demolishing God's altars, and now seeking the life of the only prophet left (1 Kgs 19:10, 14; Rom 11:3).[59] But YHWH comforted Elijah with the assurance that there would remain seven thousand who had not bowed the knee to Baal (1 Kings 19:18; Rom 11:4).

Why does Paul explicitly invoke the story and the voice of Elijah here? It is noted that in the story Elijah confronts YHWH with Israel's sin and their persecution of the prophets, and that they were seeking the life of Elijah. However, Paul makes some adjustments of Elijah's responses to YHWH. First, he omits the part, "I have been very zealous for the LORD, the God of Hosts; for the Israelites have forsaken your covenant" (see 1 Kgs 19:10, 14). Second, he inverts the two phrases "they have thrown down your altars" and "they have killed your prophets." In Rom 11:3, the phrase concerning the killing of the prophets is mentioned first (τοὺς προφήτας σου ἀπέκτειναν). It is possible that Paul attempts to emphasize

---

58. See Cranfield, *Romans*, 544. Other arguments over the reasons of Paul's self-introduction here can be found in Xue, *Paul's Viewpoint*, 184n9.

59. Xue, *Paul's Viewpoint*, 185.

the killing/suffering of the prophets here.[60] Note that the noun τοὺς προφήτας is placed at the beginning of the quotation as emphasis. In this way, Paul sees himself as being in danger of similar suffering.

Moreover, when Paul was in trouble because of the Jews' persecution, he usually drew upon his Jewish credentials. In Acts 21:27—22:21, we read that when Paul was arrested by the Jews in the temple, he resorted to his Jewish identity, saying, "I am a Jew, born in Tarsus in Cilicia, but brought up in this city at the feet of Gamaliel, educated strictly according to our ancestral law, being zealous for God, just as all of you are today" (Acts 22:3; cf. Rom 11:1c).[61] The trouble or persecution Paul experienced often occurred because he was proclaiming the resurrected and exalted Christ and his law-free gospel, which confronted the majority of his contemporary Israelites. Therefore, it can be inferred that Paul sees himself as resembling a persecuted prophet like Elijah,[62] who felt alone and threatened.[63]

In addition, according to Jerome Walsh, the prophet Elijah stands in the Mosaic succession.[64] There are some correlations between the discourse of Moses at Sinai and Elijah's interaction with YHWH at Horeb. Some scholars noticed the parallel between two stories. For example, Michael Vanlanigham says:

> While Moses passed 40 days on Mt. Horeb (Exod 34:28), Elijah took 40 days to get there (1 Kgs 19:8); Elijah is in "the cave", probably an allusion to the location in which Moses found himself in Exod 33:22; God is said to "pass by" both Moses (Exod 33:22) and Elijah (1 Kgs 19:11), and both receive a vision of God (for Moses, see Exod 34; for Elijah, see 1 Kgs 19:11–13). Furthermore, like Moses, Elijah contended on behalf of God against apostates, called for a decision to follow God, and went to Horeb for reassurance. Elijah's theophany shared with the theophany given to Moses and Israel the elements of wind, earthquake, and fire (cf. Exod 19:9; 20;18–19; Deut 4:9–10; 5:24–25).[65]

---

60. *Contra* Vanlaningham, "Paul's Use of Elijah's Mt. Horeb Experience," 225.
61. Capes, Reeves, and Richards, *Rediscovering Paul*, 27.
62. Xue, *Paul's Viewpoint*, 188.
63. Evans, "Paul and the Prophets," 120.
64. Walsh, *1 Kings*, 271–78; cf. Aernie, *Is Paul Also Among the Prophets?* 17.
65. Vanlanigham, "Paul's Use of Elijah's Mt. Horeb Experience," 227n11. See also Childs, "On Reading the Elijah Narratives," 134–35; and Walsh, *1 Kings*, 271–78.

Although Elijah is not a new Moses, for the two stories are not the same,[66] the two prophets are both in conflict with Israel[67]—they were both oppressed and persecuted by Israel. Elijah expressed the prophetic tradition by charging God's people for neglecting their covenantal obligations and warning them of the consequences of that neglect.[68] Paul continues this theme of conflict between the prophets and Israel in Romans with the voice of Isaiah. The words of Isaiah echo earlier prophetic voices when we read in Romans 11 of the conflict turning into one between God and Israel: "God gave them a sluggish spirit, eyes that would not see and ears that would not hear, down to this very day." (Rom 11:8; cf. Isa. 29:10). In sum, through the story of Elijah, Paul invokes the image of a persecuted prophet standing in the Mosaic succession; and he views himself as resembling this suffering prophet, Elijah.

Romans 11:5–10: Paul Disputes with Israel

Romans 11:5–7 explain the reasons why Paul contends, via the voice of the prophets, against some of the Israelites, because they still depend on works for God's salvation. Paul restates that it is God's gracious election that matters, otherwise grace would not be grace. The discourse format in v.7 is similar to Rom 9:30–31 (see table), which indicates Israel's failure to attain righteousness by pursing law-righteousness:[69]

---

66. Both Vanlanigham and Childs were aware of the differences of the two stories: Moses interceded for Israel, but Elijah is an accuser of Israel. See Vanlanigham, "Paul's Use of Elijah's Mt. Horeb Experience," 228; Childs, "On Reading the Elijah Narratives," 135.

67. For the conflict between Moses and Israel, Moses has cried out to the Lord, "What shall I do with this people? They are almost ready to stone me" (Exod 17:4). See Exod 17:2–4; Num 20:2–5. Note that Elijah almost lost his life in the hand of the king of Israel (1 Kgs 18–19).

68. Aernie, *Is Paul Also Among the Prophets?*, 18; VanGemeren, *Interpreting the Prophetic Word*, 37.

69. Xue, *Paul's Viewpoint*, 189. Also, cf. Wagner, *Heralds of the Good News*, 239, in which a table (figure 4.2) compares these two passages. Also see Jewett, *Romans*, 661. Note that the parallel entities in Rom 9:30–31 are Israel and the Gentiles, but here the two groups are within Israel.

Rom 11:7	Rom 9:30–31
Τί οὖν;	Τί οὖν ἐροῦμεν;
ὃ ἐπιζητεῖ Ἰσραήλ, τοῦτο οὐκ ἐπέτυχεν	Ἰσραὴλ δὲ διώκων νόμον δικαιοσύνης εἰς νόμον οὐκ ἔφθασεν
ἡ δὲ ἐκλογὴ ἐπέτυχεν	ἔθνη τὰ μὴ διώκοντα δικαιοσύνην κατέλαβεν δικαιοσύνην, δικαιοσύνην δὲ τὴν ἐκ πίστεως
οἱ δὲ λοιποὶ ἐπωρώθησαν	

Just as Paul has delineated Israel's failure in faith-righteousness, he again emphasizes the importance of God's gracious election for salvation. (Note that the word ἐκλογή appears twice and the term χάρις four times in 11:5–7.) Such preaching of a law-free gospel has caused Paul to experience some Jewish resistance. This conflict is demonstrated in 15:30–31 as well. This point has been indicated elsewhere by this author when discussing Paul's prayer request:

> Starting with an urgent request that they join in with prayers for him (παρακαλῶ δὲ ὑμᾶς [, ἀδελφοί,] ... *συναγωνίσασθαί μοι ἐν ταῖς προσευχαῖς ὑπὲρ ἐμοῦ πρὸς τὸν θεόν*),[70] Paul mentions two immediate requests for prayer shared between himself and the Roman churches. The first is about delivery from the danger of the unbelieving Jews in Judea: ἵνα ῥυσθῶ ἀπὸ τῶν ἀπειθούντων ἐν τῇ Ἰουδαίᾳ (Rom 15:31a).[71] The second relates to the hope that the Jewish Christians in Jerusalem would accept him and his collection. In other words, when Paul wrote the letter to Romans, his relationship with his kinsmen was highly tense.[72]

Seeing that some Israelites resisted the gospel of grace, and that they could not see God's way of delivering Israel in Jesus Christ, Paul brings in the voices of prophets Elijah and Isaiah in Rom 11:1–10 to contend that Israel failed in attaining God's righteousness. Johannes Munck is right to

---

70. *Italics added* to emphasize the urgent request.

71. The participle ἀπειθούντων refers to the unbelieving Jews. See Jewett, *Romans*, 935; Moo, *Epistle to the Romans*, 910. Also, cf. Acts 21:27–36 (Paul needs to be protected from the Jews' desire to kill him).

72. Xue, *Paul's Viewpoint*, 4. Some scholars indicate that Paul accepted Gentiles through a law-free Gospel, which may have challenged the distinctive Jewish way of life. In other words, Paul's controversies with the Jews were due to the law-free Gospel. See Campbell, *Paul and the Creation*, 6.

point out that Paul sees himself as a prophet, like Elijah, who "confronts a majority of the people, alone and in danger of death."[73] However, this does not mean that Israel is doomed. On the contrary, in the latter part of Romans 11, Paul articulates his hope for Israel's salvation in an eschatological future.

Romans 11:25–36: Paul's Hope for Israel's Salvation

Paul's heart is toward his people even in his Gentile ministry. Paul warns the Gentiles not to boast over Israel in Rom 11:11–15. Particularly, his ministry to the Gentiles is to make Israel jealous so as to save some of his kinsmen (11:13–14). In Rom 11:16–24 Paul expresses his hope for Israel that they can be grafted back like a broken branch is grafted back onto an olive tree.[74] Then Paul turns to speak of the final salvation of Israel in 11:25–32.

The mystery of God's salvific plan is, (1) "a hardening has come upon part of Israel" (πώρωσις ἀπὸ μέρους τῷ Ἰσραὴλ γέγονεν); (2) "until the full number of the Gentiles has come in" (ἄχρι οὗ τὸ πλήρωμα τῶν ἐθνῶν εἰσέλθῃ); and (3) "all Israel will be saved" (πᾶς Ἰσραὴλ σωθήσεται) (11:25–26). The structure of this plan is threefold, with three different time periods: the hardening of Israel in the past, the ongoing Gentile mission, and the future salvation of Israel.[75] The hardening of Israel is limited numerically by the phrase ἀπὸ μέρους ("part of") first,[76] and is limited temporally by the clause ἄχρι οὗ τὸ πλήρωμα τῶν ἐθνῶν εἰσέλθῃ ("until the full number of the Gentiles has come in"). Paul places a numerical and temporal restriction on Israel's heart-hardening, in contrast with the following statement that "all Israel" will be saved in the eschatological future.[77] The time-dimensioned structure is characteristic of a prophetic oracle.[78] Also, the phrase ἄχρι οὗ ("until then") shares the prophetic connotation in v. 25, for it corresponds with Isaiah's question ("How long,

---

73. Munck, *Christ and Israel*, 13.

74. Moo, *Romans*, 715.

75. Getty, "Paul and the Salvation of Israel," 458; Moo, *Romans*, 716; Sandnes, *Paul, One of the Prophets*, 174–75; Xue, *Paul's Viewpoint*, 217.

76. Xue, *Paul's Viewpoint*, 214.

77. Xue, *Paul's Viewpoint*, 214.

78. Sandnes, *Paul, One of the Prophets*, 174–75. See also *The Epistle of Barnabas* 1:7; Rev 1:19.

O Lord?" [Isa 6:11]), a cry of lamentation over Israel's fate.[79] Thus, Paul interprets the mystery of all Israel's salvation in terms of the prophetic tradition.

In sum, Paul indicates that, as an apostle of Christ, he was oppressed by some of the Israelites. But he still hopes for the final salvation for all Israel. He reckons that even his Gentile ministry contributes to Israel's future deliverance. Paul identifies himself as a prophet in the Mosaic succession and eagerly hopes for his kinsmen's salvation.

Conclusion: Paul's Suffering Represented in His Prophetic Identity

Romans 9–11 provides a unique perspective on Paul's suffering in his prophetic office for the sake of his kindred. Paul's self-reference of his identity in the beginning of each chapter of Romans 9–11 forms the framework of his argumentation. His Mosaic-prophetic identity validates that his authority for preaching the gospel has come from YHWH. Moreover, his heart is for the salvation of God's people, which includes both Israel and the Gentiles.

Three outstanding prophets are referred to in Romans 9–11: Moses, Elijah, and Isaiah. Moses is considered as the beginning and fountainhead of the prophetic movement, who is empowered by the Holy Spirit "to withstand the pressures of his contemporaries, to speak the word of God, and to discharge his office faithfully" for the sake of God's people.[80] Elijah lived in the tumultuous time of Ahab and Jezebel, and took a special place next to Moses as a prophetic figure in Israel's history.[81] As VanGemeren states, "if Moses is the fountainhead . . . of the prophetic stream, then Elijah shaped the *course* of the classical prophets."[82] Elijah is "the beginning of a long line of prophets who charged God's people with the breaking of the covenant,"[83] but he is also empowered by the Holy Spirit to have

---

79. Sandnes, *Paul, One of the Prophets*, 178; Xue, *Paul's Viewpoint*, 214–15. The phrase ἄχρι οὗ shares the similar meaning with ἕως (see BDF, §383), which usually appears in the prophetic lamentation over Israel's fate in the OT (Isa 6:11 ["How long, O Lord"; ἕως πότε κύριε]; Dan 9:26 (ἕως καιροῦ). Cf. Kim, *Origin of Paul's Gospel*, 96.

80. VanGemeren, *Interpreting the Prophetic Word*, 32–34.

81. VanGemeren, *Interpreting the Prophetic Word*, 36.

82. VanGemeren, *Interpreting the Prophetic Word*, 36. Emphasis in the original.

83. VanGemeren, *Interpreting the Prophetic Word*, 37.

"a concern for the spiritual condition of his people."[84] He "longed for a people whose heart would be loyal to the Lord."[85] Isaiah lived in the era of Israel's captivity. He is seen as a prophet in the footsteps of Moses, an authoritative successor to Moses (cf. 2 Kings 17–21; Deut 31–34).[86] In a word, these three figures are not only correlative to one another, but are also representative of three different eras of the history of Israel: the exodus, the dynastic period, and the captivity. Paul mirrors himself to these representative prophets, not only because he views himself as a prophet of a new era of Jesus Christ, but also because they all share the effects and characteristics of ministry in the Mosaic tradition. They all longed for the salvation of Israel and experienced oppression or persecution because of Israel's disobedience. Like Moses, Paul would suffer and sacrifice himself for the sake of his kindred. He is willing to be cursed by severing from Jesus Christ so that his kindred can come to understand God's message in the gospel.

Implications for Today

Paul's gospel message encounters resistance for various reasons. Sometimes it is based on fact, but at times it is due to misunderstanding. His law-free gospel for the Gentiles has been seen as a threat to Jewish identity. But his message to his kinsmen was similar to that of Moses, Elijah, and Isaiah: return to the Lord God in faith and righteousness. As an apostle to the Gentiles and as a Jewish prophet, with heartfelt concern for the fate of his people, Paul intercedes for Israel and is willing to give up his life for his kindred. In other words, as a prophet and pioneer in the ministry of God, Paul suffers for God's people. And, like earlier Jewish prophets, including Christ, Paul the Benjaminite thinks that his suffering carries a vicarious role.

It is understandable that many of his kinsmen did not understand or value Paul and his message. Rejecting that his prophetic message was from God, some of his Jewish contemporaries even considered his preaching as heretical, and wanted to kill him because of their zeal for God. Paul sharply criticized Israel's ignorance, but his heart's desire for

---

84. VanGemeren, *Interpreting the Prophetic Word*, 38.
85. VanGemeren, *Interpreting the Prophetic Word*, 38.
86. O'Kane, "Isaiah," 29–51.

their return to God burned so greatly within him that he was willing to sacrifice himself for them.

The suffering of Paul arose from his apostolic-prophetic vocation, for he preached a message that went counter to the prevailing cultures, both Jewish and Gentile. Paul's gospel of the cross gave birth to a new community representing a new creation in Christ Jesus. The community of God's people based on national or cultic identity faded in the light of the gospel of Christ. Such a message was perceived as counter-cultural and a dire threat to Jewish identity, particularly those aspects based on sociological identity markers, such as circumcision and food laws. This conflict of worldviews cost Paul much suffering and eventually his life.

Times have not changed all that much since the day of the apostle Paul. Even now, the preaching of the gospel of the crucified Christ often leads to suffering as worldviews collide. It is, for example, not easy to serve in the ministry of gospel in East Asia. If one is summoned to serve God, he or she must be prepared to suffer to some degree. Firstly, in today's profit-driven world, people value economic success highly. Not many are eager to embrace the value system of the gospel, which calls us to love, serve, and sacrifice for one another. In fact, people may mock or deride the message of Christ. Secondly, believers have to endure different kinds of persecution. Christian values are often viewed as opposed to traditional cultural values, and in some places the government imposes laws to regulate church activities. Followers of Jesus face social isolation and physical danger as a result.

In this context, God's servants must suffer and endure trials and tribulations as they proclaim the gospel and worship Christ. This should not surprise us, for suffering is part of the ministry of the gospel from the time of the apostle Paul till now.[87] To serve God does not guarantee a life of happiness and harmony. If we truly embrace our vocation in the world, then it is highly probable that we will endure many kinds of difficulties, emotionally, mentally, and physically. However, if we participate in the suffering of Christ, we will be glorified with him in the future manifestation of the sons and daughters of God.[88] We agree with Paul that "our present sufferings are not comparable to the glory that will be revealed in us" (Rom 8:19). So, suffering calls us to rejoice as Paul rejoiced in a Roman prison with great satisfaction, "I rejoice in the Lord greatly that

---

87. Tang, *Servant as Messenger of Gospel*, 125–69.
88. Cf. Nee, *Spiritual Man*, 951.

now at last you have revived your concern for me . . . for I have learned to be content with whatever I have. I know what it is to have little, and I know what it is to have plenty. In any and all circumstances I have learned the secret of being well-fed and of going hungry, of having plenty and of being in need. I can do all things through him who strengthens me." (Phil 4:10–13)

Bibliography

Abasciano, Brian J. *Paul's Use of the Old Testament in Romans 9.1–9: An Intertextual and Theological Exegesis*. London: T & T Clark, 2005.

Adewuya, J. Ayodeji. "The Sacrificial-Missiological Function of Paul's Sufferings in the Context of 2 Corinthians." In *Paul as Missionary: Identity, Activity, Theology, and Practice*, edited by Trevor J. Burke and Brian S. Rosner, 88–98. New York: T & T Clark, 2011.

Aernie, Jeffrey W. *Is Paul Also Among the Prophets?: An Examination of the Relationship between Paul and the Old Testament Prophetic Tradition in 2 Corinthians*. LNTS 467. New York: T & T Clark, 2012.

Campbell, William S. *Paul and the Creation of Christian Identity*. London: T & T Clark, 2006.

Capes, David B., Rodney Reeves, and E. Randolph Richards. *Rediscovering Paul: An Introduction to His World, Letters, and Theology*. Downers Grove, IL: IVP Academic, 2007.

Childs, Brevard. *Isaiah*. Louisville: Westminster John Knox, 2001.

———. "On Reading the Elijah Narratives." *Interpretation* 34 (1980) 128–37.

Clements, Ronald E. "A Light to the Nations: A Central Theme of the Book of Israel." In *Forming Prophetic Literature: Essays on Isaiah and the Twelve in Honor of John D. W. Watts*, edited by James W. Watts and Paul R. House, 57–69. Sheffield: Sheffield Academic, 1996.

Cranfield, C. E. B. *A Critical and Exegetical Commentary on the Epistle to the Romans*. ICC. Edinburgh: T & T Clark, 1979.

Dodd, C. H. *The Epistle of Paul to the Romans*. London: Hodder & Stoughton, 1932.

Dunn, James D. G. *Romans 9–16*. WBC 38. Dallas: Word Books, 1988.

Evans, C. A. "Paul and the Prophets: Prophetic Criticism in the Epistle to the Romans." In *Romans and the People of God: Essays in Honor of Gordon D. Fee on the Occasion of His 65th Birthday*, edited by Sven Soderlund, Gordon D. Fee, and N. T. Wright, 115–28. Grand Rapids: Eerdmans, 1999.

Friesen, Ivan. *Isaiah*. Scottdale, PA: Herald, 2013.

Getty, Mary Ann. "Paul and the Salvation of Israel: A Perspective on Romans 9–11." *CBQ* 50 (1988) 456–69.

Hafemann, *Suffering and Ministry in the Spirit: Paul's Defense of His Ministry in II Corinthians 2:14–3:3*. Grand Rapids: Eerdmans, 1990.

Hays, Richard B. *Echoes of Scripture in the Letters of Paul*. New Haven: Yale University Press, 1989.

Jewett, Robert. *Romans: A Commentary*. Hermeneia. Minneapolis, MN: Fortress, 2006.

Kim, Seyoon. *The Origin of Paul's Gospel*. Grand Rapids: Eerdmans, 1981.

Lim, Kar Yong. *"The Sufferings of Christ Are Abundant in Us": A Narrative Dynamics Investigation of Paul's Sufferings in 2 Corinthians.* LNTS 399. London: T & T Clark International, 2009.
Moo, Douglas J. *The Epistle to the Romans.* NICOT. Grand Rapids: Eerdmans, 1996.
Munck, Johannes. *Christ and Israel: An Interpretation of Romans 9–11.* Philadelphia: Fortress, 1967.
Nee, Watchman. *The Spiritual Man.* Taiwan: Taiwan Gospel Book Room, 1988.
O'Kane, Martin. "Isaiah: A Prophet in the Footsteps of Moses." *JSOT* 69 (1996) 29–51.
Pate, C. M. *The Glory of Adam and the Afflictions of the Righteous: Pauline Suffering in Context.* Lampeter: Mellen Biblical, 1993.
Pobee, John S. *Persecution and Martyrdom in the Theology of Paul.* JSNTSup 6. Sheffield: JSOT Press, 1985.
Porter, Stanley E. *Idioms of the Greek New Testament.* 2nd ed. BLG 2. Sheffield: Sheffield Academic, 1994.
Rahlfs, Alfred, and Robert Hanhart, eds. *Septuaginta.* Rev. ed. Stuttgart: Deutsche Bibelgesellschaft, 2006.
Sandnes, Karl Olav. *Paul, One of the Prophets?: A Contribution to the Apostle's Self-Understanding.* WUNT 43. Tübingen: Mohr, 1991.
Seeley, David. *The Noble Death: Graeco-Roman Martyrology and Paul's Concept of Salvation.* Sheffield: JSOT Press, 1990.
Shum, Shiu-Lun. *Paul's Use of Isaiah in Romans: A Comparative Study of Paul's Letter to the Romans and the Sibylline and Qumran Sectarian Texts.* WUNT 156. Tübingen: Mohr Siebeck, 2002.
Smith, Barry D. *Paul's Seven Explanations of the Suffering of the Righteous.* SBL 47. New York: Peter Lang, 2002.
Tang, Samuel Y. C. *The Servant as Messenger of Gospel: A Study of Isaiah 40–55.* Hong Kong: Christian Witness Press, 1985.
———. *Toward a Theology of Suffering.* Hong Kong: Excellence Book House, 1991.
Tillar, Elizabeth K. "Eschatological Images of Prophet and Priest in Edward Schillebeeckx's Theology of Suffering for others." *The Heythrop Journal* 43 (2002) 34–59.
VanGemeren, Willem A. *Interpreting the Prophetic Word: An Introduction to the Prophetic Literature of the Old Testament.* Grand Rapids: Zondervan, 1990.
Vanlaningham, Michael G. "Paul's Use of Elijah's Mt. Horeb Experience in Rom 11:2–6: An Exegetical Note." *TMSJ* 6.2 (1995) 223–32.
Wagner, J. Ross. *Heralds of the Good News: Isaiah and Paul "in Concert" in the Letter to the Romans.* NovTSup 101. Leiden: Brill, 2002.
Wakefield, Andrew H. "Romans 9–11: The Sovereignty of God and the Status of Israel." *RevExp* 100 (2003) 65–80.
Walsh, Jerome T. *1 Kings.* Collegeville, MN: Liturgical, 1996.
Whybray, R. N. *Thanksgiving for a Liberated Prophet: An Interpretation of Isaiah Chapter 53.* JSOTSup 4. Sheffield: University of Sheffield, Department of Biblical Studies, 1978.
Widmer, Michael. *Moses, God, and the Dynamics of Intercessory Prayer.* FAT 8. Tübingen: Mohr Siebeck, 2004.
Wiles, Gordon P. *Paul's Intercessory Prayers: The Significance of the Intercessory Prayer Passages in the Letters of St. Paul.* Cambridge: Cambridge University Press, 1974.

Windsor, Lionel J., James D. G. Dunn, and Carl Holladay. *Paul and the Vocation of Israel: How Paul's Jewish Identity Informs His Apostolic Ministry, with Special Reference to Romans*. Berlin: De Gruyter, 2014.

Wright, N. T. *The Climax of the Covenant: Christ and the Law in Pauline Theology*. Minneapolis: Fortress, 1999.

Wu, Siu Fung. *Suffering in Romans*. Eugene, OR: Pickwick, 2015.

Xue, Xiaxia E. *Paul's Viewpoint on God, Israel, and the Gentiles in Romans 9–11: An Intertextual Thematic Analysis*. Carlisle, Cumbria: Langham Monographs, 2015.

4

"The Weapons of Righteousness"

Righteousness and Suffering in 2 Corinthians

DAVID I. STARLING

Weapons of Righteousness

DISCUSSIONS OF THE THEME of righteousness in Paul's letters, as I have argued elsewhere,[1] frequently understate the importance to Paul of the active, ethical righteousness of believers. This under-emphasis has been a consequence, in part at least, of the amount of energy that has been expended across the last five centuries on the disagreements between Western Protestants and Catholics over the doctrine of justification and, in more recent years, on the debates (conducted largely though not exclusively within Protestant scholarship) over the presence or absence of retributive elements within the justice of God.

Important as those two debates are, neither should be conducted as if the terrain over which it is being fought amounts to the entire landscape of Paul's thought on the themes of righteousness, justice, and justification.[2] In Paul's letter to the Romans, for example, the account that he offers of the revelation of God's righteousness in the gospel does not

---

1. See especially Starling, "Covenants and Courtrooms," 9–12; "Meditations on a Slippery Citation," 249–54.

2. For brief surveys of that larger landscape, see Seifrid, "Righteousness, Justice, and Justification"; and Starling, "Righteousness/Justice/Justification."

terminate with the retributive judgment foreshadowed in 1:18—3:20 or the justifying verdict pronounced on believers in 3:21—4:25. The effect of God's saving work in Christ, according to Paul, is to end the dominion of death over the world, and to bring in a day when "grace . . . reign[s] through righteousness" in the life of the age to come (5:21 ESV).[3] "Justification," as Paul uses the word in Romans, implies a consistently forensic metaphor, referring to a verdict that declares believers to be free from divine condemnation (e.g., 8:33–34) and free from the oppressive dominion of sin and death (e.g., 6:7). But "righteousness" language in Romans (as elsewhere in Paul's letters) can refer to realities that take place before, during, and after the metaphorical law court in which the verdict of justification is pronounced.

For Paul, the active, ethical righteousness of the life that is transformed by obedient faith and participates in the manifestation of God's righteousness on earth is not only the evidence of salvation but an integral dimension of its content and purpose (8:4). Salvation, according to Paul, is not only from wrath (5:9) but also from sin (6:22). The purpose of that salvation is "in order that, just as Christ was raised from the dead by the glory of the Father, we too might walk in newness of life" (6:4 ESV)— a life in which believers are summoned to offer every part of themselves to God as "instruments," or better, given the warfare metaphor implied by the clash of powers between personified righteousness and personified sin, "weapons" of righteousness (6:13).

Important as that theme is, it is equally important that it be articulated in a manner that guards against the risk of propagandistic distortion. Paul's image of Christians offering themselves as "weapons of righteousness," along with his exhortation later in the same letter urging the readers to clothe themselves with "the armor of light" (τὰ ὅπλα τοῦ φωτός; 13:12), could easily be misappropriated in support of a triumphalist, utopian form of Christian activism. Christian history offers no shortage of examples of movements that have mobilized zealous Christians as foot-soldiers in campaigns and culture wars of various kinds, promising them (explicitly or implicitly) a divine guarantee of the success that their actions will have in establishing the kingdom of God or restoring the glories of a lost Christendom.[4]

---

3. Biblical quotations elsewhere in the chapter follow the NRSV translation, except where otherwise indicated.

4. For a survey of recent North American examples, see Hunter, *To Change the World*, 99–193.

The wider context of Paul's words within his letter to the Romans contains important clues that help a watchful reader to avoid this sort of misappropriation of his martial imagery. In chapter 8, for example, believers are depicted—in the present age, at least—not as invulnerable and all-conquering but as "groaning," in concert with the whole creation and God's own Spirit, waiting for the coming redemption of their bodies and the created world that they inhabit (8:18–25).[5] And in chapters 12–13, in the immediately preceding context of the apocalyptic image that urges the readers to clothe themselves with the armor of light (13:12), they are encouraged to live patiently and peaceably within a potentially hostile social order (12:14–21), recognizing even the pagan authorities as "God's servants" and paying them whatever taxes and honors are due to them (13:1–9). A triumphalist reading of the apocalyptic imagery in 6:13 and 13:12 does not sit comfortably with important elements of the eschatology and ethics that Paul teaches within the larger argument of Romans itself. But it is in 2 Corinthians, in response to the praxis and message of the super-apostles, that Paul offers a more extended exposition of his thoughts on power, weakness, and suffering, and the weaponry and warfare of the servants of righteousness.

Righteousness and Suffering in 2 Corinthians

Ministries of Righteousness

Paul's conflict with the super-apostles in 2 Corinthians is presented within the letter as a contest between two competing ministries—that of Paul and his co-workers and that of the super-apostles who have subsequently become influential in Corinth—each of which claims to be a "ministry of righteousness."[6] According to Paul, the new covenant ministry for which he has been made competent by God is a διακονία τῆς δικαιοσύνης (3:9), and his opponents are ministers of Satan who disguise themselves as διάκονοι δικαιοσύνης (11:15).[7]

---

5. See the discussion of this passage in Starling, "Life Because of Righteousness," 385–87.

6. See the larger discussion of this aspect of the letter in Starling, "Meditations on a Slippery Citation," 250–51, from which this paragraph and the next are adapted.

7. The contrast in 3:9 between the ministry of the old covenant as ἡ διακονία τῆς κατακρίσεως and the ministry of the new covenant as ἡ διακονία τῆς δικαιοσύνης offers some support to the decision of the NRSV translators to render the latter as "the

The presence of the language of δικαιοσύνη in polemical contexts such as these does not require the conclusion that Paul's opponents are "judaizing Jews,"[8] or that Paul's contest with them is, in essence, a dispute over whose gospel gives the better account of how a person attains the verdict of divine justification. His criticism of the super-apostles and their gospel is not confined to the question of whether it does the job of justifying those who believe it; in 12:19–21, when he reaches the end of his argument with the super-apostles, the motive that he identifies as the driving force behind his polemic is not his concern for the Corinthians' assurance of divine justification, but his fear that old sins of "quarreling, jealousy, anger, selfishness, slander, gossip, conceit, and disorder" have continued unchecked under the super-apostles' influence. If there is a "righteousness" that is in view here as having been undermined by the ministry of the super-apostles, it would appear from the evidence of these verses to be one that consists in (or at least includes) the present transformation of their ethical conduct by the work of the Spirit.

Paul's Apologia and Appeal

As part of the contest between the super-apostles' "ministry of righteousness" and his own, Paul offers an extended *apologia* for his ministry in 1:15—5:21. Within it, he responds to a set of inter-connected criticisms relating to questions of integrity and transparency (addressed principally in 1:15—2:13) and the shameful sufferings that he and his fellow-workers have endured (addressed principally in 2:14—5:21).[9]

The apology that Paul offers in 1:15—5:21 is followed in 6:1—7:16 by an appeal to the Corinthians to be reconciled with Paul.[10] The initial

---

ministry of justification," but the fact that the verb δικαιόω is nowhere to be found within 2 Corinthians, whereas the noun δικαιοσύνη occurs seven times, suggests that other possible meanings should at least be considered. Most English versions translate δικαιοσύνη in 3:9 as "righteousness" and leave open the question of the sense in which Paul is using the word in that verse—a better decision in my view.

8. A conclusion along these lines was famously asserted in Barrett, "Paul's Opponents," 251.

9. For a discussion of the inter-relationship between these two themes and the apologetic strategy that Paul follows in responding to them, see Starling, "We Do Not Want You to Be Unaware," 276–79.

10. As Ivar Vegge has convincingly argued (see Vegge, *2 Corinthians*, 360–75) the apologetic rhetoric of chs. 1–7 is directed toward a larger, conciliatory purpose; Paul's aim is not simply to defend his ministry, but to win back his relationship with the

extension of the appeal in 6:1 is followed immediately in 6:2 by a citation from Isaiah 49:8: "For he says, 'At an acceptable time I have listened to you, and on a day of salvation I have helped you.' See, now is the acceptable time; see, now is the day of salvation!"

This citation, as Mark Gignilliat has demonstrated, functions as a hermeneutical key for Paul's appeal to the Corinthians in this section of the letter:

> Paul understands himself to be in the midst of the eschatological now, a period of divine history witnessed to by Isaiah and brought to its fulfillment in the person and work of Jesus Christ, the embodiment of true and faithful Israel struck down by the Father for the reconciliation of the world, i.e. the Servant.[11]

Given the connections that Paul has already drawn in 5:14-21 between the Isaianic Servant texts and the person and work of Christ, it is unlikely that he intends his readers to hear the words of YHWH that he quotes in 6:2 as addressed directly to himself; here, as in the previous chapter, the Servant is Christ. Nevertheless, the pattern of redemptive suffering seen in the Servant has profound implications for Paul and his fellow-workers' ministry as θεοῦ διάκονοι (6:4) and δοῦλοι ὑμῶν διὰ Ἰησοῦν (4:5).[12]

The Peristasis Catalogue of 6:3-10

Paul goes on, in the "peristasis catalogue" of 6:3-10,[13] to paint a picture of that ministry in support of the appeal for reconciliation that he com-

---

Corinthians. In chs. 6-7 that conciliatory purpose becomes the explicit aim of Paul's rhetoric. Unlike Vegge, I would place the transition from apology to appeal for reconciliation at 6:1 rather than at 5:11. For arguments in favor of that way of reading the flow of Paul's rhetorical strategy, see Starling, "We Do Not Want You to Be Unaware," 278.

11. Gignilliat, *Paul and Isaiah's Servants*, 108.

12. Cf. Isa 54:10 and the discussion in Gignilliat, *Paul and Isaiah's Servants*, 112-13.

13. Here and in the following paragraphs, I will be referring to 6:3-10 not as a "catalogue of hardships" but (in keeping with more recent scholarly usage) as a "peristasis catalogue" (literally, a "catalogue of circumstances"). The latter term correctly reflects the fact that positive as well as negative circumstances can sometimes, as here, be included in the lists that fall within that genre, and is to be preferred for that reason. Here, strictly speaking, the contents of the list are even more variegated than the designation "peristasis catalogue" or "catalogue of circumstances" would imply, since Paul speaks not only of the circumstances (positive and negative) within which he

mences in 6:1–2 and continues in 6:11–13.[14] The depiction of the ministry of Paul and his fellow workers in 6:3–10 also functions as a recapitulation of the *apologia* in 1:15—5:21, focusing (as does the earlier *apologia*) on the inter-related themes of Paul's sufferings (6:4b–5, 8–10; cf. 2:14—5:21) and his transparency and integrity (6:6–7; cf. 1:15—2:13).

The bulk of the paragraph is made up of an intricately-constructed series of lists that Paul strings together in 6:4b–10, commencing with the phrase, ἐν ὑπομονῇ πολλῇ ("in all perseverance"),[15] which serves as a general heading for the lists.[16] To begin with, in verses 4b–7a, Paul offers a series of seventeen successive phrases, each of which is introduced by the preposition ἐν. The first nine items of the list form a sub-series of their own, with the preposition followed by a plural noun that speaks of the circumstances in the midst of which Paul and his fellow-workers minister: "in afflictions, in hardships, in difficulties, in beatings, in imprisonments, in riots, in labors, in sleepless nights, in fastings." The next eight comprise a second sub-series, in which the items of the list are singular nouns referring not to the circumstances that Paul and his fellow-workers endure but to the graces, virtues, and resources with which, by God's enabling, they minister in the midst of those circumstances: "in purity, in knowledge, in patience, in kindness, in the Holy Spirit, in unfeigned love, in the word of truth, in the power of God."[17]

---

ministers but also, in vv. 6–7, of the graces and virtues with which, by God's enabling, he conducts his ministry in the midst of those circumstances.

14. Note the way in which the participles of vv. 3–4 (διδόντες, συνιστάντες) are syntactically subordinated to the principal verb παρακαλοῦμεν in v. 1.

15. Here and throughout the following paragraphs, in my analysis of 6:3–10, I will be departing from the NRSV and following my own translation.

16. See especially the analysis and discussion in Harris, *Second Corinthians*, 465–67.

17. In my translation of the items in this second sub-series I have continued to gloss the Greek ἐν with the English "in" for the whole series in vv. 4b–7a, rather than follow the NRSV (and commentators including Thrall, *2 Corinthians*, 450; Harris, *Second Corinthians*, 467) in switching from "in" to "by" for the second sub-series. While there a clearly differences of form and meaning between the second sub-series and the first, it is an over-simplification of those differences to categorize all of the items of the second sub-series as "instruments" that Paul makes use of in his ministry, which the translation "by" risks implying. It is better, I think, to preserve the slightly greater semantic flexibility of the English word "in" for the second sub-series (as is the case, for example, in the NIV 2011 translation of these verses) and leave readers to intuit the differences of meaning and function between the first sub-series and the second.

Verses 7b–8a contain a second, much shorter series of just three items, each of which is introduced by the preposition διά (with the genitive case). Like the series of ἐν-phrases in verses 4b–7a, this series too falls into two (much shorter) sub-series, distinguished from one another by the plural or singular number of the nouns of which they are composed. The first, in verse 7b, comprises just one item, in the plural: "through the weapons of righteousness in the right hand and the left," with the διά ("through") functioning to indicate the means through which the graces and enablings of the immediately preceding sub-series in verses 6–7a (purity, knowledge, patience, kindness, the Holy Spirit, unfeigned love, the word of truth, the power of God) are exercised and manifested. The second, in verse 8a, comprises two items, each of which is a pair of contrasting singular nouns: "through glory and dishonor, through slander and praise," with the διά in this instance pointing to the items in the list as circumstances in which the weapons of verse 7b are used.

Finally, in verses 8b–10, Paul concludes the description with a series of seven contrasting pairs of items, introduced in each case by ὡς, with the items in each pair connected by either καί or δέ: "[regarded] as impostors, and yet true; as unknown, and yet well known; as dying, and yet see!—we live; as punished, and yet not killed; as sorrowful, but always rejoicing; as poor, but making many rich; as having nothing, and yet possessing everything." In each case, the first item of the pair represents the way in which Paul and his fellow-workers appear (correctly, in some cases, incorrectly in others) to human observers and the second item represents the hidden reality of their situation, as transformed by the saving work of Christ.

"Weapons of Righteousness in the Right Hand and the Left"

The item in Paul's description that is of particular interest to us in this chapter—his reference to "the weapons of righteousness in the right hand and the left" (v. 7b)—is thus positioned at a kind of hinge-point between the graces and enablings of verses 6–7a and the contrasting pairs of circumstances in verse 8a.[18] On the one hand, its focus on the means by which the graces and enablings of God are enacted in the ministry of Paul and his fellow-workers suggests an obvious thematic connection with what precedes, particularly the reference to "the power of God" that

---

18. See Guthrie, *2 Corinthians*, 332.

concludes the list in verses 6–7a.[19] On the other hand, its form (e.g., the introductory διά and the contrasting pair, "in the right hand and the left") suggests that it be read in connection with what follows.[20]

The meaning of Paul's expression has been much discussed. One topic on which the commentators focus is the intended function of Paul's reference to "the right hand and the left." Though some argue that this implies nothing more than the comprehensiveness with which believers are equipped,[21] most agree, with good reason, that Paul intends a reference to the offensive and defensive weapons that are held in the right and left hands, respectively.[22]

A second focus of discussion is the genitive construction, "weapons of righteousness." This can be understood in several different ways, chiefly: (i) "weapons characterized by righteousness," (ii) "weapons with which to fight for righteousness," (iii) "weapons consisting in righteousness," and (iv) "weapons supplied by righteousness."[23] The parallel with the closely-similar expression in Rom 6:13 counts in favor of option (ii), given the implied metaphor in that verse of a war between personified sin and personified righteousness, and the initiative that believers are urged to take in "present[ing]" the parts of their bodies to righteousness as weapons.

The parallel with Rom 6:13 is not a perfect one; whereas there it is the parts of believers' own bodies that are the "weapons" in the metaphor, here the weapons are held in the believers' hands—an image that speaks equally strongly of the active participation of believers in the war that righteousness wages against its enemies, but less directly of the self-involvement of believers, in their very bodies, as the weapons with which the war is waged. Nevertheless, the surrounding context makes it clear that the battle Paul has in mind is not fought at (metaphorical) arm's length. The hardships listed 2 Cor 6:4b–5 are all experienced bodily by Paul and his fellow-workers; the graces and enablings listed in verses 6–7a are all, in one way or another, manifested in their character, speech,

---

19. See Thrall, *2 Corinthians*, 461; Harris, *Second Corinthians*, 466–67.

20. See Seifrid, *Second Letter to the Corinthians*, 281–82; Barnett, *2 Corinthians*, 330–31.

21. E.g., Barrett, *Second Corinthians*, 188; Thrall, *2 Corinthians*, 462.

22. E.g., Harris, *Second Corinthians*, 478; Arzt-Grabner and Kritzer, *2. Korinther*, 350.

23. See the discussion in Harris, *Second Corinthians*, 477–78, including Harris's argument in favor of option (iv).

and action; and the contrasting estimations and realities in verses 8b–10 all involve their persons and the various ways in which they are regarded. Even within verses 7b–8a, a close connection is implied between the offensive and defensive actions in which believers exercise the "weapons" in their right hand and left and the fluctuating circumstances of "glory and dishonor . . . slander and praise" in which they find themselves: "the 'weapons' given to the apostle," as Mark Seifrid rightly argues, "are inseparable from the message of Christ that he bears in his own person: 'through glory and dishonor, through slander and praise.'"[24]

Seifrid is probably drawing that connection more tightly than the text requires when he goes on to imply that the "weapons" of offense and defense in verse 7b *are* the "glory and dishonor . . . slander and praise" of verse 8a.[25] He is right, however, to point out the chiasm created by the inversion of terms within the second contrasting pair in verse 8a—"through *glory* and dishonor, through slander and *praise*"—and the implication (in line with the paradoxes of ch. 4 and chs. 10–13) that the "slander" Paul encounters is as much an occasion through which the gospel advances as the "glory," and the "praise" he receives from his friends and admirers is, potentially at least, as much a threat to his ministry as the "dishonor" to which he is exposed.[26]

Seifrid is correct, too, in the emphasis that he places on the extent to which Paul's own active participation in the work that God's righteousness accomplishes in the world is framed by his depiction of "the work of God that he 'suffers,'" as it is described in verses 4–7b and verses 8b–10.[27] Agency, character, and suffering are inseparable elements of Paul's account of his ministry, as he presents it in 6:3–10, and the first of those elements is decisively framed by the second and the third.

---

24. Seifrid, *Second Letter to the Corinthians*, 281.

25. Seifrid, *Second Letter to the Corinthians*, 282.

26. See especially 2 Cor 12:1–10. Unlike Seifrid, I am interpreting the "glory" and "praise" of v. 8a as references to human estimations of Paul and his fellow-workers, rather than to the eschatological glory and praise given by God. See Harris, *Second Corinthians*, 478–79; Guthrie, *2 Corinthians*, 334.

27. Seifrid, *Second Letter to the Corinthians*, 280–81. The quotation marks that Seifrid places around the word "suffers" are a signal that his intended meaning is the broad, semi-technical sense of the word that embraces the whole range of experiences that Paul undergoes passively, as acted upon by God, rather than the somewhat narrower subset of those experiences that involve the enduring of pain and loss.

Apologia and Example

Within the immediate context of 2 Corinthians 1–7, the account of Paul's "ministry of righteousness" that he offers to the readers is principally apologetic in its function: in writing these things, he tells the Corinthians in 5:12, he is giving his readers "an opportunity to boast about us, so that you may be able to answer those who boast in outward appearance and not in the heart." But this is not the entirety of Paul's purpose in offering the Corinthians an account of his ministry; his hope is not only that the Corinthians will be able to endorse the boast that he makes about the holiness and sincerity of his ministry (1:12), but also that that he will be able to make a similar boast about them (1:14; cf. 8:24; 9:2–4; 11:2–3; 12:20–21; 13:9–10).[28] Motivated by that double hope, Paul gives his readers a description of his ministry and the mindset that informs it, which functions *both* as an argument for why the Corinthians can have confidence in him *and* (as is the case elsewhere in his correspondence with the Corinthians) as an example for them to imitate.

The particular part that Paul and his fellow-workers play within the "warfare" that the righteousness of God wages against its enemies is not in all respects identical with the part to be played by the Corinthians; there is a unique "authority" that Paul lays claim to as an apostle of Christ (13:10) and a unique task that springs from it. But the cruciform, grace-shaped manner in which he conducts his part within the larger conflict, deliberately rejecting the "earthly wisdom" that offers itself as a seductive alternative, models a pattern that is as valid for the Corinthians as it is for him (cf. 1:3–14; 6:14—7:1; 13:4–10).

To sum up: The "ministry of righteousness" (3:9; ESV) which Paul describes and defends in 2 Corinthians 1–5 is a ministry that not only speaks about God's righteousness but participates in and embodies its powerful, transformative extension in the world, manifesting and modelling the way in which it reshapes human conduct and community. But the triumph and the transformation which God accomplishes through Paul's ministry are inseparable from the sufferings that he undergoes and the character that is forged by and displayed in them, in keeping with the crucicentric message that he proclaims. If the Corinthians have believed

---

28. The translation of 1:12 departs from the NRSV to read "holiness" (ἁγιότητι) rather than "frankness" (ἁπλότητι) as original. See Harris, *Second Corinthians*, 183, for text-critical arguments in favor of this reading. If ἁπλότητι rather than ἁγιότητι is judged to be original, the substance of the point is unaffected.

the same message, received the same Spirit, and are being transformed into the same likeness, then a similar dynamic will be at work within their lives.

Implications for Today

Paul's image of the "weapons of righteousness" that he and his fellow-workers wield in their ministry, read within the context of the peristasis catalogue of 2 Cor 6:3-10 and the wider context of the letter as a whole, has obvious and important implications for Christians today.

In my own situation, within the post-Christendom West, Christians are increasingly voicing a sense of concern and anxiety about the uncomfortably marginal place that we are learning to occupy within the culture that we inhabit. Stung by a succession of incidents in which prominent and not-so-prominent Christians have been the targets of public ridicule and hostility, we feel the pull of a strong temptation to insulate ourselves from the risk of similar suffering and social shame. The temptation takes various forms, depending on our social location, our temperament, and our politics: for some, the most appealing option will be to restrict our words and actions in the public square to causes that will retain the approval of the socially progressive left; for others, it will be to throw in our lot with the lobbyists and power-brokers of the revanchist right; and for others still it will be to retreat altogether from engagement with the wider world.

The warfare images that Paul uses in 2 Cor 6:7 and 10:4-5, along with his warnings to the Corinthians against being "mismatched" (6:14) with unbelievers by assimilating their thinking and practice to the mindset of the surrounding culture,[29] speak powerfully into this context. There is no comfortable or neutral space into which Christians can retreat with integrity from the battle between "the knowledge of God" and the various arguments and obstacles that are raised up against it (10:4-5). To be a Christian is to be at war.

But the battle lines of that warfare do not coincide neatly with the battle lines inscribed by the warring factions in the power struggles and ideological conflicts of our culture. The vision of righteousness and

---

29. For an argument in support of this understanding of 6:14 and its relationship with Paul's polemic against the "earthly wisdom" of the surrounding pagan culture, see Starling, "*Apistoi* of 2 Cor. 6:14," 53-60.

justice that we have learned in the gospel will inevitably overlap at some points with the common consensus of our society and with the particular, distinctive convictions of parties and ideologies within it, but the overlap will never be complete. And the weapons with which our warfare is to be waged are radically different from the "merely human" (σαρκικά) weapons with which the culture wars of our society are typically fought (10:4). They are, as Paul goes on to say, imbued with "divine power to destroy strongholds" (10:4); but their use (as he has already stressed in 6:3–10) is inseparable from the vulnerability and integrity of the servants of Christ who wield them. "Dishonor" and "slander" are inescapable dimensions of the ministry of righteousness that Paul models in 2 Corinthians, and the perseverance and graciousness with which we endure them are integral to the way in which God's power is at work in the world. Suffering and righteousness are joined together in the vocation of the Servant, and of the servants who follow in his steps. The moment of history in which we find ourselves, like the moment in which Paul composed his second letter to the Corinthians, will prove to be a searching test of whether we have understood and embraced that conjunction.

Bibliography

Arzt-Grabner, Peter, and Ruth Elisabeth Kritzer. *2. Korinther*. PKNT. Göttingen: Vandenhoeck & Ruprecht, 2014.
Barnett, Paul. *The Second Epistle to the Corinthians*. NICNT. Grand Rapids: Eerdmans, 1997.
Barrett, C. K. *A Commentary on the Second Epistle to the Corinthians*. BNTC. 2nd ed. London: A & C Black, 1990.
———. "Paul's Opponents in II Corinthians." *NTS* 17 (1971) 233–54.
Gignilliat, Mark S. *Paul and Isaiah's Servants: Paul's Theological Reading of Isaiah 40–66 in 2 Corinthians 5:14—6:10*. LNTS. London: T&T Clark, 2007.
Guthrie, George H. *2 Corinthians*. BECNT. Grand Rapids: Baker, 2015.
Harris, Murray J. *The Second Epistle to the Corinthians: A Commentary on the Greek Text*. NIGTC. Grand Rapids: Eerdmans, 2005.
Hunter, James Davison. *To Change the World: The Irony, Tragedy, and Possibility of Christianity in the Late Modern World*. New York: Oxford University Press, 2010.
Seifrid, Mark A. "Righteousness, Justice, and Justification." In *New Dictionary of Biblical Theology*, edited by T. Desmond Alexander and Brian Rosner, 740–45. Downers Grove, IL: IVP, 2000.
———. *The Second Letter to the Corinthians*. PNTC. Grand Rapids: Eerdmans, 2014.
Starling, David I. "The *Apistoi* of 2 Cor. 6:14: Beyond the Impasse." *NovT* 55 (2012) 1–17.
———. "Covenants and Courtrooms, Imputation and Imitation: Righteousness and Justification in *Paul and the Faithfulness of God*." *JSPL* 4 (2014) 37–48.

———. "'Life Because of Righteousness': The Spirit, the Church, and the *Missio Dei* in Romans." *Mission Studies* 33 (2016) 376–90.

———. "Meditations on a Slippery Citation: Paul's Use of Psalm 112:9 in 2 Corinthians 9:9." *JTI* 6 (2012) 241–55.

———. "Righteousness/Justice/Justification." In *Brill Encyclopedia of Early Christianity*, edited by Paul van Geest and Bert Jan Lietaert Peerbolte. Leiden: Brill, forthcoming. Available online at <http://dx.doi.org/10.1163/2589-7993_EECO_SIM_00001842>.

———. "'We Do Not Want You to Be Unaware . . .': Disclosure, Concealment and Suffering in 2 Cor 1–7." *NTS* 60 (2014) 266–79.

Thrall, Margaret E. *A Critical and Exegetical Commentary on the Second Epistle to the Corinthians*. ICC. 2 vols. Edinburgh: T&T Clark, 1994.

Vegge, Ivar. *2 Corinthians—A Letter About Reconciliation: A Psychagogical, Epistolographical and Rhetorical Analysis*. WUNT. Tübingen: Mohr Siebeck, 2008.

5

Suffering, Salvation, and Solidarity in 2 Corinthians 1:3–11

Sean F. Winter

Introduction

SECOND CORINTHIANS IS REPLETE with the language of suffering.[1] Paul reminds the Corinthians of the affliction (θλίβω, θλῖψις) that characterizes his own ministry (2 Cor 4:8, 17; 6:4). The three great hardship lists of the letter (2 Cor 4:8–9; 6:4–10; 11:23–27) carefully compile a lexicon of adverse circumstances and the experience of suffering that arises from them.[2] In what looks like a summary of Paul's experience, 2 Cor 12:10 talks about learning to be content in the midst of "weaknesses, insults, hardships, persecutions, and calamities". Paul portrays his ministry in terms that suggest constant threat and danger: from his fellow Jews (2 Cor 11:24–26); from fate or providence (2 Cor 11:25–26); from the natural world (2 Cor 11:25–26); from fellow Christian leaders (2 Cor 11:26); not to mention the burden of caring for his own churches (2 Cor 11:28). Whatever the meaning of Paul's reference to receiving a "thorn in the

---

1. For the purposes of this essay I am not entering into the contested territory of literary criticism of canonical 2 Corinthians, although readers should be aware that my view closely aligns with a growing body of scholarship that considers it likely that chapters 1–13 are a unity. See, for example, Vegge, *2 Corinthians*; and Schmeller, "No Bridge," 73–84.

2. For details of the composition and rhetoric of these texts see Fitzgerald, *Cracks in an Earthen Vessel*.

flesh", the metaphor itself evokes the idea of physical pain (2 Cor 12:7). While suffering language clearly appears elsewhere in Paul's letters, the intensity of the reflections on suffering in 2 Corinthians invites exposition and explanation.[3]

It is next to impossible to determine, with any chance of accuracy, the nature of the actual experiences that lie behind these formulations. The Corinthians themselves have, of course, been a source of affliction to Paul (2 Cor 2:4; 7:4-5), but the exact circumstances that elicit that language from Paul are largely lost to us.[4] The third hardship list in 2 Cor 11:23-27 provides us with tantalizing windows into some of the likely physical hardships experienced by Paul in the course of his travels and preaching, but the details are contested.[5] We wish that we knew more about the precise nature of Paul's "thorn" (12:7), but have to be content with supposition.[6] The language of suffering in 2 Corinthians clearly relates to genuine, empirical suffering, the marks of which Paul no doubt carried physically, emotionally, and psychologically. Yet, as this essay hopes to show, the language does much more than that. An adequate understanding of the theme of suffering in 2 Corinthians must take seriously the sense in which Paul interprets his experiences in christological terms.

The importance of seeing suffering as a christological rather than simply an experiential category for Paul is clear from the verses we have just surveyed. Paul cannot talk about his own sufferings without relating his experience to his participation in the sufferings of Christ. The fragile, breakable "clay jars" of 2 Cor 4:7-9 contain nothing other than the "dying" of Jesus (4:10). As Mark Gignilliat has shown, the vocation of the "servants of God" in 2 Cor 6:4-10 is explicitly described in terms that align those "servants" to the ministry of the "Servant".[7] Paul's weaknesses are the outward manifestation of the power of Christ at work within him

---

3. For a review of the scholarship on suffering in Paul and especially 2 Corinthians see Lim, *Sufferings of Christ*, 1-15.

4. This does not stop scholars from trying to reconstruct the relational history that lies behind the composition of 2 Corinthians. The most detailed recent case is Welborn, *End to Enmity*.

5. See, for example, the discussion of synagogue discipline in Bolton, "Paul and the Whip".

6. See Wallace, *Snatched*, 269-71.

7. See the argument of Gignilliat, *Paul and Isaiah's Servants*. The extensive hardship list of 6:4-10 reaches a crescendo in language that evokes the dying and rising (6:9 cf. 4:10-14) and poverty and riches (6:10 cf. 8:9) of Christ.

(2 Cor 12:9) and so he regards his sufferings as being "for the sake of Christ" (2 Cor 12:10).

This christological framing of the experience of suffering is clearly set out in Paul's account of his experience in Damascus (2 Cor 11:30–33). In emphasizing the veracity of his account Paul appeals to "the God and Father of the Lord Jesus—blessed be he forever!" (11:31). This verse, often neglected by those who seek to separate 2 Corinthians 10–13 from the rest of the letter, seems clearly to echo the language of the letter opening (2 Cor 1:3). In what follows, I consider the ways in which those opening verses establish the main contours of Paul's understanding of suffering in the letter as a whole.[8] In particular, I argue that Paul's account of his own suffering is predicated on certain convictions about God's deliverance of Christ from death, and is directed towards establishing patterns of solidarity in suffering between Paul and his audience at Corinth. In our search for the theological dynamics at work in Paul's argument, we examine 2 Cor 1:3–11 first with reference to Christ's suffering and deliverance, and then consider how the Corinthians and Paul are together related to Christ and to each other in a relationship of mutual solidarity.[9]

The Christological Pattern: Christ's Suffering and God's Deliverance

In 2 Cor 1:5 Paul places the sufferings of Christ (τὰ παθήματα τοῦ Χριστοῦ) at the center of the *berakah* with which the letter opens (1:3–7). The phrase has caused some consternation among scholars, not least because the focus of Paul's "blessing" of God seems to relate primarily to the consolation experienced by Paul in his own suffering. What might it mean for Paul to connect his apostolic affliction to the "sufferings of Christ"? Margaret Thrall outlines the major interpretative possibilities and concludes, correctly in my view, that we encounter here the notion of participation in Christ that dominates Paul's account of apostolic and Christian identity in 2 Corinthians (and arguably elsewhere).[10] If this is

---

8. See also Lim, *Sufferings of Christ*, 28–39.

9. The exegetical discussion that follows is, in part, predicated on a wider set of conclusions about the purpose and argument of canonical 2 Corinthians. These cannot be spelled out in detail here, but are the focus of ongoing research into the letter.

10. See the survey of opinions in Thrall, *2 Corinthians 1–7*, 107–10. The objections against this view outlined by Lim (*Sufferings of Christ*, 48–49) do not convince. The lack of baptismal imagery in 2 Cor 1:3–11 does not negate the connection with

close to the mark, then Paul's reference to consolation through Christ (2 Cor 1:5) seems to refer to the "salvation" experienced by Christ in which Paul and the Corinthians come to participate. God's comfort (1:3) is, therefore, that of delivering Christ from suffering. In other words, we have here a variant articulation of the basic pattern of suffering and vindication that is the hallmark of Paul's understanding of the Christ-event.[11]

This point opens up two further possibilities for exegesis. The first concerns the possibility that this account of the Christ-event is actually a more important theme in the letter opening of 2 Corinthians than has been realized. In other words, could Paul allude to Christ's suffering and consolation elsewhere in this distinctive letter opening? The second relates to the likely meaning of the language of divine consolation used in relation to Christ. It is relatively straightforward to read suffering language related to Christ in terms of the cross. But what might it mean for Paul to talk about a consolation received through Christ? Was Christ ever the object of divine consolation? We treat each of these topics in what follows.

Christ and Divine Consolation

The adoption of a blessing, rather than a thanksgiving formula, in the opening of 2 Corinthians invites an explanation. The typical suggestion is that Paul's departure from his usual practice is the result of his decision to focus in 2 Corinthians not on the situation of his audience but on his own circumstances. Customarily, Paul uses his letter openings to give thanks for the activity of his hearers: their faithfulness (Rom 1:8), testimony to Christ (1 Cor 1:6), sharing in the gospel (Phil 1:6), faith, hope, and love (1 Thess 1:3). In the absence of such characteristics, Paul simply withdraws the thanksgiving altogether (thus Galatians). In the case of 2 Corinthians, so the usual argument runs, Paul adopts the εὐλογητός formula because it more clearly connects with his own Jewish heritage; the blessing of God came naturally to Paul. The reason for this is that Paul already has

---

Rom 6:3-11; both texts give expression to a fundamental category of Pauline thought (cf. Phil 3:10 and 2 Cor 4:7-12). More importantly, the idea that Paul's sufferings are qualitatively different from those of the Corinthians needs challenging. The purpose of the letter opening of 2 Cor is precisely to locate both forms of suffering into the christological frame that makes sense of Paul's relationship to the Corinthians.

11. At another level of abstraction this implied narrative can be described in terms of "descent" and "ascent." See Campbell, "Story of Jesus."

in mind the circumstances that he describes in 1:8–9, namely his affliction in Asia. In the minds of many commentators, it is this profound and personal experience that explains both the form (the *berakah*) and the content (the focus on consolation) of 1:3–7.[12]

But is Paul the primary recipient of divine consolation in this section of the letter? We shall argue below that the specific comfort afforded to Paul is not directly referred to until 2 Cor 1:6. The opening, generic reference to the "God of all consolation" requires closer attention, because it suggests that the christological aspect of this motif is primary. The obvious chiastic arrangement of 1:3 is usually understood as follows:

A   ὁ θεὸς
   B   καὶ πατὴρ τοῦ κυρίου ἡμῶν Ἰησοῦ Χριστοῦ
   B' ὁ πατὴρ τῶν οἰκτιρμῶν
A' καὶ θεὸς πάσης παρακλήσεως[13]

The symmetry of this arrangement is not especially neat, however, in that it includes an additional and disruptive genitive modifier in clause B. Moreover, that clause (τοῦ κυρίου ἡμῶν Ἰησοῦ Χριστοῦ) seems to modify both initial terms in A and B: θεὸς καὶ πατήρ. God is both "God" and "Father" in relation to Jesus.[14] It is therefore preferable to arrange the material so that the two nouns in clauses A and B are modified initially by reference to Jesus Christ, and subsequently by the addition of the "genitive of effect" in clauses A' and B' relating to each of the initial terms.[15] This would leave the extra clause to form the center of the chiasm, thus:

A   ὁ θεὸς
   B   καὶ πατὴρ
      C   τοῦ κυρίου ἡμῶν Ἰησοῦ Χριστοῦ
   B' ὁ πατὴρ τῶν οἰκτιρμῶν
A' καὶ θεὸς πάσης παρακλήσεως

---

12. See, for example, Furnish, *II Corinthians*, 117.

13. See Kleinknecht, *Leidende Gerechtfertige*, 243–44, for a detailed analysis.

14. See Harris, *2 Corinthians*, 142. The presence of the single article, the existence of equivalent expressions in 2 Cor 11:31 and 1 Thess 3:11 (cf. Eph 1:17) and the broader Pauline commitment to setting christological affirmations within the broader context of monotheistic convictions makes it entirely possible that he could speak of "the God of Jesus."

15. Thrall, *2 Corinthians 1–7*, 102n160. The mercy and comfort experienced by "all" has its origin in this God. See Rom 15:5 for a parallel example.

This identification "our Lord Jesus Christ" as the middle term suggests the possibility that the opening clause of Paul's blessing serves to characterize the nature of God the Father's relation to Christ, or at least that Christ is included within the comprehensive attribution of "all consolation." We can develop this in two ways. One would be to suggest that Jesus is here understood to be the primary object of divine mercy and consolation. This reading of the formula offers a clear rationale for the later notion that the consolation of Paul and the Corinthians is received διὰ τοῦ Χριστοῦ (1:5). We shall see below that the eschatological reading of Paul's consolation language here strengthens the case for the notion of divine deliverance from affliction as relating primarily to Christ as God's Servant, and the object of God's saving purpose. This leads to the second emphasis, more directly referred to in what follows, namely that any consolation experienced by the apostle or his audience can be known only in and through their participation in the sufferings of Christ. Consequently, it is Christ's suffering and consolation that orders the subsequent references to Paul and the Corinthians. Paul's general description of God as "father of mercies" and "God of all consolation" is not initially a statement about God's deliverance of him, or the Corinthians, but of the Messiah through whom that consolation is experienced by apostle and community alike. The *berakah* is less the expression of a personal thanksgiving by Paul the Jew, and more a doxological celebration of the Christ-event in which, as the rest of the section makes clear, both Paul and the Corinthians share.

The Nature of Divine Consolation

But what does the term "consolation" actually mean for Paul in the context of the letter opening of 2 Corinthians? Two possibilities present themselves for consideration. Given Paul's usage elsewhere in the letter, as a way of describing the comfort that Paul receives upon news of the Corinthians' favorable response to the "painful letter" (2 Cor 7:4, 7, 13), we might be tempted to read the language of the letter opening as referring to some form of emotional or psychological alleviation of distress; the mitigation of sorrow. The Greco-Roman *topos* of consolation in sorrow is well documented and it might be thought that it offers a potential explanatory backdrop to Paul's usage here.[16] However there

---

16. See Windisch, *Zweite Korintherbrief*, 39.

are several observations that should give us pause. First, in the Greco-Roman consolatory tradition the language of παρακαλεῖν/παράκλησις is actually rather rare. Instead the verb παραμυθέομαι and associated nouns predominate. Furthermore, the situation or set of circumstances that give rise to the need for consolation, while varied, is usually closely associated with questions of mortality, illness, or death. It is the *consolatio mortis* that dominates philosophical texts and epistles on consolation. Thus, consolation here becomes "the combating of grief through rational argument."[17] The fact that Paul speaks of divine παράκλησις for those who are ἐν πάσῃ θλίψει (2 Cor 1:4; cf. 1:6, 8) rather than offering his own λόγος παραμυθητικός suggests that another tradition forms the explanatory source for the content of his benediction. That tradition is found in the language of Paul's Bible where we find two related but distinct meanings relevant to our study.

First, there are those examples where "consolation" denotes the divine comfort offered to the individual in circumstances of suffering or affliction. This meaning is most commonly encountered in the Psalms. For example, the psalmist is confident of YHWH's deliverance in Ps 86:17 (85:17 LXX):

> Show me a sign of your favor, so that those who hate me may see it and be put to shame, because you, LORD, have helped me and comforted me (LXX = καὶ παρεκάλεσάς με).[18]

The term here clearly denotes divine intervention directed towards the individual in adverse circumstances.[19] In a number of cases the experience of the psalmist is described using the language of "affliction," θλῖψις.[20] It is clearly possible to imagine that in a moment of personal reflection, Paul has instinctively turned to the language of the Psalms as he composes his opening benediction in 2 Corinthians. Otfried Hofius has suggested that this is indeed the case. He writes that "In 2 Cor 1:3ff

---

17. Holloway, *Consolation*, 56, with a helpful summary of the consolatory tradition on pp. 56-74.

18. NRSV.

19. See also Ps 23:4 (22:4 LXX); 70:21 (LXX 71:21); 76:3 (LXX 77:2); 94:19 (LXX 93:19); 119:76, 82 (LXX 118:76, 82); 125:1 LXX only (the MT has a different sense). The sense of Ps 119:50, 52 (LXX 118:50, 52) is somewhat different. The search for consolation for the community is present in Ps 90:13 (LXX 89:13) and 135:14 (LXX 134.14). The *Thanksgiving Hymns* also use the term in this way, see *1QH* 17:13; 19:32.

20. See Ps 23:5 (LXX 22:5); 76:3 (LXX 77:2); 86:7 (LXX 85:7).

Paul speaks in the language of Israel's prayer book, familiar to him from his youth."[21]

This cannot be the whole story, however. In 2 Cor 1:3 God is named as the God of *all* consolation, not just Paul's. Paul then portrays himself as the mediator of that consolation to others (1:6–7), so it is clear that the Corinthians receive the consolation that God has afforded to Paul. Unless we assume that the Corinthians have also been "despairing of life itself" (1:8), the highly personal language of the Psalms seems inadequate as a resource for understanding how the whole community can be understood to be recipients of divine consolation through Paul's ministry. So, in view of the clear indication that divine consolation is directed not only to Paul, but also to Jesus Christ, the Corinthian community, and indeed to "those who are in any affliction" (2 Cor 1:4), it seems to me likely that Paul's language also draws significantly on the other main biblical resource, namely the tradition of eschatological consolation for Israel, first described in Deutero-Isaiah.[22]

The Isaianic vision of divine comfort for the people of God provides a further, and in my view more likely, potential background for Paul's language in 2 Corinthians. Illustrative excerpts from Isaiah 40–55 are cited below giving a translation of the LXX rather than the MT.[23] Of course, this section of Isaiah begins by striking the note:

> Comfort, O comfort my people, says God. (παρακαλεῖτε παρακαλεῖτε τὸν λαόν μου) O priests, speak to the heart of Ierousalem; comfort her (παρακαλέσατε αὐτήν), because her humiliation has been fulfilled, her sin has been done away with, because she has received from the Lord's hand double that of her sins (Isaiah 40:1–2)

YHWH promises to comfort Israel like a shepherd (Isa 40:11). God will comfort the waste places of Zion (Isa 51:3) and the prophet's question, spoken out of the experience of Israel's devastation and destruction: "Who will comfort you? (τίς σε παρακαλέσει, Isa 51:19 LXX; cf. 54:11) is met by the earlier affirmation, "I, I am he who comforts you" (ἐγώ εἰμι ἐγώ εἰμι ὁ παρακαλῶν σε, Isa 51:12 LXX; cf 57:18; 66:13). Especially notable are those occasions when the LXX replaces Masoretic imagery

---

21. Hofius, "'Der Gott,'" 251–52 (translation mine).
22. See Bieringer, "'Comfort'"; and Bieringer, "Comforted Comforter."
23. All LXX quotations are taken from Pietersma and Wright, *New English Translation*.

with the language of comfort. Thus in place of the promise to give to Jerusalem "a herald of good tidings," the LXX speaks of the divine promise of "comfort for Jerusalem on the way" (παρακαλέσω εἰς ὁδόν, Isa 41:27 LXX). Again, and in language that is very close to the characterization of God in 2 Cor 1:3, YHWH's pledge to "lead" his people in the MT of Isa 49:10 becomes in the LXX the promise that "he who has mercy on them will comfort them (ὁ ἐλεῶν αὐτοὺς παρακαλέσει). The pair of mercy/comfort reappears a few verses later:

> Rejoice, O heavens, and let the earth be glad; let the mountains break forth with joy, and the hills with righteousness, because God has had mercy on his people (ἠλέησεν ὁ θεὸς τὸν λαὸν αὐτοῦ) and he has comforted (παρεκάλεσεν) the humble of his people. (Isa 49:13 LXX)[24]

The fact that on one occasion, Isaiah can speak of YHWH's comfort as being addressed to Israel in her affliction at the hands of oppressors (see Isa 51:12-13) only serves to strengthen the connection to Paul's language in 2 Corinthians.[25]

Paul's language, then, may well derive from the portrayal of eschatological consolation in Isaiah 40–55. This claim is strengthened when we consider that these chapters provide much of the scriptural "intertext" for subsequent Pauline argumentation in 2 Corinthians. For example, G. K. Beale has argued that the motifs of new creation and reconciliation in 2 Corinthians 5–7 constitute "the inaugurated fulfilment of Isaiah's and the prophets' promise of a new creation in which Israel would be restored into a peaceful relationship with God."[26] The centrality of Isaianic themes for an overall understanding of the theology of 2 Corinthians scarcely needs justification. Isaiah 49:8 is quoted at 2 Cor 6:2 while two quotations from Isa 52:11 and 43:6 are included in the catena of 2 Cor 6:16–18. There is a further allusion to Isa 55:10 in 2 Cor 9:10. Moving beyond the boundaries of our letter, recent investigation of the use of Isaiah in Romans concludes that "Paul read large sections of Isaiah as a prophetic word concerning his own role in the eschatological restoration of Israel

---

24. Note also Is 52:9 LXX where the Hebrew is rendered with ἠλέησεν.

25. Associated ideas, although not the specific language of θλίβω/θλῖψις can be found at Isa 49:13; 51:3; 52:9; 54:11 LXX.

26. Beale, "Old Testament Background," 550-81 (here p. 551). See also Webb, *Returning Home*; and the comprehensive survey in Gignilliat, *Paul and Isaiah's Servants*.

and the extension of that salvation to Gentiles."²⁷ The notion that Isaiah therefore informs Paul's reflections here on the Christ-event, his apostolic ministry, and Corinthian participation in both is not far-fetched.

Secondly, we note that Isaiah's vision of YHWH's deliverance of Israel through the provision of consolation in affliction is picked up in later Jewish sources and thereby stands as the fount of a tradition regarding eschatological comfort that clearly existed in Paul's day. Pseudepigraphical texts use the language of παράκλησις in a general sense, but are also aware of the tradition of eschatological consolation. *Ben Sira* can refer to the Isaianic tradition specifically (*Sir* 48:24; cf. 49:10). Joseph in his *Testament* claims that "I was abandoned and the Lord showed his concern for me," a reference to his deliverance from the pit.²⁸ The epigraph to *Psalms of Solomon* 13, a chapter anticipating eschatological judgement, receives the title "the consolation of the righteous" (παράκλησις τῶν δικαίων). *Second Baruch* speaks explicitly of Israel's hope for the "consolation of Zion" in the aftermath of the first Jewish War with Rome (*2 Bar* 44:6). The tradition of eschatological consolation flourishes into the rabbinic period epitomized by the oath formula: "May I never see the consolation of Zion if . . ."²⁹ Further evidence for the *topos* of eschatological consolation is found in Luke 2:25 where Simeon is described as a man προσδεχόμενος παράκλησιν τοῦ Ἰσραήλ. It seems that the motif was utilized within the genre of *berakah* at mealtimes in Qumran.³⁰ Other Qumran fragments testify to the ongoing association of "comfort" with Jewish eschatological expectation.³¹ Finally the *targumim* offer numerous examples of the *topos* in relation to eschatological hopes.³²

---

27. Wagner, *Heralds*, 32–33.

28. *T. Jos* 1:6, cf. 2:6, my translation.

29. See *b. Sanh.* 37b; *b. Sebu.* 34a (R. Simeon b Shatah); *b. Makk.* 5b; *b. Hag.* 16b (R. Judah b. Tabbai); *b. Ketub.* 67a (R. Eleazar b. Zadok) for the formula. Other relevant references include *b. Pesah.* 54b; *b. Taan.* 11a. For a full discussion see Strack and Billerbeck, *Kommentar*, 2:124–26.

30. See *4Q434a* 1, alluding to Isa 54:11.

31. See *4QBarki Napshi (4Q436)* 1i: "to console those oppressed in the epoch of their anguish"; *1QLitPr (1Q34) = 4QPrFetes (4Q509)* 1iii.1: "For you console us from our distress and you gather together our exiles for the time . . . our scattered ones for the age of . . ." See also *11QMelch (11Q13)* where the Messiah is portrayed as the one who comforts the afflicted.

32. For example, the Targum of Isaiah 49:13 emphasizes the imminence of the prophet's eschatological hope and Targum Hosea 6:2 prophesies that "He will give us life *in the days of the consolations that will come*."

Of course, Paul is perfectly able to draw directly on the Isaianic material in his reflection on the "God of all consolation" in 2 Corinthians 1. Nevertheless, the presence of this ongoing tradition in some eschatological texts in Second Temple Judaism serves to reinforce the likelihood that Paul has in view not simply God's intervention in his own life, to deliver him from personal suffering, but also God's decisive intervention in salvation history, to inaugurate the new age in the death and resurrection of Jesus as Messiah. The connection between "consolation" and "salvation" in 2 Cor 1:6 would suggest as much. The implications of this background for the exegesis of 2 Cor 1:3–7 and its rhetorical function in relation to the rest of the letter can now be considered.

Suffering and Consolation for the Corinthians and Paul

The most obvious implication of the discussion of the motif of divine comfort in the previous section is that, in blessing the God of all consolation, Paul alludes to the message of salvation that lies at the heart of his theology. The comfort that "we" receive in affliction is the consequence of God's prior deliverance of the Messiah from suffering. If this is the case, it is unlikely that Paul regards himself exclusively as the only recipient of divine comfort. Second Corinthians 1:5, with its references to Christ's sufferings being abundant "for us," and "our consolation" being abundant through Christ, makes best sense as a construal of the shared experience of Paul and the Corinthians.

In my view, this "inclusive" reading of the first person plural terms in 1:5 extends back into 1:4. There Paul directly connects the divine consolation in suffering experienced by Christ to that received by "us in all our affliction." We do not have the space here to discuss the thorny question of Paul's use of the first person plural in 2 Corinthians, but can pause to consider one version of the more commonly held view: that Paul here is referring only to himself or to a limited group of apostolic co-workers.[33]

Murray Harris argues that the verbs and pronouns of 2 Cor 1:4–7 "afford an instance of the sustained use of the epistolary plural."[34] He offers three arguments in support of this conclusion. First, that the con-

---

33. The most comprehensive recent treatment of this question is Berge, *Faiblesse*, 11–224.

34. Harris, *2 Corinthians*, 140. Note however that in n. 6 Harris immediately qualifies this conclusion by admitting that in 1:4 Paul "enunciates a Christian principle of universal application, derived from his reflection on his own particular experience."

tents of 1:4–7 are explained by reference to Paul's account of his affliction in Asia in 1:8–11. Second, and following on from this, 1:8–11 clearly is an account of Paul's specific experience, and thereby is by definition exclusive of the experience of others. Third, Paul is able to alternate between the singular and plural when describing the same events in 2:12–13 and 7:5–6.[35]

These arguments are far from convincing. Although 2 Cor 1:8–11 does refer to Paul's experience, there is no reason to conclude that this experience is the dominant explanatory factor for the choice and content of the *berakah* in 1:3–7. We have argued that the first note to be struck in Paul's blessing relates not to Paul's deliverance from affliction, but Christ's, thus establishing the christological ground for the participatory language of 1:5. We note that in 1:4 there is, as yet, no explicit contrast made between Paul and his audience.[36] The distinction between Paul and the Corinthians is not made until 1:6 where Paul speaks of the way that apostolic affliction and consolation is directed towards the consolation and salvation of the Corinthians in their suffering. But this is to claim that Paul, as apostle, mediates the consolation of Christ which is "abundant" and inclusive of the Corinthians in their suffering. Just as the ἡμῶν of 1:2–3 is clearly referring to Paul and the community of the church, I propose that we retain the inclusive sense for the pronouns in 1:4–5. The "liturgical" tone of the *berakah* form would suggest the incorporation of the Corinthians into the blessing that Paul offers. Secondly, even if Paul's use of the plural is "literary" in some sense, or exclusively "apostolic" (i.e., referring only to Paul and his "co-authors" or "co-workers") the communicative function of such language is "to associate the readers with the writer, or the listener with the speaker."[37] On either interpretation, Paul blesses God in such a way as to locate his own ministry, and the Corinthian community, within the more fundamental story of God's deliverance of his Messiah.

It is often noted that in doing this Paul establishes a "chain of consolation" that is usually understood to move from God (1:3) to Paul (1:4a) to the Corinthians (1:4b) who through Paul's ministry experience God's comfort (1:4c). The reading suggested above modifies this pattern.

---

35. Harris, *2 Corinthians*, 140.

36. See Furnish, *II Corinthians*, 110. The presence or absence of second-person verbs and nouns is a crucial factor in determining the nuance of Paul's use of the first-person plural. See Byrskog, "Co-Senders," 230–50, especially 232–33.

37. Thrall, *2 Corinthians 1–7*, 105.

Instead, we have consolation moving from the God and Father of our Lord Jesus Christ to Jesus himself, who in his death and resurrection experiences the deliverance from affliction that inaugurates the new creation (1:3). This eschatological consolation thus comes to Paul and the Corinthians (1:4a), equipping both apostle and community to offer it to others (1:4b). The purpose clause of 1:4b is general (παρακαλεῖν τοὺς ἐν πάσῃ θλίψει) and suggests a shared missional vocation to offer divine consolation to parties besides the speaker and the audience in the epistolary situation. Moreover, the letter reminds us elsewhere that just as Paul can offer that consolation to the Corinthians (see 1:6–7), so the Corinthians can be the source of consolation to Paul (see 1:11; 7:4, 12–13). Paul is not the sole mediator of God's consolation. This helps to explain why Paul uses the present participle in 1:4 (ὁ παρακαλῶν ἡμᾶς). He is not just referring to his own past experience, but to the ongoing experience of all who have received this divine comfort. Any equivalence between Paul's affliction and that of the Corinthians is grounded not in the precise nature of their experience, but in their common participation in Christ. As Tannehill puts it "continuing participation in Jesus" death is characteristic not only of the life of the apostle, but of the Christian life in general. . . . Their lives take on a structure corresponding to the *founding events of the new dominion*."[38]

The christological basis for the mutual suffering and consolation of both Paul and the Corinthians prompts us to consider the possibility that the afflictions of which Paul speaks are shared by apostle and congregation. In 2 Cor 1:6–7 Paul is explicit: the Corinthians experience divine consolation, mediated through Paul, at that point where they "in patience" undergo the *same suffering* as Paul.[39] Paul expresses this solidarity in suffering and consolation using the form κοινωνοί ἐστε. English translations almost invariably render this as a verbal construction: "you share in . . . " But the nominal form makes Paul's point clear: the Corinthians are "partners" in Paul's apostolic suffering and consolation. Partnership with Paul is the main focus of their solidarity with him in the sufferings and consolation that apostle and congregation experience together in and through Christ.[40] This leaves, as a final issue to be explored, the

---

38. Tannehill, *Dying and Rising*, 98. Emphasis mine.

39. The syntax of 1:6 is awkward, with multiple possible nuances. I read the participle τῆς ἐνεργουμένης as possibly passive, indicating that it is the "God of all consolation" who is at work in the apostle's ministry of consolation to the Corinthians.

40. Paul uses the same term to denote Titus as coworker in the task of the

question of the precise nature of this suffering solidarity. How can Paul speak about the Corinthians in such a way as to bind them to himself not just as *recipients* of apostolic affliction and comfort, but as *partners* in it?

The answer is twofold. First, as we have seen, there is solidarity in suffering by virtue of the common participation of Paul and the Corinthians in the suffering and vindication of Christ. Margaret Thrall helpfully points to Paul's statements in Rom 8:17-18 where suffering with Christ, here met by the hope of future glorification, is cast in general and inclusive terms.[41] The "sufferings of the present time" constitute the condition of a creation and a community anticipating final redemption (Rom 8:21-25). This, for Paul, is the ground of true hope (Rom 8:25; 2 Cor 1:7).[42]

But Romans 8 also hints at another point of solidarity in suffering. There Paul points to the conviction that the suffering of "the children of God" in some ways serves to secure the redemption of creation. Creation itself waits with expectation (ἀποκαραδοκία) for the revelation of God's children (Rom 8:19). This allows for the possibility that Paul is aligning his audiences with his own apostolic vocation in such a way as to include them within it. Suffering is a form of missional solidarity. The Corinthians, with Paul, are therefore called to "console those who are in any affliction" (2 Cor 1:4) with the consolation that they have received through Christ.

This pattern of solidarity may also be present in Paul's brief account of his experience in Asia in 1:8-11. In the light of the investigation above, this passage now stands not as the singular experience that generated the strong theology of the blessing period. It is instead Paul's account of an experience that illustrates the truth of what he has just been saying about the solidarity between Christ, the Corinthians, and himself. Paul's specific "affliction," the exact nature of which it is difficult to surmise, directs the apostle to the identity of God as the one who "raises the dead," a description that, while perhaps derived from Jewish liturgical traditions and so connected to the *berakah* of 1:3-7, finds its focal referent in Paul's convictions about the resurrection of Christ.[43] On this basis Paul is able

---

Collection in 2 Cor 8:23.

41. Thrall, *2 Corinthians 1-7*, 111.

42. The motif of suffering in Rom 8 is explored in detail in Wu, *Suffering in Romans*.

43. For an extensive discussion of the issues raised by Paul's narration of his experience in Asia see Harris, *2 Corinthians*, 164-82. The identification of God as the one "who raises the dead" is found in the second benediction of the *Amidah* in Jewish

both to discern the reality of divine rescue in the past, and to anticipate it for the future. Paul clearly did not die, but the reference to "many times on the point of death" (ἐν θανάτοις πολλάκις) in 2 Cor 11:23 leads us to think that Paul's affliction in Asia was the result of his work as an apostle, and thus a repeatable event as he contemplated his ongoing labor.

To this work the Corinthians are "joined" (συνυπουργέω 1:11) through prayer on Paul's behalf. The purpose clause that immediately follows in 1:11b is difficult to interpret. The implicit meaning is surely to invite the Corinthians to continue their support for Paul by means of their prayers, and the force of Paul's request "seeks to engage the readers immediately with Paul's own situation and to accentuate their need to be active participants in the partnership of suffering and comfort of which he has just written."[44]

Suffering and Solidarity Today

I have noted on several occasions that Paul's treatment of suffering in 2 Cor 1:3–11 lacks empirical detail. We can only guess at the exact circumstances that lie behind Paul's use of the language of "affliction" or "suffering," and scholars continue to debate what is being referred to by phrases such as "utterly, unbearably crushed," "despairing of life," or "sentence of death." Yet, as I have argued, the lack of precision may be partly the point, because Paul wants to place past, present, and future hardship into a theological framework that directs his readers back to the centrality of the Christ-event and forward to the hope of eschatological consummation.

This suggests strongly that Paul's attitude to suffering is more theological than it is therapeutic. Consolation for Paul is nothing less that the promise of God to vindicate those who suffer for the cause of righteousness; those who bear witness to the truth of God's presence in the world. The challenge is not to go searching for what will make us feel better in

---

daily prayer.

44. Furnish, *II Corinthians*, 125. The textual variants in relation to this verse are attempts to sort out the obvious grammatical ambiguity. We should avoid identifying the "many" from whom the thanksgiving comes ἐκ πολλῶν προσώπων ... εὐχαριστηθῇ too closely with the "many" through whom Paul has experienced the gift of divine deliverance. In other words, the Corinthians' prayers for Paul enable the apostolic ministry to continue and be extended to others who will then turn their faces to God in thanksgiving. For similar sentiments see Guthrie, *2 Corinthians*, 86.

the midst of affliction, but to see in that affliction the truth about the God "who raises the dead." It is in Christ that this truth is revealed, and it is through Christ that all Christian believers experience the hope to which Paul's words bear witness. The proper response to all of this is "blessing" and "thanksgiving" directed to God as the source of all comfort and mercy.

Of course, suffering and hardship are usually experienced unequally. Paul seems to have come close to death. The same could not be said of the Corinthians. But in their identification with Paul, and their partnership in his apostolic ministry, they come to share the "same suffering" and thus know the "same consolation." In considering the question of solidarity it is, therefore, worth pausing to ask the question: where is the apostolic witness to Christ's suffering and vindication most obviously displayed today? Where do we see the visible embodiment of the form of solidarity with Christ and Christ's body that Paul explores in the opening of 2 Corinthians and in the letter as a whole? How do we express our solidarity with those whose lives bear witness to the good news of "consolation in affliction"?

John Flett has written that "apostolicity is the community's participation in Jesus Christ's own history, a history of resurrection from the dead."[45] This participation in Christ's own history, so Paul suggests, makes possible a mutual solidarity in which Christian believers come to participate in one another's history and experience of suffering and hope. The God of all consolation, who raised Jesus from the dead, calls us to solidarity in suffering, in celebration and in anticipation of the comfort that is promised to us through Christ.

Bibliography

Beale, G. K. "The Old Testament Background of Reconciliation in 2 Corinthians 5–7 and Its Bearing on the Literary Problem of 2 Corinthians 6.14–7.1." *NTS* 35 (1989) 550–81.

Berge, Loïc P. M. *Faiblesse et force, présidence at collégialité chez Paul de Tarse: Recherche littéraire et théologique sue 2 Co 10–13 dans le contexte du genre épistolaire antique.* NovTSup 161. Leiden: Brill, 2015.

Bieringer, Reimund. "'Comfort, Comfort My People' (Isa 40,1): The Use of ΠΑΡΑΚΑΛΕΩ in the Septuagint Version of Isaiah." In *Florilegium Lovaniense: Studies in Septuagint and Textual Criticism in Honour of Florentino García*

---

45. Flett, *Apostolicity*, 335.

Martínez, edited by H. Ausloos, B. Lemmelijn, and M. Vervenne, 57–70. BEThL 224. Leuven: Peeters, 2008.

———. "The Comforted Comforter: The Meaning of παρακαλέω or παράκλησις Terminology in 2 Corinthians." *HTS* 67 (2011) Art. #969.

Bolton, David. "Paul and the Whip: A Sign of Inclusion or Exclusion?" In *Theologizing in the Corinthian Conflict: Studies in the Exegesis and Theology of 2 Corinthians*, edited by Reimund Bieringer, Marilou S. Ibita, Dominika A. Kurek-Chomycz, and Thomas Vollmer, 363–77. BTS 16. Leuven: Peeters, 2013.

Byrskog, Samuel. "Co-Senders, Co-Authors and Paul's Use of the First Person Plural." *ZNW* 87 (1996) 230–50.

Campbell, Douglas A. "The Story of Jesus in Romans and Galatians." In *Narrative Dynamics in Paul: A Critical Assessment*, edited by Bruce W. Longenecker, 97–124. Louisville: Westminster John Knox, 2002.

Fitzgerald, John T. *Cracks in an Earthen Vessel: An Examination of the Catalogues of Hardships in the Corinthian Correspondence*. SBLDS 99. Atlanta: Scholars, 1988.

Flett, John G. *Apostolicity: The Ecumenical Question in World Christian Perspective*. Downers Grove, IL: IVP Academic, 2016.

Furnish, Victor Paul. *II Corinthians: A New Translation with Introduction and Commentary*. AB 32A. New York: Doubleday, 1984.

Gignilliat, Mark S. *Paul and Isaiah's Servants: Paul's Theological Reading of Isaiah 40–66 in 2 Corinthians 5:14–6:10*. LNTS 330. London: T & T Clark, 2007.

Guthrie, George H. *2 Corinthians*. BECNT. Grand Rapids: Baker Academic, 2015.

Harris, Murray J. *The Second Epistle to the Corinthians*. NIGTC. Grand Rapids: Eerdmans, 2005.

Hofius, Otfried. "'Der Gott allen Trostes': παράκλησις und παρακαλεῖν in 2Kor 1,3–7." In *Paulusstudien*, 244–54. WUNT 51. Tübingen: J. C. B. Mohr (Paul Siebeck), 1989.

Holloway, Paul A. *Consolation in Philippians: Philosophical Resources and Rhetorical Strategy*. SNTSMS 112. Cambridge: Cambridge University Press, 2001.

Kleinknecht, Karl Theodor. *Der leidende Gerechtfertige: Die alttestamentlich-jüdische Tradition vom 'leidenden Gerechten' und ihre Rezeption bei Paulus*. WUNT 2.13. Tübingen: J. C. B. Mohr (Paul Siebeck), 1984.

Lim, Kar Yong. *"The Sufferings of Christ Are Abundant in Us": A Narrative Dynamics Investigation of Paul's Sufferings in 2 Corinthians*. LNTS 399. London: T & T Clark International, 2009.

Pietersma, Albert, and Benjamin G. Wright, eds. *A New English Translation of the Septuagint*. Oxford: Oxford University Press, 2007.

Schmeller, Thomas. "No Bridge Over Troubled Water?: The Gap Between 2 Cor 1–9 and 10–13 Revisisted." *JSNT* 36 (2013) 73–84.

Strack, Herman Leberecht, and Paul Billerbeck. *Kommentar zum Neuen Testament aus Talmud und Midrash*. Vol. 2. Munich: Beck, 1922–1928.

Tannehill, Robert C. *Dying and Rising with Christ: A Study in Pauline Theology*. BZNW 32. Berlin: Töpelmann, 1966.

Thrall, Margaret E. *The Second Epistle to the Corinthians*. Vol. 1, *Introduction and Commentary on II Corinthians I–VII*. ICC. Edinburgh: T & T Clark, 1994.

Vegge, Ivar. *2 Corinthians—A Letter About Reconciliation: A Psychagogical, Epistolographical and Rhetorical Analysis*. WUNT 2.239. Tübingen: Mohr Siebeck, 2008.

Wagner, J. Ross. *Heralds of the Good News: Isaiah and Paul "in Concert" in the Letter to the Romans*. Leiden: Brill Academic, 2003.

Wallace, James Buchanan. *Snatched Into Paradise (2 Cor 12:1–10): Paul's Heavenly Journey in the Context of Early Christian Experience*. BZNW 179. Berlin: Walter de Gruyter, 2011.

Webb, William J. *Returning Home: New Covenant and Second Exodus as the Context for 2 Corinthians 6.14–7.1*. JSNTSup 85. Sheffield: JSOT, 1993.

Welborn, L. L. *An End to Enmity: Paul and the "Wrongdoer" of Second Corinthians*. BZNW 185. Berlin: De Gruyter, 2011.

Windisch, Hans. *Der zweite Korintherbrief.* 9th ed., KEK. Göttingen: Vandenhoeck & Ruprecht, 1924.

Wu, Siu Fung. *Suffering in Romans*. Eugene, OR: Pickwick, 2015.

6

Participating in Christ's Suffering and Being Conformed to the Image of the Son

Siu Fung Wu

Introduction[1]

IN A DENSE STATEMENT containing three σύν-compounds, in Rom 8:17 Paul speaks of co-heirship, co-suffering, and co-glorification with Christ. What is the relationship between suffering and glory here? And what does the σύν prefix signify? Constantine Campbell thinks that the words συμπάσχομεν and συνδοξασθῶμεν signify a "dynamic participation in the events of Christ's experience."[2] According to Michael Gorman, suffering and glory are inseparable in Paul, and the grammar of the statement in Rom 8:17 "clearly conveys Paul's conviction that suffering is the necessary condition for glory."[3] Campbell and Gorman alert us to the fact that Paul sees suffering with Christ as participation in him, and that suffering and glory are interconnected.

---

1. I am grateful to Professor Michael Gorman and Professor Timothy Gombis for reading an early version of this essay and giving me their valuable comments. I have incorporated many of their suggestions into this essay, but of course I alone am responsible for the flaws.

2. Campbell, *Paul and Union*, 231. Campbell says that the συγκληρονόμοι indicates a "stative union with Christ."

3. Gorman, *Cruciformity*, 326. Here I want to acknowledge the inspiration given by Professor Gorman through his writings on cruciformity and theosis. I will not be surprised if traces of his influence find their way into this essay.

Given that the overall objectives of their studies lie elsewhere, Campbell's and Gorman's discussions are quite brief.[4] In this chapter, I will expand on their studies and propose that participating in Christ's suffering is an essential and integral part of the lives of Christ-followers, both individually and corporately. Additionally, I want to suggest that, for Paul, suffering is ultimately about sharing in Christ's suffering and being conformed to his image. Indeed, sharing in the cross-shaped affliction of Christ is the Christ-community's vocation and an integral part of participating in his glory.[5] The discussion below will focus on selected passages in Philippians, 2 Corinthians, and Romans that refer to both suffering and participation in Christ, particularly when Paul uses the language of conformity and transformation.

Philippians: Sharing in Christ's Cross-Shaped Pattern of Suffering

Suffering is an important theme in Philippians.[6] As we will find, Paul sees sharing in Christ's suffering and conformity to his death as an essential part of his present existence—and that of the Philippians. At the same time, he anticipates his own and the Philippians' sharing of Christ's glory at the future transformation of their bodies.

Phil 1:12–30

As will become clear, Phil 1:12–30 introduces several key themes that are pertinent to our study, not least the connection between suffering and participation in Christ. Paul refers to his chains (δεσμοῖς) four times in Phil 1:7, 13, 14, 17. In 1:15–18a he mentions his opponents, who proclaim Christ from envy, rivalry, and selfish ambition. But nonetheless he

---

4. The discussion on Rom 8:17 by Davey, "Sight," 97–98, is surprisingly brief, given the fact that the subject matter of the author's dissertation is on "suffering as participation with Christ." Having said that, I want to say that Davey's work does offer many valuable insights into the topic. I highly recommend it.

5. I note the valuable contributions of Blackwell, *Christosis*, 143–73, 179–96; Gorman, *Inhabiting*, 9–104; Gorman, *Becoming*, 279–86; Campbell, *Paul and Union*; Davey, "Sight," 93–98; 104–7; 150–58; Jervis, *At the Heart*, 97–116, to this topic. I hope this chapter is able to offer a fresh perspective on the matter.

6. For helpful discussions on suffering in Philippians, see Jervis, *At the Heart*, 42–63; Oakes, *Philippians*, 77–99.

rejoices, for he knows that through the prayers of the Philippians and the help of the Spirit even his suffering and imprisonment will turn out to be for his σωτηρία (1:18–19). Paul expresses his eager expectation that he will not be put to shame, but that Christ will be exalted in his body, *whether by life or death* (1:20). His reasoning is that, for him, living is Christ, and dying is gain (1:21). By implication, the same is true of the Philippians, who share in his suffering for Christ (1:29–30). Several comments are in order.

First, the suffering of Paul and of the Philippians is an important driving force behind 1:12–30. No matter what form of imprisonment Paul was experiencing at the time, it would have been socioeconomically degrading and emotionally depressing to be in a Roman prison, which was infamous for its abject condition.[7] There was also a danger of impending death, as 1:22–26 indicates. Combining this with the trials caused by his opponents (1:15–18a), Paul's hardship would have been severe. His suffering and possible death almost certainly lie behind the difficult choice between life and death in the passage. Furthermore, Paul's determination to live was for the sake of the Philippians (1:23–26, 30), who were likewise graciously granted to suffer for Christ (1:29). Although it is hard to determine with precision what suffering the Philippians faced, a combination of religious oppression, social isolation, and economic hardship as a consequence of their allegiance to Christ is likely.[8]

Second, for Paul, his whole existence, including suffering, has everything to do with Christ. In 1:20b–21 Paul states his desire for Christ to be magnified in his body, whether by life or by death, and that, for him, living is Christ and dying is gain.[9] Quite clearly Paul has determined that his suffering, even to the point of death, is for the sake of Christ. For Paul, his imprisonment means that the gospel, the message about Christ, is made known through his suffering (1:12–13). Also, he reckons that his trials benefit the Philippians, as they are encouraged to conduct their lives worthy of the gospel in their own suffering (1:24–30). Alternatively, if he does die, which is in itself a form of suffering, Paul wants God to be

---

7. As Fowl says, "Being in chains was dangerous and degrading, in which one became utterly dependent and easily victimized, in which control over one's future was taken out of one's own hands." Fowl, *Philippians*, 10. See also Cassidy, *Paul in Chains*, 36–54; and Wansink, *Chained in Christ*, 27–95.

8. See the helpful reconstruction by Oakes, *Philippians*, 89–96.

9. Unfortunately, space does not allow a discussion of the different interpretive options here.

exalted nonetheless (1:20). All of these aspects of Paul's life are for the sake of Christ and the gospel concerning him.

Third, Paul believes that the Philippians are to suffer *for* Christ. A more literal translation of 1:29 can be "for to you has been graciously given on behalf of Christ not only to believe in him but also to suffer for him."[10] The christocentric construction "ὑπὲρ Χριστοῦ ... εἰς αὐτὸν ... ὑπὲρ αὐτοῦ" should be noted.[11] Paul seems to be saying that, as far as the Philippians' lives are concerned, everything is for Christ, not least the opportunity to suffer for him, or, as a representative of him.

Fourth, Paul and the Philippians suffer in partnership. This is made clear by the τὸν αὐτὸν ἀγῶνα ἔχοντες (having the same struggle) in 1:30. Moreover, the σύν-compound συναθλέω in the phrase μιᾷ ψυχῇ συναθλοῦντες (striving side-by-side with one mind; NRSV) in 1:27 further indicates the partnership in their struggles, especially in the face of the opponents mentioned in 1:28.

In light of the preceding observations, suffering can be seen as a shared experience between Paul and his audience. Suffering is where their life stories intersect. And suffering is for the sake of, and on behalf of, Christ. Indeed, it seems that Paul sees suffering as participation in Christ, for the whole existence of the believing community (as individuals and corporately) has everything to do with Christ's death and life.

Phil 2:5-11

The Christ-hymn in Philippians is one of the most important passages concerning the identity of Christ.[12] But my focus here is to highlight how Phil 2:5-11 paves the way for our later discussion on participation in Christ's suffering and cruciform death.

The word μορφή in 2:6 most likely refers to the form and character of God. Hence the ἐν μορφῇ θεοῦ refers to the fact that Christ is characterized by the qualities essential to being God.[13] But despite that—and perhaps also because of that—Christ emptied himself and took on the μορφή of a slave (2:7a).[14] This means that he took on the shape and the

---

10. My translation.
11. Fee, *Philippians*, 171; Hellerman, *Philippians*, 85.
12. The amount of study devoted to this passage is voluminous.
13. Fee, *Philippians*, 205; and Witherington, *Philippians*, 140.
14. The standard translation, "though he was in the form of God," is Phil 2:6 and

features that were essential to the reality of being a slave. Then 2:7b says that Christ was born in human likeness, being found in human form. There are debates about the exact meanings of the words ὁμοίωμα and σχῆμα here. But I find Susan Eastman's article helpful.[15] The term ὁμοίωμα denotes "likeness" and hence not sameness. The word σχῆμα can be translated as "form," but with special reference to outward appearance. But Eastman alerts us to the occurrences of these terms in Greek and Roman philosophical discussion, theatres, and public performance, where σχῆμα and ὁμοιόω are used to describe mimetic impersonation.[16] For example, Plato speaks of "mimetic assimilation" as a way of "becoming as much *like* God as possible."[17] It is thought that mimetic representation has the power to "transform its practitioners."[18] Also, "Plutarch advised politicians to order both their public and private lives well," because outward appearance, including their attire and demeanor, was all-important.[19] Whether or not one agrees with the entirety of Eastman's interpretation, the following statement below deserves attention:

> Thus, taken together, ὁμοίωμα and σχῆμα emphasize both the perceptible and the participatory aspects of Christ's downward movement into the condition of human enslavement, humiliation, and death.[20]

It is important to note that Christ's human enslavement culminates in his death, specifically in crucifixion (2:7–8). The cross, of course, was a symbol of shame, defeat, and humiliation. Crucifixion involved excruciating physical pain, and was a publically degrading punishment for the politically inferior subjects of the Roman Empire. Therefore, the end point of the movement in the Christ-hymn is not Christ's participation in humanity, but his participation in a humiliating and extreme form of

---

can also been translated as "because he was in the form of God." See the discussion in Gorman, *Inhabiting*, 22–25. Gorman comments, "It is not just *although* Christ, Paul, and all believers possess a certain identity . . . that their story has a certain shape. . . . It is also *because* they possess that identity." (p. 25)

15. Eastman, "Philippians 2:6–11," 1–22.

16. Eastman, "Philippians 2:6–11," 12.

17. Eastman, "Philippians 2:6–11," 12–13 (emphasis original). Here Eastman refers to *Phaedrus* 253A–B.

18. Eastman, "Philippians 2:6–11," 13.

19. Eastman, "Philippians 2:6–11," 9.

20. Eastman, "Philippians 2:6–11," 15.

human suffering, namely, death on the cross. The exaltation of Christ and his lordship in 2:9–11 hinges on this.[21]

It should also be pointed out that the immediate context of the Christ-hymn (Phil 2:1–5) indicates that Paul uses it to exhort his audience to foster a communal mindset and lifestyle that is modeled after Christ,[22] which includes humility and thus the possibility of suffering and even death. Therefore, we may say that the hymn serves to call the Philippians to be, in Gorman's words, "Christ-like, which is to be Godlike, which is to be kenotic and cruciform."[23] As we will see, the Christ-hymn, especially Christ's cross-shaped suffering, provides crucial interpretative clues for our discussion on Phil 3:10–11, 21.[24]

Phil 3:10–11, 21

In Phil 3:8 Paul says that he considers all things as loss because of the surpassing value of knowing Christ Jesus his Lord (κύριος). The one whom God exalted to the highest place to be Lord (κύριος), according to the Christ-hymn (2:11), is the one Paul wants to know. This desire to know Christ appears again in 3:10–11, which can be read via the following chiastic structure:

τοῦ γνῶναι αὐτὸν

καὶ

  A τὴν δύναμιν τῆς ἀναστάσεως αὐτοῦ

      B καὶ [τὴν] κοινωνίαν [τῶν] παθημάτων αὐτοῦ[25]

      B' συμμορφιζόμενος τῷ θανάτῳ αὐτοῦ

  A' εἴ πως καταντήσω εἰς τὴν ἐξανάστασιν τὴν ἐκ νεκρῶν[26]

21. I should mention that Christ does not cease to be God in such movement. As Hill rightly puts it, "Jesus' sharing the form of God and being equal with God is expressed in his self-emptying—his taking the form of a servant and being found in the likeness of humans." Hill, *Paul and the Trinity*, 91.

22. Gorman, "New Translation," 104–21, provides an excellent discussion on this.

23. Gorman, *Inhabiting*, 39.

24. For a recent discussion on the crucial role of the Christ-hymn in the whole letter, not least the relationship between suffering and participation in Christ, see Davey, "Sight," 140–45.

25. The τὴν and the τῶν are most likely not in the original. See Fee, *Philippians*, 311 n. 2; cf. Hellerman, *Philippians*, 189–90.

26. This chiastic structure follows closely the one in Fee, *Philippians*, 329. See also Thompson and Longenecker, *Philippians and Philemon*, 110; Flemming, *Philippians*, 174.

Along with others, I take the first καί as epexegetical,[27] in the sense that the "participating in his suffering" and the "being conformed to his death" (lines B–B'), in addition to the resurrection (lines A–A'), serve to explain what Paul wants to know regarding Christ. The κοινωνία here denotes sharing in common, or better still, participating in Christ's sufferings.[28] The συμμορφιζόμενος modifies the subject τοῦ γνῶναι,[29] and it should probably be taken in a passive sense ("being conformed"), rather than middle ("taking the form of").[30] Here, the intertextual links to the μορφή in 2:6–7 should be noted. Christ, who was in the form of God, emptied himself, took on the form of a slave and died a cruciform death. Paul reckons that, in order to know Christ, he must be conformed to the same cruciform pattern. This does not necessarily mean that Paul has martyrdom in mind, although, of course, suffering for the gospel may well include that.[31]

As is often noted by scholars, suffering and the power of the resurrection are two sides of the same coin—they coexist, paradoxically.[32] For Paul, knowing the power of Christ's resurrection cannot be separated from participating in Christ's sufferings and conformity to his death.[33] This is likened to the pattern of Christ in 2:6–11, where Christ's suffering

---

27. Hellerman, *Philippians*, 189; Fee, *Philippians*, 328; O'Brien, *Philippians*, 402; Flemming, *Philippians*, 173–4.

28. Commentators often see the parallel to the κοινωνοί ἐστε τῶν παθημάτων in 2 Cor 1:7. For example, Fee, *Philippians*, 331; Hellerman, *Philippians*, 191.

29. Varner, *Philippians*, 78.

30. Varner, *Philippians*, 78. Fee, *Philippians*, 333–34; Hellerman, *Philippians*, 191. But see also Bockmuehl, *Philippians*, 215–17. Note that the συμμορφίζω appears only here in the NT, and is not attested before Paul (See Bockmuehl, *Philippians*, 216). I will discuss the uses of the cognate σύμμορφος in Phil 3:21 and Rom 8:29 later.

31. But see the discussion in Witherington, *Philippians*, 206.

32. Fee, *Philippians*, 314; Flemming, *Philippians*, 174; Cohick, *Philippians*, 172. As Hellerman says, "The two concepts (δύναμιν τῆς ἀναστάσεως αὐτοῦ and κοινωνίαν παθημάτων αὐτοῦ)—now governed by a single art. [i.e., article] and joined by καί—are to be taken closely together, as alternate aspects of the same experience." Hellerman, *Philippians*, 189–90.

33. The σύν prefix in συμμορφίζω probably serves to reinforce Paul's emphasis of participating in Christ in Phil 3:10—that is, it denotes "being conformed *with* Christ." The comment by Flemming is helpful: "Knowing Christ intensely involves a profound identification with the Christ who suffered—a sharing of his very life and experience. There is a close parallel to this thought in 1 Peter 4:13." ("But rejoice insofar as you are sharing Christ's sufferings, so that you may also be glad and shout for joy when his glory is revealed" [1 Pet 4:13; NRSV].) Flemming, *Philippians*, 175.

and cruciform death are intrinsically linked to his exaltation. And this, in turn, is the pattern that Paul wants to follow. In other words, the pattern of Paul's suffering takes on the form and essential characteristics of Christ's humiliating death at the cross.

In Phil 3:21 Paul says that Christ "will transform (μετασχηματίσει) the body of our humiliation" so that it may "be conformed (σύμμορφον) to the body of his glory." The apostle is speaking of the eschatological transformation of the body at the resurrection (see 1 Cor 15:35–58), where the body of the believer will be transformed into a form that is in conformity with that of Christ's body of glory. That is, the appearance and the form of the body will be changed from one of humiliation to one of glory, in accordance with the glory of Christ. The words μετασχηματίζω, ταπείνωσις, σύμμορφος, and δόξα here echo the language in the Christ-hymn (σχῆμα, ταπεινόω, μορφή, and δόξα; 2:6–8, 11). Here we may say that it is the pattern of Christ—the movement from humiliation, suffering, death, to exaltation and the glory of God—that both provides the pattern for believers' life and gives them hope. Their present body (σῶμα) of humiliation will be transformed to a body of glory.

In summary, in Philippians we find that, for Paul, suffering is thoroughly about participating in the suffering of Christ, and it is a shared experience between the apostle and the Philippians.[34] This experience is patterned after the cruciform suffering of Christ, and it will eventually result in the transformation of the body into one that shares in Christ's glory.[35] But does it mean that Paul sees no glory in the present suffering of believers? Unlikely, as the discussion below will show.[36]

Second Corinthians:
Being Transformed into God's Image Through Suffering

As in Philippians, suffering is an important theme in 2 Corinthians. Our interest lies in the texts that refer to the relationship between suffering

---

34. Cf. Davey, "Sight," 157–58.

35. It should be noted that, while the focus of Phil 3:21 is the *future* bodily resurrection, apparently Paul thinks that he can experience the power of resurrection *here and now*, according to 3:10a (τοῦ γνῶναι αὐτὸν καὶ τὴν δύναμιν τῆς ἀναστάσεως αὐτοῦ).

36. I tend to agree with Haley Goranson Jacob's study on Philippians in this volume ("Suffering and Glory in Philippians"), where she argues for the paradoxical co-existence of suffering and glory in the present life of believers.

and participation in Christ, namely 3:18 and 4:10, 11–12. As we will see, Paul understands his suffering as a visible manifestation of God's glory, and it is by participating in Christ's cross-shaped suffering that one is transformed into Christ's image.

2 Cor 3:18

The notion of transformation into the image of Christ in 2 Cor 3:18 is important for our study because it lays the foundation for 4:10–12, which, in turn, concerns suffering and participation in Christ's death and life. There are, however, many exegetical issues to deal with concerning 3:18, and the debates are endless. Space only allows a brief outline of my own reading of the text, which will take the form of responses to a series of questions.

First, what do the four occurrences of κύριος stand for in 3:17–18? Do they refer to God, Christ, or the Spirit? The first κύριος in 3:17 is the Spirit, as Paul states.[37] Given the (almost certain) allusion to Exod 34:34 in 2 Cor 3:16 and the LXX's frequent use of πνεῦμα κυρίου for the Spirit of YHWH, it is most likely that the second κύριος in 3:17 refers to YHWH.[38] With this, I understand the next κύριος (the first in 3:18) as a reference to YHWH as well, or "God," in Paul's language.[39] This is especially the case given the fact that in Exodus Moses was in the presence of YHWH when he beheld his glory. The last κύριος (the second in 3:18), on the other hand, is a reference to the Spirit (hence πνεύματος is a genitive of apposition), which harks back to the usage of the first κύριος in 3:17.[40] Of course my view here is subject to critique, but it seems to fit well with Moses' experience in the presence of YHWH in Exod 34:34.[41] This will assist our interpretation of 2 Cor 3:18 below.

---

37. Fee, *God's Empowering Presence*, 311; Guthrie, *2 Corinthians*, 225. Note especially the extended discussion of Thrall, *Corinthians*, 274, 278–81.

38. Fee, *Presence*, 312; Thrall, *2 Corinthians*, 274.

39. See the detailed discussion by Thrall, *2 Corinthians*, 282–83. Cf., Fee, *God's Empowering Presence*, 317; Guthrie, *2 Corinthians*, 227.

40. See Fee, *God's Empowering Presence*, 318–19; Guthrie, *2 Corinthians*, 229; Long, *II Corinthians*, 74.

41. Of course, we should not be too rigid about the identifications of the κύριος here. Given the fact that elsewhere Paul says that the Spirit is the "Spirit of God" (Rom 8:14) and the "Spirit of Christ" (Rom 8:9; Cf. John 20:22; Acts 16:18).

Second, how does the mirror imagery (indicated by the κατοπτριζόμενοι) work? The complexity of the matter is well summarized by Ben Blackwell's lucid study, *Christosis*, and I will not go into detail here.[42] My view is that in 3:18 Paul refers to the beholding of God's glory by believers (Paul, his co-workers, and the Corinthians).[43] Just as Moses beheld YHWH's presence with unveiled face, believers behold the glory of God through the Spirit's transforming power under the new covenant (see 3:1–16).[44] I do not, however, believe the metaphor should be pushed so far as to identify each metaphorical detail. But Blackwell's remarks here are worth noting.

> As believers encounter God with unveiled faces, directly like Moses, they serve as the mirrors that reflect the glory of the Lord. In distinction to Moses' illuminated face, Paul's emphasis is now upon changed hearts and lives that embody Christ.[45]

Blackwell's point about the embodiment of Christ in the changed hearts and lives of believers is important, and I will return to that later.

Third, how do we understand the terms εἰκών and δόξα in 3:18? The reference to Christ as the image of God in 4:4 indicates that in 3:18 Paul is saying that believers, by beholding God's glory with unveiled faces, are being transformed into "the same image" (τὴν αὐτὴν εἰκόνα) of God that Christ bears.[46] It is probable that Paul has in mind Gen 1:26–27 in referring to the image of God, and hence the glory refers to the image-bearer's reflection of God's glory.[47] But we must also note that the immediate context of 2 Cor 3:18 does not refer to Genesis. Rather, the presence of YHWH in Exod 34:29–35 and the new covenant (hence Jer 31:31–34 and Ezek 36:25–27) are in view in 3:1–18. In light of that, the glory in 2 Cor 3:18 is also likely to be the return of the presence of YHWH under the

---

42. Blackwell, *Christosis*, 181–93.

43. Note the "all" in ἡμεῖς δὲ πάντες in 3:18 here.

44. The Spirit's work in the Hebrew Bible is often characterized by the presence of YHWH. Note that here I use the word "behold" instead of "reflect," in agreement with Fee, *God's Empowering Presence*, 317; Thrall, *2 Corinthians*, 282, 292. The verb κατοπτρίζω can denote beholding as in a mirror or reflecting like a mirror.

45. Blackwell, *Christosis*, 187–88.

46. The chiastic structure suggested by Long, *II Corinthians*, 76, puts τὴν αὐτὴν εἰκόνα in the middle, which, in turn, indicates the importance of the "image" in 2 Cor 3:18.

47. This is supported by the reference to Christ being God's image and the allusion to Gen 1:3 in 2 Cor 4:4, 6.

new covenant when a renewal of hearts takes place.⁴⁸ Having said that, we must note that scholars have found in Genesis 1 a picture of creation that is likened to a cosmic temple, where humans, as image-bearers of God, are his vice-regents.⁴⁹ Moreover, the εἰκών of the emperor was often found on Roman coins and temple statues. And the emperor was, according to Roman propaganda, understood as an agent of the gods, for he brought victory and peace to the Empire. I think it is important to take into account all of these backgrounds when interpreting 2 Cor 3:18. For believers to display the image of Christ, they are to be God's human representatives (vice-regents), showing the world what God is like through the life-giving Spirit. At the same time, their Spirit-transformed hearts and life pattern are an embodied manifestation of God's glory and presence under the new covenant.⁵⁰

Fourth, what kind of transformation does the μεταμορφούμεθα refer to? Several observations can be made here. To start with, clearly this transformation is empowered by the life-giving Spirit. Also, the transformation takes place when believers behold the glory of God under the new covenant. This is precisely the goal of the freedom (ἐλευθερία) that 3:17 refers to. The veil has been removed so that believers are free to behold God's glory and be transformed.⁵¹ In addition, the μεταμορφόω indicates a change of μορφή, that is, a change of form, quality, and reality. If the above analysis of the Christ-hymn is any guide, the transformation in 2 Cor 3:18 refers to a pattern of change modeled after Christ's humiliation and cruciform death. (Our study of 2 Cor 4:10–12 below will support this.) Furthermore, the transformation is about being changed into the same image of God that Christ bears (4:4). Just as Christ bears God's

---

48. For a discussion of the background of glory in the New Testament, see Macaskill, *Union*, 110–14.

49. See Wu, *Suffering in Romans*, 170–73; Middleton, *Liberating Image*, 58–60; Watts, "New Exodus," 21; Walton, *Genesis 1*, 192; Beale, *Temple*, 81; Levenson, "Temple and the World," 297.

50. I should mention the helpful argument by Kilner, *Dignity and Destiny*, especially 174–76, 312, that it is problematic to say that the image of God was damaged as a result of Adam's disobedience in Genesis 3. The Scripture does not explicitly say that the image of God was damaged. Rather, it is better to speak of the "renewal, conformation, and transformation of humanity into God's image" (p. 252). Although I do not always fully agree with Kilner's interpretation of the Pauline texts, I value his insistence on humanity dignity, which, of course, has huge implications for today, not least when we seek to walk with the poor and marginalized, as well as those living with mental illnesses and disabilities.

51. Fee, *God's Empowering Presence*, 313–14.

image and displays his glory, believers are empowered by the Spirit to exhibit God's glory through transformed hearts under the new covenant (2 Cor 3:6; Jer 31:33; Ezek 36:26–27). This brings us to the meaning of the phrase ἀπὸ δόξης εἰς δόξαν. On one level, this phrase denotes a progressive transformation so that believers become more God-like.[52] On another level, it is by beholding the δόξα of God through the Spirit that believers may bear God's image and display his glory.[53]

If my interpretation above is close to the mark, then the transformation into the image of God in 2 Cor 3:18 is about the believers' display of his glory in their transformed hearts and lives under the new covenant, which is empowered by the life-giving Spirit.[54] This understanding will aid our analysis of 2 Cor 4:10–12, which is a passage about Paul's view of participating in Christ's death in suffering. To this passage we now turn.

2 Cor 4:10, 11–12

Immediately after mentioning the Spirit-empowered transformation, Paul refers in 4:1 to his ministry (διακονία), which is a ministry of the πνεῦμα and of the δικαιοσύνη (3:8, 9), for he is a minister (διάκονος) of the new covenant (3:6). In 4:5 Paul says that he does not proclaim himself. Instead, he proclaims Jesus Christ as Lord and himself as the Corinthians' slaves for the sake of Jesus (διὰ Ἰησοῦν). Again, using the Christ-hymn as our guide, then, the lordship of Christ is understandably the center of Paul's proclamation (see Phil 2:11). Also, it can explain Paul's reference to δοῦλος in 2 Cor 4:5. It seems that the apostle is modeling his ministry after Christ's taking on of the form of a slave (Phil 2:7). Paul's christocentric thinking is further reinforced by his remarks in 2 Cor 4:4, 6. The allusion to Gen 1:3, the glory of God in the face of Christ (ἐν προσώπῳ Χριστοῦ), the notion of light shining in the hearts in 2 Cor 4:6, as well as Christ being the image of God in 2 Cor 4:4, may all be understood as intertextual and thematic links to 2 Cor 3:18 and its intertexts. (Note the πρόσωπον, the allusion to Gen 1:26–27, and the notion of beholding God's glory in 2 Cor 3:18.) This signifies the fact that Paul sees

---

52. Cf. Thrall, *2 Corinthians*, 286.

53. For the different options for interpretation, see Thrall, *2 Corinthians*, 285–88; Blackwell, *Christosis*, 189–90; Guthrie, *2 Corinthians*, 229.

54. In his work concerning the role of the Spirit in 2 Cor 3:18, Rabens concludes that when believers are transformed into the same image of Christ, "their lives portray more of the characteristics of Christ." Rabens, *Holy Spirit*, 202–3.

his ministry as based on God's revelation of the knowledge of his glory displayed by Jesus, who is God's image. The outworking of this ministry is the transformation of believers.

Then in 2 Cor 4:7–9 Paul speaks of the extraordinary power of God that manifests itself in his afflictions, which leads to the statement in 4:10.[55]

> Always carrying the death of Jesus in the body, so that the life of Jesus may also be made visible (φανερωθῇ) in our body.[56]

It seems, then, that Paul believes that he is participating in Christ's death when he suffers from bodily afflictions.[57] As he participates in Christ's death, God works powerfully in his afflictions, and in that process Paul also participates, paradoxically, in the life of Christ. This, in turn, means that the life of Christ is made visible in his body, despite the suffering he experiences.

In 4:11–12 Paul elaborates on what he has just said.[58]

> For we who are alive are always given over to death for the sake of Jesus, so that the life of Jesus may also be made visible (φανερωθῇ) in our mortal flesh. So then, death is at work in us, but life in you.[59]

Verse 11 repeats and adds new elements to the themes in 4:10. Paul says that he is handed over to death for Jesus' sake. The παραδίδωμι appears in Rom 4:25, Rom 8:32, and Gal 2:20. Twice in Romans the term refers to Jesus' being handed over (by God) for *believers* and for *their* trespasses, and Gal 2:20 says that *Christ* handed over himself for *Paul*. In these cases, Christ suffered death for humans. But in 2 Cor 4:11 it is *Paul* who is handed over for the sake of *Christ*. As he suffers, he *participates in Christ's death*. And as in 4:10, Paul's suffering in the mortal body

---

55. Although the δέ in 4:7 indicates a new development in the argument of the letter, the section 4:7—5:10 does flow from the previous section. See, e.g., the discussions in Matera, *II Corinthians*, 105; Guthrie, *2 Corinthians*, 249.

56. My translation.

57. There is no need, in interpreting the death of Christ in 4:10, to make a sharp distinction between the "process of dying" of Christ (e.g., Long, *II Corinthians*, 83) and the state of his death. (See the discussion in, for example, Guthrie, *2 Corinthians*, 259–60.) By Christ's death here I refer to the suffering of Christ that took place in the process leading to his death on the cross.

58. Note the γάρ in 4:11.

59. My translation.

makes visible the life of Christ.⁶⁰ In this way, he *participates in the life of Christ*, with *his afflictions* providing the opportunity to do so.⁶¹ Then in verse 12 Paul brings a new dimension to the purpose of his suffering: his participation in Christ's death is at work so that life may be at work in the Corinthians, which is a logic already found in 1:3–7.⁶² For Paul, his Spirit-empowered new-covenant ministry involves participation in Christ's death and life, which, in turn, brings life to the Corinthians (see also 4:14).

Therefore, Paul sees suffering as the visible manifestation of God's glory. This may sound counterintuitive, but it is not surprising. The cruciform death of Christ happened before his exaltation. Since participation in Christ is central to Paul, the Spirit-empowered new-covenant ministry that brings about transformation into God's image must involve cruciform suffering—which is accomplished by beholding God's glory and displaying his image as his vice-regents. Through this, God's glory is made known in Paul's afflictions, which, in turn, are for the benefit of the Corinthians. If Christ suffered and died for the believers, so Paul suffers for the Corinthians. In all this, the life of Christ—and hence, the glory of God—is manifest.

Romans: Participating in Christ's Suffering and Being Conformed to His Image

When it comes to understanding Paul's thought and theology, Romans is arguably the most important book in the Pauline corpus. And it does not disappoint when we come to the topic of suffering and participation in Christ. Our focus here will be on Rom 8:17, 29, and 12:2. I have discussed 8:17 and 8:29 in detail in my book, *Suffering in Romans*. Here I will highlight my findings, as well as add new arguments that are particularly relevant to the present discussion.

A few comments on Romans 5–8 are needed to set the stage for interpreting 8:17 and 8:29. First, the most important texts concerning suffering in Romans, namely, 5:3–5 and 8:17–39, are found in Romans 5–8. Second, as is often recognized, God has created a new humanity in Christ

---

60. Note that the φανερωθῇ appears in both 4:10 and 4:11.

61. Cf. Matera, *II Corinthians*, 110–12.

62. As Collins says, "Paul experiences his hardships so that the Corinthians might live." Collins, *Second Corinthians*, 102.

out of Adamic humanity, according to 5:12–21.⁶³ Third, the prominent themes of Adam and creation in 5:12–21 and 8:18–23 suggest that Genesis 1–3 is an important background for reading Romans 5–8.⁶⁴ Fourth, my analysis in *Suffering in Romans* shows that Rom 5:12–21 "provides the ultimate reason" for suffering.⁶⁵ Sin and death are cosmic powers that introduce "evil and chaos into the cosmos," with the result that "social, economic and political power relationships are not orderly, but infiltrated by anti-God powers."⁶⁶ Also, "Gen 1–3 affirms the cosmic nature of humanity's struggles.... The deceit of the serpent in Gen 3 symbolizes an anti-God power that seeks to destroy humanity, even before Adam rebelled.... The primordial stories in Genesis help to explain how the dominion of sin and death leads to affliction and pain in the world."⁶⁷

Suffering, then, is inevitable due to the presence of anti-God powers and the failure of human beings to overcome the power of sin. But God sent his Son to participate in a humanity under sin (8:3). He defeated sin through the death of his Son, and reconciled humans to him (5:10–11). In Christ, Spirit-led believers are the children of God (8:14). They have received the Spirit of adoption, through whom they cry "*Abba* Father" (8:15). The creation awaits its liberation from the bondage of decay, which will take place when the children of God are raised and glorified (8:21, 23). But at present they suffer and indeed they groan with the entire creation (8:18, 22, 23). In this process, the children of God are being conformed to the image of the Son (8:29). In other words, in a world where suffering abounds, God sent his Son to be a human being so that humans might become his children, and be transformed and renewed as his image-bearers through the Spirit. With this in mind, we are in a position to examine 8:17 and 29.

Rom 8:17

Romans 8:17 contains the first reference to suffering since 5:5, and it paves the way for the extended discussion of suffering in 8:18–39. With three

---

63. Wu, *Suffering in Romans*, 63–66.

64. See Wu, *Suffering in Romans*, 70–75; 165–74. This is also supported by the cosmic scale of God's victory over evil in Rom 8:31–39.

65. Wu, *Suffering in Romans*, 67.

66. Wu, *Suffering in Romans*, 67.

67. Wu, *Suffering in Romans*, 74–75.

σύν-compounds loaded in one verse (συγκληρονόμοι, συμπάσχομεν, and συνδοξασθῶμεν), the notion of participation in Christ is exceptionally prominent in Rom 8:17. The Spirit-led children of God are joint-heirs with Christ, share in his suffering, and will be glorified with him. While the theme of participation in Christ in 6:1–11 focuses on being united with his death, burial, and life, here in 8:17 the emphasis is on heirship, suffering, and glorification. It should be noted that there is no hint in 8:17–39 that the suffering here is restricted to persecution for the sake of Christ. Instead, most likely Paul has in mind all types of suffering, as the affliction-list in 8:35 indicates.[68] Having said that, I want to focus on two things in Romans that help us to understand the suffering mentioned in 8:17. First, as mentioned above, the ultimate force behind suffering is the anti-God power of sin and death. But, although in this world groaning is inevitable, through Christ's death and resurrection God has defeated sin and death and nothing can separate believers from God's love (8:31–39). Second, the suffering in 8:17 should be understood in terms of Christ's cross-shaped pattern of suffering, given what we have learned in Philippians and 2 Corinthians.

Along with several scholars, I think the εἴπερ in Rom 8:17 carries a hortatory and conditional sense,[69] and that the ἵνα indicates both purpose

---

68. See Moo, *Romans*, 511; Wu, *Suffering in Romans*, 119; and most recently, Davey, "Sight," 174–75. Cf. Shen, *Cardinal Truth*, 300. Of course, the suffering in Rom 8:17–39 includes the afflictions that result from persecution (as Paul and the believing community experience opposition because of their proclamation of the gospel and/or their transformed lifestyle in a hostile world), but not exclusive of it. (For example, the first item in the list in Rom 8:35, θλῖψις, does not have to refer to persecution—see 2 Cor 8:2, where the word refers to financial hardship.) Note also that the contexts of Philippians and 2 Corinthians are different, and the types of suffering in these two letters are more specifically about persecution. In his comments on Rom 8:35, Dunn notes the parallels between the affliction-list in 8:35 and the one in 2 Cor 11:23–27; and says that Paul would have thought of his experience of suffering for the sake of the gospel as "typical for all his fellow believers." Dunn, *Romans 1–8*, 505. This is true to the degree that persecution would have been a common experience for all believers. But I would argue that Paul had much wider scope of suffering in mind. Given the context of the groaning of creation, the list of afflictions in Rom 8:35 should include all manner of suffering, inclusive of persecution. (I should mention here that in this essay I refer to three works that are written in Chinese, and they are, as far as I know, not available in English: Fung, *Commentary on Romans*; Huang, *Romans*; and Shen, *Cardinal Truth*.)

69. See Wu, *Suffering in Romans*, 116–18. Cf., Dunn, *Romans 1–8*, 456; Byrne, *Romans*, 253–54; Schreiner, *Romans*, 428; Moo, *Romans*, 506; Fung, *Commentary on Romans 5–8*, 646–47.

and result.⁷⁰ But this does not mean that 8:17 is a warning for believers, as if they are unwilling to suffer with Christ. Rather, Paul is "urging his audience to join him in following Christ's pattern."⁷¹ So, there is a strong sense in which believers are *called to participate in the suffering of Christ*.⁷² To be more specific, the υἱοί of God are to suffer with the υἱός of God. Just as God's Son suffered and died for humanity, his children suffer with the Son. And just as the Son was glorified at his resurrection and exaltation, God's children will also be glorified with the Son at the renewal of the entire creation. Indeed, as I have argued elsewhere, the glorification of the children of God has a present dimension, for their suffering is a visible display of Christ's glory.⁷³ The "purpose of God glorifying his people will stand, and suffering with Christ is an important part of that purpose."⁷⁴

Rom 8:29

The second half of Rom 8:29 is of particular interest to us because it speaks of the believers' conformity to the image (εἰκών) of the Son. We have already come across the adjective σύμμορφος and the cognate συμμορφίζω in Phil 3:10, 21. I have proposed elsewhere that in Rom 8:29 the conformity that the word συμμόρφους "denotes is not simply a general likeness or similarity in form. Rather, it is about participation in Christ's existence."⁷⁵ But what existence are we talking about here? The clue is found in the term εἰκών. Given our earlier discussion of the term, and given the likely echo of Genesis 1–3 in Romans 5–8, the εἰκών of the Son here is best understood to refer to Christ being God's representative, who displays God's glory as his vice-regent. To partake in the Son's image-bearing means that the children of God participate in exhibiting the glory of God as fellow image-bearers—as truly human, just as God intends. Also, along with not a few scholars, I believe that the aorist ἐδόξασεν in 8:30 refers to a process of transformation (into glory) that

---

70. Cf. Wallace, *Greek Grammar*, 474.
71. Wu, *Suffering in Romans*, 117.
72. Wu, *Suffering in Romans*, 120, 123–24.
73. Wu, *Suffering in Romans*, 122–23.
74. Wu, *Suffering in Romans*, 117.
75. Wu, *Suffering in Romans*, 161. Also, the use of the adjective συμμόρφους with the genitive εἰκόνος suggests that the συμμόρφους carries a substantival force (160–61). I am indebted to Gieniusz, *Romans*, 272; Byrne, *Romans*, 272, here.

has already begun.⁷⁶ If I am right, then the co-glorification in 8:17 most likely refers to the same thing, in that it is not merely about the *future* glorification of God's children (although that is certainly included), but also about participating in the glory of Christ at the *present* time.

So, God's purpose has always been that (as indicated by the προέγνω and προώρισεν in 8:29a) believers will be conformed to the image of the Son. But the goal of this is that he may be the πρωτότοκον ἐν πολλοῖς ἀδελφοῖς.⁷⁷ In the Exodus tradition, the people of God, Israel, is said to be YHWH's firstborn (Exod 4:22, 23), and so the Son's being the "firstborn among many brothers and sisters" in Rom 8:29 probably refers to Christ being the firstborn of a new people of God. But Campbell and Fee have rightly alerted us to the allusion to Ps 89:26–27 here, noting that the πατήρ and the πρωτότοκος appear in 88:27–28 LXX.⁷⁸ Assuming such an allusion, then, given the anointing of David in Ps 89:20, most likely Jesus' messianic Davidic sonship is in view (cf. 2 Sam 7:10–15).⁷⁹ Thus, Jesus is the Davidic Son of God, which reflects Paul's opening statement in Rom 1:3–4. What should also be noted are the motifs of cosmic battle, and God's righteousness and faithfulness, in Ps 89:5–14.⁸⁰ YHWH is depicted as the creator (89:11–12), and his primordial victory over chaos seems to be presupposed in 89:6–10.⁸¹ And in 89:14 the psalmist affirms YHWH's righteousness, justice, steadfast love, and faithfulness, which are, of course, key themes in Romans concerning God and his faithfulness through Christ. So, one may say that the allusion to Ps 89 implies that Christ assumes the Davidic anointed kingship, which in turn actualizes the kingship of YHWH in the cosmos.⁸²

---

76. See Wu, *Suffering in Romans*, 163–64, as well as Jewett, *Romans*, 530; Byrne, *Romans*, 270. Cf. Fee, *Pauline Christology*, 251 n. 33; Cranfield, *Romans I-VIII*, 433; Huang, *Romans*, 206.

77. For a recent discussion on the divine sonship of Christ, see Kincaid and Barber, "Conformed to the Image," 41–50. I am, in board terms, in agreement with Kincaid and Barber that being "conformed to the image of the Son, those 'in Christ' share in the suffering that is necessary for the redemption of the cosmos, ushering in the eschatological age" (41). Cf. Wu, *Suffering in Romans*, 137–51.

78. Campbell, "Story of Jesus," 116; Fee, *Pauline Christology*, 250–51.

79. Campbell, "Story of Jesus," 116; Fee, *Pauline Christology*, 250–51.

80. Middleton, *Liberating Image*, 246–47.

81. Middleton, *Liberating Image*, 246–47.

82. Commenting on Ps 89:26–27, Goldingay says, "David's kingship actualizes Yhwh's kingship in the world. It is the agency through which Yhwh's rule is extended from heavens to the earth." Goldingay, *Psalms 42–89*, 679.

Yet this needs to be read together with the fact that humans are made in God's image. The reference to Adam in Rom 5:12–21 and the theme of creation in 8:19–23 strongly indicate that the εἰκών in Rom 8:29 should be read in light of Gen 1:26–27. The Son is God's image (2 Cor 4:4; cf. Col 3:15), and the children of God are to be conformed to the same image (Rom 8:29). With this in mind, it is likely that the πολλοῖς ἀδελφοῖς in Rom 8:29 refers to the new humanity that comprises the children of God in Christ, who are going through a process of transformation to be representatives of God (vice-regents) by being conformed to the image of the Son, who is the Davidic Son of God. To put this differently, the Son is God's true image-bearer and is simultaneously the messianic Davidic king. As Spirit-led children of God are being conformed to his image, a worldwide family (of diverse ethnicities; cf. 15:7–13) is being gathered to the glory of God the Father.[83]

Romans 8:29, of course, must be read in terms of the sufferings of the present time, for 8:18–30, and indeed, the whole of 8:17–39, is about suffering. The theme of suffering and the συμμόρφους here tie 8:29 to 8:17 (which has the first mention of suffering in Romans 8 and three συν-compounds) together.[84] As I have argued elsewhere, 8:17 is pivotal within the development of the argument in Romans 8 about suffering, and 8:28–30 is a climactic celebration of glory for those who suffer with Christ.[85] The process of transformation has everything to do with participating in Christ's suffering, in order that believers may be glorified with him (8:17).[86] That is to say, *the vocation of suffering with Christ is an integral part of conformity to the Son's image, and hence of displaying God's glory as his image-bearers.*

---

83. I welcome the question raised by Davey, "Sight," 56–57, on my statement in *Suffering in Romans*, which says, "A large royal family of God is formed, and God's program of transforming humanity and renewing creation is being completed in this process" (p. 162). Davey questions why I do not clarify *how* the cosmic renewal comes about. My response is simply that the limited space in my book means that my exegesis of Rom 8:29 cannot deal with everything concerning the cosmic renewal. (I also note that Davey's exegesis on Rom 8:29 ["Sight," 106–7] is actually quite brief.)

84. Dunn, *Romans 1–8*, 483.

85. Wu, *Suffering in Romans*, 113–24, 155–64.

86. See Wu, *Suffering in Romans*, 159–64, for a longer discussion on this. Cf., the brief discussion by Davey, where he says that there is a connection between 8:17 and 8:29, and that the conformity in 8:29 is "conformity to the *suffering* Christ" ("Sight," 106–7; emphasis original).

Rom 12:2

Our primary interest in Rom 12:2 lies in its reference to the transformation of the mind. The imperative μεταμορφοῦσθε indicates Paul's strong desire for his audience to be transformed by the renewal of the mind. This is reinforced by the prohibitive μὴ συσχηματίζεσθε, urging the audience not to be conformed to this age. We have already discussed the only other occurrence of μεταμορφόω in the Pauline corpus in 2 Cor 3:18, where the transformation is primarily about the Spirit-empowered image-bearing of believers under the new covenant. Here in Romans, however, the notion of transformation is best understood in terms of the σύμμορφος in Rom 8:29 (because of the shared theme and vocabulary of transformation between 8:29 and 12:2),[87] where the emphasis is not so much the new covenant but the image-bearing of God's Spirit-led children. Having said that, I also note that the transformation in Romans is similar to 2 Cor 3:18, in that it is about displaying God's glory by participating in Christ's suffering.

The rest of Romans 12 outlines what this transformation looks like in the Christ-community. For our purposes, we note the afflictions of the members of this community, which is clearly indicated by the word θλῖψις in 12:12. The references to persecution and to being cursed, and the exhortation to weep with those who weep (12:12, 14), point to the specific forms of affliction in the community. The call to hospitality and association with the lowly in 12:13, 16 speaks of sharing of hardship within the community and with outsiders. Most importantly, the fourfold mention of evil (κακός) in 12:17, 21 strongly implies that Paul calls for the audience to endure suffering. All of these are part and parcel of the transformation that Paul urges the Roman Christ-followers to undertake. As they endure hardship, share the pain of others, and overcome evil with good, they participate in Christ's suffering; and together they display God's glory as co-image-bearers with the Son.

---

87. We should also note the shared contextual theme of suffering in 8:17–39 and 12:12–14, 16–17, 21.

Conclusion[88]

For Paul, suffering and conformity to Christ's cruciform death are intertwined.[89] Participation in Christ's suffering is an integral part of Christian existence. Suffering and glorification are also inseparable. Sharing in Christ's suffering is the vocation of the believing community and is intrinsically connected with participating in his glory. The Son of God participated in humanity, and the children of God (both individually and corporately) participate in his image-bearing. Conformity to the image of the Son includes partaking in his cross-shaped suffering. By beholding the glory of God in his glorious presence through the Spirit, believers are being transformed to exhibit the glory of God as co-sufferers with Christ in conformity to his image. This transformation takes place as they embody Christ in their hearts and lives—when they share one another's affliction and pain in the Jesus-community and with outsiders, and when they overcome evil with good by living out Christ's cruciform pattern of suffering. In this light, Blackwell is right to see suffering as an important part of Christosis (the christo-form embodiment of Christ).[90] And once we take into account the fact that Christ-likeness is at the same time God-likeness, then Gorman's use of the term "theosis" (becoming like God by

---

88. Space limitations do not allow me to study Gal 4:19, where Paul says, "My little children, for whom I am again in the pain of childbirth until Christ is formed [μορφωθῇ] in you" (NRSV). But the comments by Susan Eastman are perceptive and worth citing at length, for they cohere with much of my conclusion here.

> As the climax of his appeal to "become like me," it tells them that, just as his participation in Christ involves suffering for the sake of the gospel, so the formation of Christ in them will take a cruciform shape. Just as the transforming and sustaining power of God is paradoxically displayed through Paul's "weakness," so it will be with the Galatian congregations. In this way, Paul's maternal imagery evokes the relational matrix through which the apocalyptic gospel intersects with and realigns the narrative of God's children—a set of relationships characterized by the sacrificial, proactive and boundary-crossing love of the "Son of God, who loved me, and gave himself for me" (2:20). Eastman, *Recovering Paul's Mother Tongue*, 126.

89. I would like to briefly respond to the critique of Davey, "Sight," 55–56, against my audience-focused methodology in *Suffering in Romans*. I hope this essay shows that I value author-focused studies highly, for I do not focus on the audience at all in this chapter. I will not repeat the reasons for my audience-focused approach in *Suffering in Romans* (see pp. 2–9), except to say that the approach is by no means a superior methodology, or the only valid one.

90. Blackwell, *Christosis*, 155–57, 167, 261–62, 264–65. Blackwell says, "His [Christ's] suffering and glory are both the means and model of life for believers as they reproduce his image" (p. 261).

participating in the life of God) to describe Paul's soteriology should be taken seriously.[91]

A Reflection

In a world where the whole creation groans and God's children groan with it, suffering is inevitable. But the good news is that, if we faithfully live for Christ in our suffering through the empowerment of the Spirit, then our lives exhibit the glory of God by being conformed to the image of his Son. I have seen this again and again in the faithful followers of Jesus today. I belong to a Christian community where there are many refugees and low-income Australians. Their suffering—financial hardship, emotional distress, life-threatening physical danger, displacement from homeland, and prolonged separation from close family members—is beyond my imagination. But their resilience and tenacity in affliction is inspiring. To me, those who suffer much are the ones who display God's glory in great measure. The testimony of my friend Sung Sung Lian Hrang, a former refugee from Myanmar, is powerful.

> Suffering is necessary in our new life in Christ as we give our lives to God and for others. This is something we have in common with Christ in order to know the purpose of God in our lives. Since God has restored our relationship with him through the suffering of Christ, our calling, or our vocation, is the same as Christ's, who suffered and died for humanity.[92]

For me, this is a vivid example of how God's glory is reflected in the life of someone who has suffered immensely.

---

91. See Gorman, "Romans," 27. A few comments on Free, "Suffering in Paul," 75–92, are in order here. Regardless of whether one agrees with her conclusions, Free raises good questions about the scale of persecution against Christians when he wrote his letters. Her questions around whether suffering represents a cataclysmic apocalyptic event in Paul are also worth considering. But it seems that her article tends to undermine the significance of suffering in Paul. The extended treatment of suffering in chapter 8 of Romans—an important letter in the Pauline corpus—indicates strongly that it is an important topic for the apostle. And I hope my conclusion above provides further evidence that suffering is an essential element of Paul's thought.

92. From the transcript of Sung Sung Lian Hrang's speech at the launch event of my book, *Suffering in Romans*, on October 22, 2015, at Whitley College, Australia. Used with her permission.

Bibliography

Beale, Greg K. *The Temple and the Church's Mission: A Biblical Theology of the Dwelling Place of God.* Leicester: Apollos, 2004.
Blackwell, Ben C. *Christosis: Pauline Soteriology in Light of Deification in Irenaeus and Cyril of Alexandria.* WUNT 2.314. Tübingen: Mohr Siebeck, 2011.
Bockmuehl, Markus. *The Epistle to the Philippians.* London: A & C Black, 1997.
Byrne, Brendan. *Romans.* SP 6. Collegeville, MN: Liturgical, 1996.
Campbell, Constantine R. *Paul and Union with Christ: An Exegetical and Theological Study.* Grand Rapids: Zondervan, 2012.
Campbell, Doug. "The Story of Jesus in Romans and Galatians." In *The Narrative Dynamics in Paul*, edited by Bruce W. Longenecker, 97–124. London: Westminister John Knox, 2002.
Cassidy, Richard J. *Paul in Chains.* New York: Crossroads, 2001.
Cohick, Lynn H. *Philippians.* SGBC. Grand Rapids, MI: Zondervan, 2013.
Collins, Raymond F. *Second Corinthians.* Paideia. Grand Rapids, MI: Baker, 2013.
Cranfield, C. E. B. *A Critical and Exegetical Commentary on the Epistle to the Romans: Introduction and Commentary on Romans I–VIII.* ICC. London: T & T Clark, 1975.
Davey, Wesley Thomas. "Sight in the Tempest: Suffering as Participation with Christ in the Pauline Corpus." PhD diss., Southeastern Baptist Theological Seminary, 2016.
Dunn, James. *Romans 1–8.* WBC 38A. Dallas: Word, 1988.
Eastman, Susan. "Philippians 2:6–11: Incarnation as Mimetic Participation." *JSPL* 1.1 (2010) 1–22.
———. *Recovering Paul's Mother Tongue.* Grand Rapids, MI: Eerdmans, 2007.
Fee, Gordon D. *God's Empowering Presence.* Peabody, MA: Hendrickson, 1994.
———. *Pauline Christology.* Peabody, MA: Hendrickson, 2007.
———. *Paul's Letter to the Philippians.* NICNT. Grand Rapids: Eerdmans, 1995.
Flemming, Dean. *Philippians: A Commentary in the Wesleyan Tradition.* New Beacon Bible Commentary. Kansas City: Beacon Hill, 2009.
Fowl, Stephen E. *Philippians.* THNTC. Grand Rapids: Eerdmans, 2005.
Free, Marian. "Suffering in Paul: A Case for Exaggeration." *St Mark's Review* 239 (2017) 75–92.
Fung, Ronald Y. K. *Commentary on Romans 5–8.* Taipei, Taiwan: Campus Evangelical Fellowship, 2001.
Gieniusz, Andrzej. *Romans 8:18–30—Suffering Does Not Thwart the Future Glory.* Atlanta: Scholars, 1999.
Goldingay, John. *Psalms 42–89.* BCOT 2. Grand Rapids: Baker Academic, 2007.
Gorman, Michael J. *Becoming the Gospel: Paul, Participation, and Mission.* Grand Rapids: Eerdmans, 2015.
———. *Cruciformity: Paul's Narrative Spirituality of the Cross.* Grand Rapids: Eerdmans, 2001.
———. *Inhabiting the Cruciform God.* Grand Rapids: Eerdmann, 2009.
———. "A New Translation of Philippians 2:5." In *Conception, Reception, and the Spirit*, edited by J. Gordon McConville and Lloyd K. Pietersen, 104–21. Eugene, OR: Cascade Books, 2015.
———. "Romans: The First Christian Treatise on Theosis." *JTI* 5.1 (2011) 13–34.
Guthrie, George H. *2 Corinthians.* BECNT. Grand Rapids: Baker, 2015

Hellerman, Joseph H. *Philippians*. EGGNT. Nashville: B & H Academic, 2015.
Hill, Wesley. *Paul and the Trinity*. Grand Rapids: Eerdmans, 2015.
Huang, Caleb K. *Romans*. Fountain Valley, CA: Christian Digest, 2005.
Jervis, L. Ann. *At the Heart of the Gospel: Suffering in the Earliest Christian Message*. Grand Rapids: Eerdmans, 2007.
Jewett, Robert. *Romans: A Commentary*. Hermeneia. Minneapolis: Fortress, 2007.
Kilner, John F. *Dignity and Destiny: Humanity in the Image of God*. Grand Rapids: Eerdmans, 2015.
Kincaid, John A., and Michael Patrick Barber. "Conformed to the Image." *Letter and Spirit* 10 (2015) 35–64.
Levenson, Jon D. "The Temple and the World." *JR* 64 (1984) 275–98.
Long, Fredrick J. *II Corinthians*. Waco: Baylor University Press, 2015.
Macaskill, Grant. *Union with Christ in the New Testament*. Oxford: Oxford University Press, 2013.
Matera, Frank J. *II Corinthians*. Louisville, KY: Westminster John Knox, 2003.
Middleton, J. Richard. *The Liberating Image: The Imago Dei in Genesis 1*. Grand Rapids: Brazos, 2005.
Moo, Douglas. *The Epistle to the Romans*. NICNT. Grand Rapids: Eerdmans, 1996.
Oakes, Peter. *Philippians: From People to Letter*. SNTSMS 110. Cambridge: Cambridge University Press, 2001.
O'Brien, Peter T. *The Epistle to the Philippians*. NIGTC. Grand Rapids: Eerdmans, 1991.
Rabens, Volker. *The Holy Spirit and Ethics in Paul: Transformation and Empowering for Religious-Ethical Life*. WUNT 2.283. Tübingen: Mohr Siebeck, 2010.
Schreiner, Thomas R. *Romans*. BECNT. Grand Rapids: Baker, 1998.
Shen, Paul. *Cardinal Truth—A Study on Romans*. Hong Kong: Tien Dao Publishing, 2002.
Starling, David. "'For Your Sake We are Being Killed All Day Long': Romans 8:36 and the Hermeneutics of Unexplained Suffering." *Themelios* 42.1 (2017) 112–21.
Thompson, James W., and Bruce W. Longenecker. *Philippians and Philemon*. Grand Rapids: Baker, 2016.
Thrall, Margaret E. *2 Corinthians 1–7*. ICC 47A. Edinburgh: T & T Clark, 1994.
Varner, William. *Philippians*. Waco: Baylor University Press, 2016.
Wallace, Daniel. *Greek Grammar Beyond the Basics: An Exegetical Syntax of the New Testament*. Grand Rapids: Zondervan, 1996.
Walton, John H. *Genesis 1 as Ancient Cosmology*. Winona Lake, IN: Eisenbrauns, 2011.
Wansink, Craig S. *Chained in Christ*. JSNTSup 130. Sheffield: Sheffield Academic, 1996.
Watts, Rikk E. "The New Exodus/New Creational Restoration of the Image of God: A Biblical-Theological Perspective on Salvation." In *What Does It Mean to Be Saved*, edited by John G. Stackhouse Jr., 15–42. Grand Rapids: Baker, 2002.
Witherington, Ben, III. *Paul's Letter to the Philippians*. Grand Rapids: Eerdmans, 2011.
Wu, Siu Fung. *Suffering in Romans*. Eugene, OR: Pickwick, 2015.

7

Suffering and Glory in Philippians

Haley Goranson Jacob

Introduction

THE CONCEPT OF SUFFERING is woven throughout Paul's letter to the Philippians. Paul describes his own suffering, the suffering of the Philippians, and that of Christ on the cross. Yet throughout the letter, Paul's descriptions of suffering are closely linked with the concepts of glory and exaltation. The Father's glory, Christ's exaltation and glory, and believers' conformity to that glory stand in tandem with their suffering, humiliation, and death. Nevertheless, the relationship between the two concepts is not immediately obvious. Suffering is commonly assumed to be a precursor to eschatological glory: suffering and humility in this life, glory and exaltation in the next. But does humility lead to exaltation, or, rather, is humility an expression of exaltation? Does such a reading coalesce with either Paul's understanding of God's self-revelation in suffering (Phil 2:6–8) or the weight Paul places on the Philippians' communal identity as those in union with both the crucified and resurrected Christ? Such questions will occupy our attention in this chapter.[1] Rather than

---

1. These are complex questions that demand an investigation into a field of literature larger than this brief chapter can accommodate. My goal here is simply to raise the questions and offer a potential avenue for yet one more line of questioning, especially with regard to Phil 2:5–11. I intentionally refrain from providing extended footnotes and histories of research that are detailed at length elsewhere; see esp. Martin, *Carmen Christi*; Martin and Dodd, *Where Christology Began*, in addition to the majority of

understanding suffering as an earthly reality which somehow leads to heavenly glory, this chapter will explore the possibility that in Philippians Paul viewed suffering as a paradoxical demonstration of glory: God's glory and believers' glory "in Christ" are both revealed in suffering.

The Nature of Suffering and Glory in Philippians

Suffering and glory are fundamental themes in the Christian experience. Yet what Christians today mean by the use of the two terms often varies from one Christian's experience to another's. And, more importantly, what Christians in the twenty-first century mean by suffering and glory, particularly those living in the West, can be drastically different from the meaning used by Paul in his various letters. Before discussing the relationship between the two themes, therefore, it is important for us first to plant them in their historical and literary context.

No person is a stranger to suffering by the end of their life. Suffering wrought by disease, death, terrorism, natural disasters, and systemic injustices afflict people without bias; it is a common element to the human experience. And while many western Christians today do experience suffering as a result of their Christian faith, what we might call "persecution,"[2] they are more typically persecuted for their willingness to oppose injustice as a result of their faith in Christ. One might think here of the life and death of Dietrich Bonhoeffer.[3] But the suffering that Paul encouraged the Philippian church to endure is, I suggest, not a suffering that is common to the human experience or even purely a suffering that stems from a participation in overturning the injustices of the world. Rather, the suffering which the Philippian believers experienced stemmed directly from their profession of faith in Jesus Christ as Lord—what Paul calls their "participation in the gospel" (1:5) or their "sacrifice and the offering of [their] faith" (2:17).[4] Two reasons in particular lead to this conclusion, and both stem from 1:27–30.

---

recent commentaries.

2. Broadly speaking, any form of physical, economic, or social injustice that results from one's declaration of faith in Christ.

3. I will return to some of these thoughts at the end of this chapter when I reflect on the persecuted church living throughout the world today.

4. This is not to suggest that Paul's encouragement to endure suffering does not therefore also apply to forms of suffering beyond that of persecution. Certainly, it does. For the sake of the focused discussion of this chapter, however, I will limit the term to

First, Paul identifies the Philippians' suffering most clearly in 1:29–30, where he writes, "For he has graciously granted you the privilege not only of believing in Christ, but of suffering for him as well—since you are having the same struggle that you saw I had and now hear that I still have."[5] Paul himself is in prison as a result of preaching the gospel,[6] and though the Philippians themselves are not also in prison (as far as we know), their "struggle" (ἀγών) resembles that of Paul's. The natural conclusion, then, is that the Philippians, like Paul, are experiencing persecution as a result of their struggle in the defense of the gospel.

Second, this reading is confirmed by the fact that the suffering is produced by a group of opponents who are the cause of both fear and disunity amongst the Philippian believers (1:27–28).[7] Such opponents are destined for destruction, Paul states, clearly underscoring their rejection of Christ. It is impossible to articulate with any level of certainty the identity of such opponents or the nature of their tactics used to foster fear and disunity amongst the Philippians.[8] But the politically charged environment of Philippi may indicate that the opponents mentioned in 1:27–28 are on some level socio-political opponents.[9] Philippi was populated in part by military veterans in the years 42 BCE and 30 BCE and declared a Roman colony by Caesar Augustus, thus offering its people Roman citizenship and guaranteeing their devotion to the Empire. By the mid-first century CE, such devotion to the Empire would have also included civic devotion to the emperor as one's lord and savior.[10] For the average resident in Philippi, "love of god and country" would be less an overflow of the heart and more a civic obligation—an obligation which would prove impossible for Philippian believers and thus result in their

---

its likely original context.

5. NRSV. Scripture translations elsewhere in this chapter are my own, unless otherwise noted.

6. Phil 1:7, 12–14, 19–21.

7. This may also be the cause of Paul's later encouragement in 4:4–7 to rejoice, to let their gentleness be evident to all, to not be anxious but rather to pray, and to let the God of peace guard their hearts.

8. Fee, *Philippians*, 7–10, notes that there are upwards of eighteen hypotheses for accounting for the various "opponents" in the letter, including those in 1:15–17; 2:21; 3:2–3; and 3:18–19, in addition to those in 1:27–28.

9. See Flemming, *Philippians*, 84; and Oakes, *Philippians*, 79–82. Silva, *Philippians*, 82, suggests that it is "reasonable to assume" that Paul is referring to the Judaizers of 3:2–3. I am unpersuaded.

10. See Crossan, *God and Empire*, 141.

persecution within the politically charged community.[11] Hence, Paul's use of πολιτεύεσθε ("live out your citizenship") in 1:27 is not inadvertent. Such a stance within that socio-political environment would guarantee such absenters dishonor and social ostracism, at a minimum, but likely also significant persecution and suffering.

With this understanding of suffering as persecution, let us now turn our attention to the notion of glory. One of the great oddities to date within discussions of Christian theology is that, while so much emphasis is placed on believers' hope of glory, so few have actually articulated the nature of this glory. This discussion formed the heart of my doctoral work, particularly as it relates to Paul's letter to Rome. Some space, though, was dedicated to Paul's use of glory in Philippians, especially Phil 3:18–21. It is there that Paul refers to the glory of humans: of Jesus, Christians, and pagans. I can only summarize here what I detailed at length there and refer my reader to that work.[12] Three things need to be noted here, each of which will (I have no doubt) leave my reader asking for more qualification.

First, the resurrection body of glory which Jesus has and into which believers' bodies will be transformed is not one characterized locally as being in the presence of God, but one characterized by possessing the status of glory—which is to say, a status of rule.[13] In and through his resurrection body, Jesus fulfills Psalm 8, subjecting all things to himself as the new Adam, the son of man crowned with glory and honor and given dominion over all things (Phil 3:21; Ps 8:5–6; see 1 Cor 15:21–28). At the return of Christ, believers' bodies will be transformed to share that similar status of glory and honor as vicegerents of God and as redeemed humans in Christ, thus also fulfilling their vocational calling described in Genesis 1 and Psalm 8.

---

11. See Cohick, "Philippians and Empire," 166–82, on the presence of and Paul's engagement with the imperial cult in Philippi. See also Fee, *Philippians*, 24–32, for an excellent summary of these political realities that form the historical occasion for the letter.

12. Jacob, *Conformed to the Image*, 140–51.

13. See Hellerman, *Philippians*, 225, who does not suggest a "status of rule" *per se* but, because of its contrast with (a) the status of humility in 3:21 and (b) the contrast with the pseudo-glory of those whose minds are set on earthly things in 3:19, rightly suggests that the genitive should be taken as a possessive ("our body of glory") rather than an attributive ("our glorious body"). This insight applies also to the second and third points in this section.

Second, this understanding of believers' future status of glory is demonstrated by Paul's use of ταπείνωσις here in Phil 3:21 in reference to the present low status experienced by believers. A parallel comparison is found in 2:6–8 where Paul uses ταπεινόω (2:8) in reference to Christ's voluntary acceptance of that low status and contrasts that position with his exalted (i.e., glorified) status in 2:9–11. I will return to this conversation anon.

Third, Paul contrasts the citizenship and the current and future status of the Philippian believers in 3:20–21 with the implied citizenship and current and future status of those who are enemies of the cross of Christ in 3:18. Such enemies' minds are set on earthly things, their glory is their shame, and their end is said to be destruction in 3:19. With Cohick, "any firm conclusions on the enemies' identity outruns the evidence."[14] Nevertheless, in the midst of the various suggestions offered by scholars, I suggest that, at a minimum, Paul's use of πολιτεύομαι in 1:27, πολίτευμα in 3:20, ἀπώλεια in 1:28 and 3:19, and also σωτηρία in 1:28 and σωτήρ in 3:20 link the "enemies" in 3:18–19 with the "opponents" in 1:28.[15] Linking the two groups also clarifies the logic behind the transition to 3:20–21: the hope of glory is the natural theme that arises from a situation of present suffering. Given this connection between 1:28–30 and 3:18–21, it is reasonable to assume that the Philippians' suffering is one which leads them to experience a low status, a status without power or control (i.e., persecution), in contrast to the status of their opponents who currently enjoy a status of power, authority, and rule (i.e., persecutor). Such tides will one day be turned, when the true Lord and Savior returns and establishes his kingdom. On that day, citizens of his kingdom—people who have lived the way of the cross—will be shown to have the true glory, and their enemies—people who have lived as enemies of the cross—will be destroyed.

With these definitions of "suffering" and "glory" in place, we are now in a position to think through more closely how Paul understands

---

14. Cohick, *Philippians*, 197.

15. Against Fee, who suggests that "they are almost certainly to be understood as . . . professing Christians from their own point of view, despite how Paul views them" and, thus, "since they are 'believers' after a fashion, they can scarcely be the same as those mentioned in 1:28." Fee, *Philippians*, 374. I am unpersuaded that such an identity of the opponents in 3:18–19 can be gleaned from the text. Other suggestions have included the Judaizers of 3:2–3, Christians who reject the call of the cross and indulge in pagan practices, and general pagans who have a lifestyle that Paul says leads to destruction.

their relationship in Philippians. On the surface, it seems that the glory possessed by believers will be a future glory, one into which they are transformed at the time of the resurrection. But is it possible that Paul understood believers' present suffering to be an expression of their present glory, a glory that will be expressed clearly and completely in the resurrection? To answer these questions, we must return—as all discussions in Philippians do—to the Christ hymn in 2:6–11.

God's Expression of Glory in Humility: Phil 2:6–11

In order not to get swept up in the currents of discussions on this critical text, we will need to anchor ourselves only to those questions that will impact our investigation in this chapter. Such questions will come down to these two: (1) Does Paul intend the hymn to be read with ethical or kerygmatic implications? (2) What is the relationship between Jesus' lordship before and after his incarnation and resurrection?

Rethinking the Kerygmatic Reading

Whether Paul intended the hymn to be read ethically (i.e., with Jesus' demonstrations of humility as an example for the Philippian believers to follow: "that *was* in Christ Jesus"[16]) or kerygmatically (i.e., as the example of what is the Philippians' new reality/identity in Christ: "which *is* yours" in Christ Jesus"[17]), depends on how one reads 2:5: Τοῦτο φρονεῖτε ἐν ὑμῖν ὃ καὶ ἐν Χριστῷ Ἰησοῦ. An ethical reading is certainly the most common approach, especially given Paul's call to humility and service of others in 2:3–4.[18] What does it look like to consider others better than yourself (2:3) or to look out for the interests of others (2:4)? Jesus offers an excellent example (2:5): he demonstrated such humility and sacrifice for others in his cruciform life (2:6–8).

---

16. NRSV. Emphasis added.
17. ESV. Emphasis added.
18. For an ethical reading, see: Bockmuehl, *Philippians*, 123–24; Hellerman, *Philippians*, 109, "with reservations"; O'Brien, *Philippians*, 258. For a kerygmatic reading, see esp. Barth, *Philippians*, 59–60.

A number of weaknesses exist in this reading. Most commonly noted is the lack of obvious relevance for the inclusion of 2:9–11.[19] What kind of example does Jesus' exaltation offer to the Philippians struggling with issues of unity? But a more significant weakness of the reading is that it makes Paul's sub-points in 2:3–4 the focus of the entire section of the letter. Rather than reading 2:5 as an extension of 2:4, one should understand it as a return to his admonition in 2:2, which itself is a return to his primary admonition for the entire section in 1:27: Conduct yourselves as citizens [of heaven] worthy of [the death and resurrection] of Christ. Do this by:

1. Standing firm in one spirit (στήκετε ἐν ἑνὶ πνεύματι) and striving together with one mind (μιᾷ ψυχῇ συναθλοῦντες) (1:27);

2. Be of the same mind, having the same love, being in full accord and of one mind (τὸ αὐτὸ φρονῆτε, τὴν αὐτὴν ἀγάπην ἔχοντες, σύμψυχοι, τὸ ἓν φρονοῦντες) (2:2); and

3. Let the same mind be in you which you have/is in Christ Jesus (Τοῦτο φρονεῖτε ἐν ὑμῖν ὃ καὶ ἐν Χριστῷ Ἰησοῦ) (2:5).

When this theme of being united in mind in the midst of enduring persecution is recognized in 1:27–30 and is thus traced to 2:2 and then to 2:5, it becomes more obvious that the mindset which Paul speaks of in 2:5 is not one merely of humility and self-sacrifice as demonstrated by Christ. It is, rather, the fundamental identity which defines both them and their persecutors. Paul admonishes the Philippian believers to live their civic lives in a manner worthy of the gospel: as those whose identity is in the crucified *and* exalted Christ and, as he will write in 3:20, whose citizenship *currently exists* in heaven (ἡμῶν γὰρ τὸ πολίτευμα ἐν οὐρανοῖς ὑπάρχει). These realities are not recognized by the pagan world, and in the midst of persecution are difficult even for the Philippians themselves to recognize. But they are realities nonetheless.

Partially to blame for the lack of support given to the kerygmatic reading is the inadequate recognition of the importance of the theme of participation with Christ in Philippians. There is now greater acceptance of participation with Christ as a key concept in understanding Paul's theology, especially in Galatians and Romans. Yet this thematic appreciation seems to have remained on the periphery within the context of

---

19. See Kreitzer, "When He at Last Is First," 113–18, for an overview of the various functions assigned to 2:9–11 within ethical readings of the hymn.

Philippians (other than in 3:9–10). Undoubtedly the letter is written in part to encourage unity and endurance in the midst of persecution. But below the surface stands the theme of the Philippians' identity "in Christ."

I will return to the importance of this conversation in the next section, but here I simply note the places in which the motif of union/participation appears, whether explicitly or implicitly. Paul uses the typical construct ἐν Χριστῷ (2:1), ἐν Χριστῷ Ἰησοῦ (1:1, 26; 2:5; 3:3, 14; 4:7, 21), or ἐν αὐτῷ (3:9) throughout the letter. He also uses two σύμ-compounds: συμμορφίζω in 3:10 and σύμμορφος in 3:21. Additionally, Paul uses κοινωνία in 2:1 and 3:10 to indicate much the same idea: a participation or sharing in the identity of Christ/Spirit. Though infrequently noticed, participation with Christ/Spirit is at the heart of Philippians; joy and unity in the midst of persecution comes as a result of believers' new identity in Christ.

Undoubtedly, an ethical component does lie below the surface; unity is possible only through humility and self-sacrifice. With Cohick, who helpfully balances the readings: Phil 2:5 "serves to introduce the Christ hymn, and it signals to the reader whether he or she should see Christ primarily as their example or as their Redeemer. Of course, Christ is both, but the point is where the accent lies."[20] She goes on to write, "Both dissolve when we emphasize participation or union with Christ, our Redeemer, who redeems us that we might be an example of his holiness to the world."[21] Cohick holds the two in balance, but her ethical scale is altered from the typical rendering. Holiness is far more comprehensive than humility and self-sacrifice; holiness includes that which comes *after* the hymn in 2:12–15.

But even this call to holiness is a sub-theme of Paul's larger admonition, which he returns to in 2:16–18 and where he forms an *inclusio* with 1:27–30. He describes the Philippian believers as "holding fast to the word of life" (2:16; λόγον ζωῆς ἐπέχοντες) and their lives being a "sacrifice and offering of [their] faith" (2:17; θυσίᾳ καὶ λειτουργίᾳ τῆς πίστεως ὑμῶν).[22] In both texts, then, Paul admonishes the Philippians to persevere in the midst of suffering, to stand fast as those who *are* united

---

20. Cohick, *Philippians*, 96.

21. Cohick, *Philippians*, 96. Bockmuehl, *Philippians*, 123–24, includes the present verb ("which *is* also in Christ Jesus") in his translation, thus also providing a more balanced approach.

22. See Fee, *Philippians*, 219.

in Christ, living out as one body the reality that *is* theirs in both the death and exaltation of Christ, even when persecution veils that reality.[23]

Rethinking Jesus' Exaltation

The second question we must wrestle with is more difficult: How do we make sense of διὸ καὶ ὁ θεὸς αὐτὸν ὑπερύψωσεν in 2:9? In other words, what is the relationship between Jesus' lordship before and after his incarnation and resurrection? Does Jesus' exaltation to the highest place indicate that God gave him a new status he did not previously possess? Was it somehow consequentially dependent on his humility? These questions are important not only christologically, but they are also critical to how we understand the relationship between suffering and glory in Philippians. The space here certainly is not adequate for a full investigation, but a dip into the murky waters will nonetheless prove useful.

Most scholars rightly deny that the exaltation added in any way to Jesus' divinity, essence, character, or person. Given this, one possible approach is that of Bockmuehl, who writes that, "While there is no suggestion of a change of *being*, there is nevertheless a change of *name* and of *function*: at his exaltation Christ becomes Lord of all and receives the name above all."[24] More typically, however, scholars suggest that the exaltation is the Father's vindication or divine approval of Christ.[25] Fee is representative when he notes that, "[It is] God's 'yes' to *this* expression of 'equality with God'"[26] and does not imply that Jesus was "given a *higher* 'position' than he had heretofore."[27] Since the verb usually means to "magnify or express excess," Fee argues, its use in the hymn indicates that God exalted Jesus to the "highest possible degree."[28] But his use of "degree" reveals how, even still, the waters remain quite murky.

---

23. In this way, then, the kerygmatic reading *is* an ethical reading, but one that is based fundamentally on the entirety of the hymn and, more importantly, believers' union with Christ rather than imitation of Christ.

24. Bockmuehl, *Philippians*, 144 (emphasis original). Similarly, though also denying a change in status elsewhere, O'Brien writes, "in his exalted state Jesus *now* exercises universal lordship" (*Philippians*, 233; emphasis mine).

25. See Flemming, *Philippians*, 120; and O'Brien, *Philippians*, 234.

26. Fee, *Philippians*, 220.

27. Fee, *Philippians*, 221 (emphasis original).

28. Fee, *Philippians*, 221.

While this notion of vindication might be accurate, a more helpful option is that posited by Thielman:

> Since it is difficult to imagine a station higher than that of "being in very nature God" and "equality with God" (v. 6)—the place Christ occupied before his condescension—the term *exalted* is better understood as a reference to God's exaltation of Jesus to a position of recognizable superiority over all creation. Although he was acting in a way that was fully consistent with his divine status when he humbled himself, his resurrection and ascension to the Father's right hand make his superiority more fully evident to the creation over which he rules.[29]

This also explains the purpose clause, ἵνα ἐν τῷ ὀνόματι, in 2:10. When God exalted Jesus, which is to say, "gave him the name that is above every name"[30] (2:9; ἐχαρίσατο αὐτῷ ὄνομα τὸ ὑπὲρ πᾶν ὄνομα), "the process began by which the equality with God that Jesus always possessed would be acknowledged by all creation."[31] It is not, therefore, that Jesus was given a new status or a new function; he did not *become* Lord. As the early church recognized in its abundant use of Psalm 110, he was always Lord.[32] But what did change is the world's recognition of that status. And, moreover, now that Jesus is recognized as the Lord he always was, Caesar is recognized as the lord he could never be. God made clear to the world that Jesus is, in fact, the true Lord and Savior. He is the LORD himself of Isaiah 45:23, and to him, not Caesar, will every creature one day bend the knee.[33]

If Jesus was not given a new status or position in being given the divine name, but rather maintained the same exalted position as always, how then does one make sense of the seeming progression the hymn

---

29. Thielman, *Philippians*, 120 (emphasis original).

30. NRSV.

31. Thielman, *Philippians*, 120. See also Flemming, *Philippians*, 121.

32. Matt 22:44; Mark 12:36; Luke 20:42; Acts 2:36; Heb 1:13.

33. Gorman notes that at least five scriptural echoes and at least three cultural allusions have been identified in the hymn. Echoes include: pre-existent Wisdom, the form and/or glory of God, Adam, the Isaianic suffering servant and Israel's "'eschatological monotheism' within the framework of Isaiah 40–55 more generally." Cultural allusions include: "the reality and ideology of slavery," "the Roman ideology and pursuit of honor," and "the theology and practices of the imperial cult." Gorman, *Inhabiting the Cruciform God*, 14–15. On the cultural allusions more specifically, see Goldingay, *Biblical Theology*, 355; and Hellerman, *Philippians*, 152–53.

makes from suffering/humility to exaltation/glory?³⁴ The answer, I suggest, lies in Karl Barth's reading of the text. In his commentary, Barth writes:

> There is good reason for what the ancient painters did when, in their representations of Christ ascending to heaven and throned in heaven, they left the wounds from the cross. That is the meaning of the *dio* (therefore). It does not say that he who was humbled and humiliated was afterwards exalted, was indeed . . . rewarded for his self-denial and obedience. But what it says is that precisely he who was abased and humbled, even to the obedience of death on the cross, is also the Exalted Lord.³⁵

The διὸ καὶ ὁ θεὸς αὐτὸν ὑπερύψωσεν, then, according to Barth, does not constitute a new status for Christ, whether in the form of a reward or vindication. But rather, it reveals the true identity of Christ: he is both exalted and abased, and this two-sided identity is present in Christ in *both* the form of a servant (2:6–8) and as the risen Lord (2:9–11). The resurrected Christ is the crucified Christ, and the crucified Christ is the glory of God. Barth goes on to write, "God's Equal has found his right in this—that *in* his abasement and humiliation he is *Lord* over all. God has found his glory in this—that he prepares his kingdom in incomprehensible condescension."³⁶ Barth therefore rejects the two-part process of obedience and vindication, suffering and then glory, humiliation and then exaltation.³⁷

For some, Barth's reading places too much emphasis on suffering, especially a currently suffering Christ.³⁸ But this view of Christ finds plenty of precedence in John's Gospel and in the Apocalypse. In the latter, the throne room vision specifically includes a vision of Christ: he is *called* the "Lion of the tribe of Judah," the one who "has conquered," but he is *viewed* as a "Lamb standing as if it had been slaughtered" (Rev 5:6).³⁹

---

34. Though the word "glory" is not used to describe Jesus' exalted position as Lord in 2:11, it is the entire context of Isa 45.

35. Barth, *Philippians*, 66.

36. Barth, *Philippians*, 68 (emphasis original).

37. In contrast with most modern commentators who, though they also reject the notion of reward, nevertheless maintain a two-part reading, replacing the notion of reward with that of vindication.

38. See Thielman, *Philippians*, 126. For a more general response to Barth's reading, see Martin, *Carmen Christi*, 232–33; and O'Brien, *Philippians*, 234.

39. NRSV.

Christ is depicted as both exalted and crucified. This paradoxical glory in suffering is also present throughout the entirety of John's Gospel. On this paradox in the Gospel, Bauckham writes:

> John uses *hypsoō* in a series of cryptic sayings that refer both to the physical elevation of Jesus on the cross and to the exaltation to heavenly glory that this entailed (3:14; 8:28; 12:32–34). Since *doxazō* accompanies *hypsoō* in Isa. 52:13, John uses this verb similarly to refer to the death-and-exaltation of Jesus, but he also multiplies its meaning by using it both of Jesus's glorification of his Father and the Father's glorification of Jesus, two movements of glorification that occur simultaneously.[40]

Moreover, the servant's exaltation (aka suffering in Isaiah 53) is the means by which God makes his name known (Isa 52:6), his salvation seen (Isa 52:10), and his kingship declared (Isa 52:7). Or, as Barth describes it: "Jesus Christ, the Lord as Servant" is at the same time "Jesus Christ, the Servant as Lord."[41] In a similar vein, Goldingay writes that "Jesus' execution was . . . an event over which he was Lord. [His execution] pointed to the fact that it was actually his exaltation, a manifestation of his majesty and of his Father's majesty."[42] Making sense of the resurrection, then, Goldingay continues: "[The resurrection] offered a more conventional demonstration of his majesty. While his submission to death was a paradoxical kind of glorious triumph, it was his rising from death that showed it to be so."[43] If such sentiments are correct, and I believe they are, then what one finds in Phil 2:6–11 is not a progression of Jesus from the state of humility to a new state of exaltation, and especially not to a status of Lord which he did not previously possess. Rather, one finds an expression of the paradoxical identity of Jesus Christ as both humble and exalted, and thus what the nature of reality is for those whose own identity and thus mindset is in *that* Christ, *that* Lord and Savior. The way in which this works itself out, especially in 3:9–10 and 3:20–21, is what must occupy our focus for the rest of this chapter.

---

40. Bauckham, *Gospel of Glory*, 59.
41. Barth, *Church Dogmatics* IV.1, 135.
42. Goldingay, *Biblical Theology*, 354.
43. Goldingay, *Biblical Theology*, 354.

The Case for a Two-Part Glory

Given the importance of the motif of participation with Christ in Paul's theology, it can be argued that in Philippians Paul is not describing a two-step process in the life of the believer, at least not in the way that it is often communicated. Certainly, Paul understood that the resurrection of the body and the believer's complete change of status from humility to glory had not yet occurred. But this did not limit his recognition of some level of participation in the exalted status of Christ in the present, even if that participation took the form of suffering. For Paul, participation in Christ this side of the new heaven was both a participation in the Servant as Lord and the Lord as Servant. The two places where humanity's humility/suffering and exaltation/glory are described are in 3:8–16 and 3:18–21.

Phil 3:8–16

In 3:8 Paul describes the surpassing value of knowing Christ Jesus as his Lord. He then describes in 3:9 his desire to "be found in him" (εὑρεθῶ ἐν αὐτῷ), and in 3:10 his desire to "know Christ and the power of his resurrection and the sharing of his sufferings by participating in his death" (τοῦ γνῶναι αὐτὸν καὶ τὴν δύναμιν τῆς ἀναστάσεως αὐτοῦ καὶ [τὴν] κοινωνίαν [τῶν] παθημάτων αὐτοῦ, συμμορφιζόμενος τῷ θανάτῳ αὐτοῦ). These verses, along with 3:14 where Paul writes, "I press on toward the goal for the prize of the heavenly call of God in Christ Jesus"[44] (ἐν Χριστῷ Ἰησοῦ), contain the bulk of Paul's participatory language in Philippians. And they are rife with this recognition of participation in both the life of Christ in humility and the life of Christ in glory at the same time.

Unequivocally, Paul does have a future focus in this passage. But the prize for which he presses on toward is not the opposite of earthly suffering; it is the physical, resurrected body—the completion of the status in Christ in which he currently exists. Thus he can write in 3:12–13: I have not attained this; I have not arrived at that final goal [of resurrection], but I press on toward it. Cohick notes here that, "if we understand God's call more broadly as the salvation brought by Christ and accomplished in the final judgment, the prize is eternal life with God, with *resurrected* bodies in the new heavens and new earth."[45] Being found in Christ,

---
44. NRSV.
45. Cohick, *Philippians*, 179 (emphasis mine).

knowing Christ Jesus as his Lord, and having been claimed by Christ as his own (3:12; καὶ κατελήφθην ὑπὸ τοῦ χριστοῦ Ἰησοῦ), all make Paul look forward to the prize that is the completion of glory revealed in physical resurrection for those already raised to new life in Christ. But part of knowing Christ this side of heaven is also knowing the power of his resurrection this side of heaven: a power demonstrated or expressed by suffering, humility, and death. For Paul, being in Christ and knowing Christ this side of heaven means participation in the Lord as Servant and Servant as Lord—the Christ exemplified in 2:6–11.

In fact, Paul continues in 3:16, "Only let us hold fast to what we *have* attained"[46] (πλὴν εἰς ὃ ἐφθάσαμεν, τῷ αὐτῷ στοιχεῖν). O'Brien rightly notes that, "as Christians they need to be united in the contest in which all are engaged."[47] I am inclined to take it a step further and suggest that the phrase refers *first to the position they have attained in Christ*, and thereafter the unity that should stem from such a position.[48] They belong to Christ (3:12), their identity is in Christ (2:5), and, as such, they should live as citizens of the kingdom over which he rules as Lord (2:9–11; 3:20). Their position as exalted citizens of another kingdom may not yet be revealed while the kingdom of Caesar persists and while their earthly bodies remain, but it is *the* reality into which they were baptized and declared to be new creations nonetheless.[49] This should be the reality that compels them to remain united to one another, to serve in humility, and to endure through suffering together as those who are one with the risen Christ.[50]

46. NRSV. Emphasis added.

47. O'Brien, *Philippians*, 442.

48. This reading accounts for the textual variants which include τὸ αὐτὸ φρονεῖν at the end of 3:16 (so KJV, "let us mind the same thing"), thus linking Paul's statements in this section with those in (1:27); 2:2, 5; 3:15, 19.

49. See also 2 Cor 5:17; Gal 6:15; Rom 6:3–11. Lydia and her family were, of course, the first to experience this new reality in Philippi, followed by the jailor and his family (see Acts 16:15, 33).

50. Perhaps this is why Paul echoes the words of Dan 12:3 in Phil 2:15 (ἐν οἷσ φαίνεθε). For Daniel, shining like the stars was about the future resurrection, when the people of God currently oppressed by Babylon/Greece would be resurrected to new life and thus find victory and vindication over their enemies. Paul picks up this theme but says that the Philippians are *currently* shining like the stars in the world. They are vindicated; they are victorious. But they shine as they suffer, or, perhaps more accurately, their suffering is their shining; it reveals their glory, their victory, their resurrection life in Christ. It reveals that they are, in fact, the children of God and that God is, in fact, in the midst of their sufferings, demonstrating that he is, in fact, the

Phil 3:18–21

In 3:18 Paul describes a group of unidentified people as those who "live as enemies of the cross." Earlier I identified them as those whom Paul calls "opponents" in 1:28. "Their end is destruction, their god is their belly, and they glory in their shame, with minds set on earthly things" (3:19).[51] Such traits identify them as those who live as citizens of the earthly kingdom, who follow and impose the rules of Caesar. Believers, on the other hand, live as citizens of a different kingdom, an empire not ruled by and defined by Rome. And while they currently exist in a physical state of humility, they will one day also share in Christ's physical resurrection state of glory (3:21). This transformation will be inaugurated at the return of the true Savior, the true Lord, Jesus the true King (3:20). But, in all of this, does Paul seek to draw a contrast between believers suffering now and receiving glory later? Well, not entirely.

Whereas for those living in the first century Roman world, those who exist for their own honor, whose "god is their stomach and glory is their shame," suffering is the opposite of glory. A willingness to suffer might depict weakness, dishonor, and what Paul describes as humility. This mindset would have been no different in Roman Philippi, situated along the *via Egnatia* with a strong presence of Roman military veterans and with, at least on some level, the presence of an established imperial cult.[52] The contrast Paul makes is not between believers' present suffering and future glory, but rather *what glory looks like in Caesar's kingdom vs. what glory looks like in God's kingdom*, as described in 2:6–11. Some live as enemies of the cross, thinking that glory looks quite the opposite of the cross. But in the kingdom of God, true power, true glory is demonstrated in one's willingness to take the lowest position, to be subjected to enemies even to the point of death. Christians are called, therefore, to lead lives worthy of the gospel of Christ—lives characterized by glorious suffering, paradoxical though it is. In their suffering, they demonstrate a new and greater reality: not only are they redeemed humans in Christ, who is their righteousness through the cross; but because of the cross, the fundamental reality to which the entire Roman world ascribes is utterly false. Caesar is not Lord and Savior. Rome is not the seat of judgment.

---

true Lord of the world.

51. ESV.

52. See again Cohick, "Philippians and Empire," 166–82.

Glory is not discovered or displayed in cruelty, esteem, and domination. What does glory look like? It looks like the Suffering Servant.

Undoubtedly there is a strong link between 2:6–11 and 3:18–21. Therefore, to read the hymn either purely ethically or to read in it a progression of Christ from a state of humility to a vindicated state of exaltation weakens the magnificence of the hymn itself and minimizes the necessity for its inclusion in the letter. This is why Flemming, while right to connect 2:6–11 to 3:20–21 (though, better yet to include 3:18–19), misinterprets that connection. Because of the helpful contrast he makes with my suggestion here, I quote him at length:

> How might Christ's exaltation offer an example to follow? Here the analogy between the story of Christ and those who are in Christ is less direct. Nevertheless, the parallels with 3:20–21 noted above suggest that Paul views the Philippians' own future through the lens of the drama of Christ. The passage implies that just as God vindicated Jesus in response to his obedience unto death, so also the Philippians, if they remain faithful to the gospel in the face of suffering, will be exalted by God in the end (see 1:6). Put differently, if they are *conformed* to his likeness in humility now, they will be *transformed* into his glorious likeness in the future (3:21; see 3:10–11). Furthermore, Paul has already assured his readers that their present opposition and suffering is a sign that they are genuine followers of Christ and that they will indeed be saved by God (1:28–29).[53]

Ultimately, the only correlation Flemming can make between the exaltation of Christ in 2:9–11 with that of believers is that, *if* they faithfully endure their suffering, *then* they will be assigned glory in the future. They will be "exalted by God in the end."[54] Their present suffering is a sign that they *will* be saved by God. But nothing indicates that the salvation promised in 1:28 must be limited to a *future* salvation. More importantly, no language of conditionality exists in 3:21 to suggest an if-then construct. In contrast with Flemming's ethical reading of the hymn, in which he limits any practical application for believers to what he sees in 2:6–8, the point of connection between the hymn and 3:18–21 is the fact that in Christ they are already citizens of heaven, a kingdom ruled by the Messiah as Lord and in which they participate as redeemed humans. Their exaltation currently takes the same shape as that of Christ's; they

---

53. Flemming, *Philippians*, 111.
54. Though one might also question this reading of 1:6.

are already participating in the paradoxical state of glory. Just as the "rulers of this age" did not know they were crucifying the "Lord of glory" (1 Cor 2:8), so also the world might not yet know the true status of those whose identity is in that Lord of glory. But one day the world will know, when the true Lord and Savior returns to establish the true kingdom on earth. On that day he will subject all things to himself and every knee will finally bend.

Making Sense of the Separation

It might be worth reflecting for a moment on why these twin concepts of suffering and glory have been so separated within Christian theology and understanding. I see two factors that bear at least some culpability. The first is the lack of understanding or awareness of the motif of participation/union with Christ amongst laity. Certainly, within the scholarly realm this discussion has made its impact. But how often does the average lay reader of Scripture take notice of seemingly insignificant words such as "in" and "with"? No reason exists for why they should, of course, unless it is instilled in them from the pulpit or in serious biblical and theological studies offered by churches.

But what happens when lay readers of Scripture begin to understand the motif of participation with Christ? What happens when they recognize that baptism is not just a public proclamation of faith "about" Christ but also a participatory incorporation into the death and resurrection of Christ? Perspectives change. It is no longer us and Christ, but us in Christ. It is no longer Paul telling the Philippians they ought to be sacrificial toward one another because, well, look at Jesus, he was certainly sacrificial toward us. Rather, it is Paul telling the Philippians to stand firm, to stand united because they are united in Christ. They ought *therefore* to live out the reality that was put into place both by Jesus' death and resurrection but also by their own death and resurrection *in him*.

The second factor is the ingrained escapist/rapture theology pervasive within the American Christian church.[55] The goal of our salvation is often presented to us as an escape from the dreary suffering of this world.[56]

---

55. As an example, after teaching an "Introduction to the Bible" course, a student wrote in a course evaluation something to the point of: "Haley's a great teacher and she's fun and she knows her stuff, but she doesn't believe that the rapture described in Revelation is necessarily going to happen. I thought this university hired Christians."

56. Not that most American Christians have experienced the kind of suffering Paul

And, while we struggle to articulate precisely what or where heaven is, we can at least say that it is "up there" opposed to "down here" and it is "spiritual" rather than "physical." Such views find less support than they once did, but thanks to Plato, Tim LaHaye, and a slew of writers between them, many Christians still have a lot of unlearning to do.

But what if, as many have now argued,[57] the *parousia* of Christ is not about him returning to snatch us all away from this earth? What if, instead, he is going to return to earth and transform it, along with us and the whole lot of creation, to be the cosmic temple we get a glimpse of in Genesis 1? And, moreover, what if the kingdom that he will establish is already inaugurated on earth as it is in heaven? If that kingdom is here now but is not yet fully, just as we are dead to sin and alive to Christ, but not yet fully, and just as Jesus is currently exalted as Lord but every knee has not yet bended to him, then we are glorified now but not yet fully. We live here on earth and have new life in a new kingdom in a new creation as redeemed humans and adopted children of God. Our sanctification is our glory: it is our being made wholly human, able to live out completely the human vocation described in Genesis 1 and Psalm 8—the same vocation that is expressed in the lordship of Christ. And if we recognize *that* reality launched by Christ on the cross and *that* glory displayed by Christ on the cross, then we will also recognize that we are part of that same new reality, here and now.

Implications for Contemporary Christianity

After graduating from college, I spent one year in Kyrgyzstan teaching English at a local university. There my twenty-two-year-old self was introduced to the physical, social, and political dangers Christians around the world experience as a result of their country and culture's religious regulations. One woman of my age whom I knew was baptized that year, knowing full well that it would mean rejection from her family, and likely far worse. The underground church exists throughout the globe, with countless brothers and sisters now, in this very moment, sitting in prison

---

is typically emphasizing.

57. Perhaps most emphatically by N. T. Wright. See esp. *Surprised by Hope*, but also *Resurrection and the Son of God*, 229–36, for the same themes specifically applied to Phil 3:20–21.

as a result of preaching and defending the gospel. Many of them will die as a result of it, and their families will face starvation.[58]

How are these believers to understand their suffering? Where are they to find their hope to endure, to press on and finish the race? According to Paul, that needed hope is not based on a conditional future glory, something that will come if one suffers well on earth. Rather, their persecution is a sign of their salvation, an indication that they are citizens of the heavenly kingdom and that they are participants in the resurrection life of the true Lord. This does not mean that such suffering is inherently good or something to be sought after. Quite the opposite. It is a sign that the new has come but not yet in full, and that "Caesar's reign" is not yet fully destroyed. Darkness still exists. But the darkness in which some believers live is the same darkness in which God demonstrated his own glory; it is a darkness in which glory reveals a new reality.[59] The Lord is Servant, and his position was and is one of exaltation and glory. This paradoxical definition of suffering as glory in Philippians should encourage contemporary Christians who suffer for the gospel to live and suffer in a broken and dark world not only for the anticipated glory but also as an expression of their current life in the crucified and exalted Lord.

There is also a challenge here to those of us who are not persecuted for the gospel to remember the unity we share with these believers. Their suffering is all but forgotten by most in the West. Major news networks are unconcerned. Even in the western church, only the rare sermon will highlight their plight. And, while prayers offered on behalf of Bob finding a job or Sally's upcoming exam are undoubtedly good things to pray for, the prayers offered on behalf of our brothers and sisters whose meeting place is a forest, who have never touched a bible, whose families starve while they sit in prison, but who count it a privilege to suffer in such ways for the gospel, well, those prayers occur about as often as the sermons on the same topics. The call to be united in Christ is not for the local church community alone, but for the entire body of Christ. We are all citizens of heaven now, and that means that we in the West share more in

58. Several organizations exist to make the plight of the persecuted church known around the world and to bring relief to their suffering where possible, including: The Voice of the Martyrs (www.persecution.com), International Christian Concern (www.persecution.org), and Christian Aid (www.christianaid.org).

59. For this reason, this reading that I am proposing of the relationship between suffering and glory in Philippians should not be read as either an over-realized, triumphalist eschatology, or an under-realized, life-this-side-of-heaven = suffering eschatology.

common with these brothers and sisters than many of us do with our own neighbors. Paul's charge to the Philippians to stand firm in one spirit, in one mind, as those whose identity is in the Lord who is Servant and the Servant who is Lord, is the same charge to those of us who have perhaps never experienced the Lord as Servant in such ways. If we take seriously the reality of believers' union with Christ, through which we are made the body of Christ, then failing to remember our persecuted siblings is not an option.[60]

Bibliography

Barth, Karl. *Church Dogmatics IV.1: The Doctrine of Reconciliation*. Translated by G. W. Bromiley. New York: T & T Clark, 2004.

———. *Epistle to the Philippians*. Translated by James W. Leitch. 40th Anniversary ed. Louisville: Westminster John Knox, 2002.

Bauckham, Richard. *Gospel of Glory: Major Themes in Johannine Theology*. Grand Rapids: Baker, 2015.

Bockmuehl, Markus. *The Epistle to the Philippians*. Black's New Testament Commentary. Peabody, MA: Hendrickson, 1998.

Cohick, Lynn H. *Philippians*. The Story of God Bible Commentary. Grand Rapids: Zondervan, 2013.

———. "Philippians and Empire: Paul's Engagement with Imperialism and the Imperial Cult." In *Jesus Is Lord, Caesar Is Not: Evaluating Empire in New Testament Studies*, edited by Scot McKnight and Joseph B. Modica, 166–82. Downers Grove, IL: IVP Academic, 2013.

Crossan, John Dominic. *God and Empire: Jesus Against Rome, Then and Now*. San Francisco: Harper Collins, 2007.

Fee, Gordon D. *Paul's Letter to the Philippians*. New International Commentary on the New Testament. Grand Rapids: Eerdmans, 1995.

Flemming, Dean. *Philippians: A Commentary in the Wesleyan Tradition*. New Beacon Bible Commentary. Kansas City: Beacon Hill, 2009.

Goldingay, John. *Biblical Theology: The God of the Christian Scriptures*. Downers Grove, IL: IVP Academic, 2016.

Gorman, Michael J. *Inhabiting the Cruciform God: Kenosis, Justification, and Theosis in Paul's Narrative Soteriology*. Grand Rapids: Eerdmans, 2009.

Hellerman, Joseph H. *Philippians*. Exegetical Guide to the Greek New Testament. Nashville: Broadman and Holman, 2015.

Jacob, Haley Goranson. *Conformed to the Image of His Son: Reconsidering Paul's Theology of Glory in Romans*. Downers Grove, IL: IVP Academic, 2018.

Kreitzer, Larry J. "'When He at Last Is First!': Philippians 2:9–11 and the Exaltation of the Lord." In *Where Christology Began: Essays on Philippians 2*, edited by Ralph P. Martin and Brian J. Dodd, 111–27. Louisville: Westminster John Knox, 1998.

Martin, Ralph P. *Carmen Christi: Philippians 2:5–11 in Recent Interpretation and in the Setting of Early Christian Worship*. Rev. ed. Grand Rapids: Eerdmans, 1983.

---

60. See also Heb 13:3.

Martin, Ralph P., and Brian J. Dodd, eds. *Where Christology Began: Essays on Philippians 2*. Louisville: Westminster John Knox, 1998.

Oakes, Peter. *Philippians: From People to Letter.* Society for New Testament Studies Monograph Series 110. Cambridge: Cambridge University Press, 2007.

O'Brien, Peter T. *The Epistle to the Philippians: A Commentary on the Greek Text.* The New International Greek Testament Commentary. Grand Rapids: Eerdmans, 1991.

Silva, Moisés. *Philippians.* Baker Exegetical Commentary on the New Testament. 2nd ed. Grand Rapids: Baker, 2005.

Thielman, Frank. *Philippians.* The NIV Application Commentary. Grand Rapids: Zondervan, 1995.

Wright, N. T. *The Resurrection of the Son of God.* Christian Origins and the Question of God 3. Minneapolis: Fortress, 2003.

———. *Surprised by Hope: Rethinking Heaven, the Resurrection, and the Mission of the Church.* New York: Harper One, 2008.

8

"The Fellowship of Christ's Sufferings" (Phil 3:10)

Politics, Sufferings, and Social Identity Formation in Philippians

Kar Yong Lim

Paul, Caesar, and the Politics of His Days[1]

Much has been said about politics in the New Testament, and particularly within the Pauline corpus, in recent years.[2] Driven partly by the rise in postcolonial reading of the New Testament, there has been a surge of interest in imperial cult studies in the last two decades. However, this recent interest is not a new discovery. In fact, over a century ago in 1908, Adolf Deissmann reminded us with these words:

> The deification of the Caesars was an abomination to Christianity from the beginning. . . . It must not be supposed that St. Paul and his fellow-believers went through the world blindfolded,

---

1. I would like to thank the trustees and donors of the Theological Research Scheme, a small private initiative set up to assist publication by Malaysian scholars, for awarding me a grant in 2017 to acquire the resources needed for this essay that are not available in our theological libraries.

2. For a brief introduction, see the compendium of essays in Porter and Westfall, *Empire in the New Testament;* and Winn, *Introduction to Empire in the New Testament.*

unaffected by what was then moving the minds of men in great cities. These pages [referring to his book *Light from the Ancient East*], I think, have already shown by many examples how much the New Testament is a book of the Imperial age. We may certainly take it for granted that the Christians of the early Imperial period were familiar with the institutions and customs that the Empire had brought with it.[3]

Deissmann then proceeded to provide a host of illustrations drawn from the daily life of those living under the shadow of the Empire. He demonstrated that people living during the era of early Christianity would have been thoroughly familiar with the imperial cult and how this served as a great challenge to the early Christ-followers.[4]

It is rather strange that what Deissmann had already described over a century ago did not generate the kind of interest seen in studies on the imperial cult since the 1990s. On the one hand, we see the dominant view made popular by Richard Horsley, Neil Elliott, Ian Rock, and others that suggest Paul's primary message is one of socio-political protest against the tyranny, arrogance, and brutality of the Empire.[5] According to this view, the interpreters of Paul paint a picture of the apostle as one who was less interested in "theology" and more in his attempt to subvert the rule of Rome under the lordship of Jesus the Messiah with the aim of challenging Rome's claim to hegemony. As rightly noted by N. T. Wright,[6] much of this reading traces its roots to various postcolonial readings, exemplified in the works of Christopher Stanley.[7] Taking this reading to an extreme, one may be left wondering whether Paul's epistles are indeed some form of subversive writings attempting to start a resistance movement against the Roman Empire rather than occasional writings that address the concerns, issues, and problems confronting the Christ-community.

---

3. Deissmann, *Light from the Ancient East*, 343–45.

4. Deissmann, *Light from the Ancient East*, 345–46.

5. See the multi-volume works edited by Horsley, *Paul and Empire*; *Paul and Politics*; and *Paul and the Roman Imperial Order*. See also Horsley and Silberman, *Message and the Kingdom*; and Horsley, *Hidden Transcripts*. For further discussion, see Elliott, *Liberating Paul*; and *Arrogance of Nations*; Rock, *Paul's Letter to the Romans*; Hardin, *Galatians and the Imperial Cult*; and Walsh and Keesmaat, *Colossians Remixed*.

6. Wright, *Paul and the Faithfulness of God*, 1273n5. See his wider discussion on the relationship between Paul's gospel and Caesar's world in pages 1271–319. See also his *Paul: Fresh Perspectives*, 59–79.

7. Stanley, *Colonized Apostle*.

On the other hand, not everyone is convinced that such enthusiasm in the political reading of Paul is warranted. Proponents of the alternative view argue that the imperial cult was much less important or significant in Paul's thought.[8] According to them, Paul's primary purpose was to turn people from worshipping idols to the one true God, and the battles he fought had more to do with the spiritual battles and war against the rulers and principalities of the cosmos, rather than the political powers of his day. After all, Paul was concerned with establishing his community that would be ready for the imminent *eschaton*. Read in this way, Paul's letters are simply writings for building up the faith of the fledging communities towards spiritual maturity. If Paul's letters are "spiritual" writings, then unearthing his theology and mining for spiritual truth will be the ultimate goal of the interpreters of Paul. This reading naturally has less to do with subverting Rome and its hegemony. Such an apolitical reading of Paul is not uncommon particularly among certain quarters of Evangelicals today.[9] Having considered the two extreme readings of Paul and the politics of his day, I will return to consider a possible way forward later in this essay.

Paul and Sufferings

A cursory reading of Philippians reveals the dominant theme of suffering in this short letter. Paul refers to his imprisonment (Phil 1:12–18), his sufferings (Phil 4:10–14), and his desire to share in the fellowship of Christ's sufferings (Phil 3:10). He speaks of the sufferings of his coworkers (Phil 2:19–30). He also mentions the sufferings of the Philippians (Phil 1:27–30) and indicates that they also share in his sufferings (Phil 4:14). Finally, Paul uses the language of suffering in describing the humiliation and exaltation of Christ (Phil 2:6–11).

The theme of suffering in Philippians has received some form of treatment throughout the history of interpretation, particularly from the

---

8. See especially the works of Kim, *Christ and Caesar*; and Bryan, *Render to Caesar*.

9. I am reminded of an interview carried out by a Malaysian daily some years ago with one of the prominent Christian leaders representing the National Evangelical Christian Fellowship, a member of the World Evangelical Alliance. During the interview, this representative publicly declared that the church is apolitical (see http://www.thestar.com.my/opinion/columnists/cafelattechat/2008/01/20/the-christian-perspective/). I attempted to reach this leader seeking clarification of what he meant by the church being apolitical. Unfortunately, my attempt was unsuccessful.

perspective of martyrdom, as reviewed by Bloomquist.[10] According to Bloomquist, the earliest interpretation of sufferings took on the position that suffering brought about perfection and bore witness to one's faith. This reading, most commonly reflected in the writings of the early Church Fathers, developed partly due to the historical reality of martyrdom in the early church. However, after the period of Constantine martyrdom receded into the historical past, there was a shift in the understanding of suffering. Whereas it had been given a spiritualized interpretation, suffering was now seen from the perspective of the daily life and activities of Christians battling with the evils of the flesh. Moving forward to the post-enlightenment period, suffering took on a different understanding where it was viewed from the perspective of Christ-mysticism developed by Albert Schweitzer.[11] Since then, suffering has been largely interpreted from a theological perspective and various models of interpretation continue to be developed. I have already reviewed some of these models such as exegetical studies, salvation-history, imitation of Christ, historical and background studies, and thematic studies elsewhere and highlighted some of their strengths and weaknesses.[12]

What can be briefly summarized here is that the theme of suffering has been largely interpreted from historical-critical and theological perspectives. There is no denying that much insight could be gleaned from these perspectives. However, it is unfortunate that these models of interpretation do not sufficiently take into consideration the political and historical realities of the minority Pauline community within the Roman Empire, more so that Paul's sufferings in Philippians were either directly related to imprisonment imposed by the Roman Empire (see Phil 1:12–18) or stated in language that is politically loaded and motivated (see Phil 2:6–11 and 3:18–20).

Is There a Nuanced Way Forward?

Two Extremes to Be Avoided

What appears from this very brief survey is that there seem to be two extremes in the political reading of the Pauline corpus. Notwithstanding my

---

10. Bloomquist, *Function of Suffering*, 18–70.
11. See Schweitzer, *Mysticism of Paul*.
12. See Lim, *Sufferings of Christ*, 1–15.

mild criticism of the task of interpreting Paul from a political perspective, it is in my opinion that this reading does, in fact, bring into sharp focus a very rewarding and refreshing understanding of Paul's letters. This reading reminds us as interpreters of Paul that his writings did not come to us in a vacuum. There is no doubt that Paul's writings were occasional letters. At the same time, these extant writings were also letters written within the πολιτεία of Caesar and the Roman Empire, as acknowledged by Deissmann. It is therefore reasonable to anticipate some form of political engagement with the Empire in Paul's letters.

Moving forward, I would like to suggest in this essay that a more nuanced reading of a political Paul might be warranted, especially in reading passages dealing with Paul and suffering in Philippians. I will attempt to avoid an approach drawn from either of the extremes in the political reading of Paul as I have briefly highlighted above. Rather, I hope to bring both extremes into a *via media*, and the litmus test is whether this approach will bring a more nuanced and balanced reading of Paul, showing that the early Pauline ἐκκλησίαι were indeed both political and spiritual entities. In order to do so, I will examine five passages where the dominant theme of suffering is present: Phil 1:12–18; 1:27–30; 2:5–11; 3:10–18; and 3:20–21. But first, I will outline the methodology I will use by reading these passages from the perspective of social identity formation.

Where Do We Go from Here? Exploring Social Identity Formation

The fledging Pauline community comprising predominantly Gentiles who were fairly recent converts to the Christ-movement would have undergone some form of identity crisis within the new religious structure. What is clear from his letters is that Paul went to great length to instruct them to abandon their previous way of life and to embrace a new way of living that conformed to the norms established in the Scripture of Israel.[13] As such, social identity formation plays a significant role within the letters of Paul.

Social identity formation, a branch of social psychology, has been employed as a useful interpretative framework in investigating Paul's

---

13. For example, see Gal 4:8—6:10; Eph 4:1—6:9; Phil 1:27–30; 3:15–21; Col 3:1—4:6.

letters in recent years. According to Henri Tajfel, the process of social identity formation primarily involves three dimensions in establishing the ethos, values, status, and boundaries for a particular group as against other groups in a society—the cognitive, emotional, and evaluative dimensions.[14] The cognitive dimension provides the group members with a strong sense of belonging and distinctiveness as compared to other groups. The emotional dimension involves various rituals and practices that enhance the emotional ties in group dynamics in order to establish a strong sense of solidarity, identity, and belonging to the group. The evaluative dimension deals with how the members of the group rate themselves in relation to other groups, and this often involves positive evaluation of the in-groups against negative evaluation of the out-groups. Social identity formation theory, initially developed by Tajfel and further explored by Turner, has been widely employed in New Testament and Pauline studies.[15] The massive *T&T Clark Handbook to Social Identity Formation in the New Testament* is strong testimony to the successful adoption of this approach.[16]

Having considered these methodological issues, I will read the suffering passages from a political perspective in order to explore how Paul could have used the notion of suffering to construct social identity of a fledging Christian community in Roman Philippi. This interdisciplinary approach is one area that has yet to be fully explored within the context of Philippians.

The City of Philippi

The city of Philippi was named in honor of Philip II of Macedonia who seized it from the Thracians around 356 BCE. The city, rich in natural resources, flourished under the rule of Philip II and also subsequently under his son, Alexander the Great. However, the fortune of Philippi faded away after this era until it was conquered by the Romans in 167

---

14. Tajfel, *Differentiation between Social Groups*, 28.

15. See Turner, *Rediscovering the Social Group*; Esler, *Conflict and Identity in Romans*; May, *Body for the Lord*; Darko, *No Longer Living as the Gentiles*; Barentsen, *Emerging Leadership in Pauline Mission*; Tucker, *You Belong to Christ*; and Tucker, "Remain in Your Calling". See also Lim, "If Anyone is in Christ"; and *Metaphors and Social Identity Formation*. For reviews of recent scholarship on social identity in Pauline studies, see Tucker, *You Belong to Christ*, 87–124.

16. Tucker and Baker, *T&T Clark Handbook to Social Identity*.

BCE. Following the Roman conquest, construction of the main highway, *Via Egnatia*, commenced. This highway linking Rome to the East completed around 130 BCE sealed the future of Philippi as a strategic establishment for decades to come. Philippi was also subsequently established as a Roman colony under the reign of Anthony (42 BCE) and Octavian, later known as Augustus (30 BCE). This ensured that the city continued to enjoy Roman interest and embraced a distinctly Roman flavor. The renaming of the city as *Colonia Julia Augusta Philippensis* in 27 BCE to commemorate the victory of Augustus at Actium and the resettlement of veterans in this city further established the city's alignment with Rome. Finally, in the mid-forties CE, Claudius conquered Thrace and made it a Roman province, thus further ensuring the significance and importance of the city of Philippi. The Romanness of the city of Philippi is further evidenced by the prominence of its imperial cult worship, as well as the archaeological evidence and numerous inscriptions that testified to the close relationship between the city and Rome.[17] This setting makes the letter to the colony's Christians an excellent test case to be read through a political lens, to examine the place of suffering in the formation of social identity.

Politics, Suffering, and Social Identity Formation

In order to achieve a political reading of Paul within the context outlined above, I have selected five passages that directly address suffering and social identity formation.

Phil 1:12–18: Paul in Prison but the Proclamation of the Gospel Cannot Be Thwarted

Philippians situates Paul in an imperial imprisonment as evidenced by references to the most elite group of Roman soldiers, πραιτώριον (imperial guard), in Phil 1:13 and Καίσαρος οἰκίας (Caesar's household) in Phil

---

17. For further discussion, see Verhoef, *Philippi*, 1–24; Bakirtzis and Koester, *Philippi at the Time of Paul*; Oakes, *Philippians*, 1–54; Hellerman, *Reconstructing Honor*, 64–87; and Nebreda, *Christ Identity*, 119–83. For a discussion on ritual and cults in Philippi, see Lamoreaux, *Ritual, Women, and Philippi*, 20–100. Note also the discussion on coins excavated in Philippi in Reasoner, *Roman Imperial Texts*, 136–38.

4:22.[18] Paul clearly indicates that he was in chains for Christ in Phil 1:13 (τοὺς δεσμούς μου φανεροὺς ἐν Χριστῷ γενέσθαι) and further mentions his chains twice in Phil 1:14 and 17. This casts before Paul's audience an apostle who suffered for the sake of the gospel. Paul's imprisonment and his suffering are central to his narrative and life, and have been referenced numerous times in his writings.[19] However, strangely, throughout his letters (and also in Acts), the reason for his imprisonment is not explicitly made known, except that Paul merely describes it as a direct result of his identification with Christ and his proclamation of the gospel. It has been generally acknowledged that the most likely reason for Paul's imperial imprisonment was *maiestas*, or treason: promoting and proclaiming another Lord, Savior, and Son of God who was above Caesar himself, to whom these titles had also been ascribed.[20]

Paul's imprisonment was more than being placed within a confined space with limited movement and freedom. When such restricted spatial boundary was imposed by Rome, it carried with it the notion of "territoriality." The function of territoriality is "the attempt by an individual or group to affect, influence, or control people, phenomena, and relationships, by delimiting and asserting control over a geographical area."[21] Seen in this way, the spatial boundary imposed on Paul not only curtailed his freedom for physical movement, it also subjected him to shameful punishment that violated a person's dignity.[22] More importantly, the spatial boundary was also a powerful and effective tool to silence Paul so that he could not continue to proclaim the gospel. Ultimately, territoriality meant that Paul had been defeated, shamed, and silenced when he was placed under the spatial control of Caesar. Not only did Paul suffer physically, he also endured emotional and mental anguish for not being able to fulfil his divine calling as an apostle.

If Paul's imprisonment with chains was meant to be a severe punishment for treason, intimidation, and a tool to silence him, then any

---

18. For comments on the use of πραιτώριον and Καίσαρος οἰκίας, see Hansen, *Philippians*, 67–68.

19. For further treatment on Paul's sufferings, see Lim, *Sufferings of Christ*.

20. So Fee, *Philippians*, 120. See also Stanhartinger, "Letter from Prison," 107–40, for a detailed description on the conditions of prisons in the days of Paul.

21. Sack, *Human Territoriality*, 16. For further discussion, see Neyrey, "Spaces and Places," 60–74.

22. For further treatment on imprisonment and the negative impact of imprisonment in the days of Paul, see Wansink, *Chained in Christ*; and Cassidy, *Paul in Chains*.

attempt by Rome in placing territoriality on him not only failed but worked against Rome itself.

Firstly, Paul clearly states that Caesar's bodyguards could not intimidate him for he served a higher power than Caesar: who is, Christ. The πραιτώριον viewed chains on a prisoner as evidence of Caesar's power. Hansen argues that in the case of Roman prisoners, "(t)hese chains were Caesar's chains, demonstrating that Caesar was Lord, binding the prisoner for Caesar to fulfill Caesar's will."[23] But in Paul's case, Hansen suggests that these palace guards saw his chains "as evidence of Christ's power" and they even realized that he "was in chains because he was in Christ."[24] If Hansen is right, the irony becomes clear—Caesar had no power to hold Paul in prison and even his elite troops acknowledge it.

Secondly, instead of impeding the proclamation of the gospel, the spatial boundary imposed by Rome through Paul's imprisonment actually served to advance the gospel. Paul states that more people were now boldly declaring the word (Phil 1:12–14), the message of Jesus Christ the crucified Messiah as the Son of God, the Lord and the Savior. If this is not already a sufficient insult to the efforts of Rome to imprison and to silence him, Paul further adds salt to the injury. He insists that even his friends and rivals were proclaiming the gospel without fear (Phil 1:15–18). The final straw would have been the fact that even Caesar's household heard the gospel being proclaimed and they were the very people requesting Paul to send their greetings to the Philippians (Phil 4:22). This satirical tone and ironical force of Paul's language in undermining the power of Rome could not have been missed by the recipients.

In other words, while Rome may be in control and the imprisonment was seen as the ultimate expression of the power of Rome on Paul's life by inflicting sufferings on the apostle, in reality, that power was not only nullified but also replaced by another more powerful Lord and Savior whose message of the gospel could not be contained and controlled even by Rome. That Paul was able to assert his confidence in Christ and the gospel arises out of his cognitive understanding of his social identity as a Christ-follower, as it provides Paul with a very strong sense of belonging to Christ, the true Lord and Savior, and not Caesar. While Paul may have been placed under arrest, this imprisonment further reinforced his social identity as an apostle, the bearer of the good news. He could

---

23. Hansen, *Philippians*, 68.
24. Hansen, *Philippians*, 68.

take comfort that instead of silencing him, his imprisonment and sufferings served to advance the gospel, and freed others from being fearful of proclaiming the gospel. In the final analysis, the effects of his imprisonment were quite the opposite of what was expected. The proclamation of the gospel could not be thwarted by Caesar, and the Philippians would have grasped the significance of Paul's sufferings.

Phil 1:27–30: The Philippians Suffer for the Sake of Christ in the Midst of Opposition

In Phil 1:27, Paul turns to address the Philippians by exhorting them with these words: Μόνον ἀξίως τοῦ εὐαγγελίου τοῦ Χριστοῦ πολιτεύεσθε. His choice of the imperatival πολιτεύεσθε is highly unusual. First, the verb itself is not used anywhere else in his letter and only once elsewhere in the New Testament in Acts 23:1. Second, this is a departure from the more common imperative used to exhort his readers for ethical conduct: περιπατεῖτε.[25] The use of πολιτεύεσθε instead of περιπατεῖτε suggests that Paul was not simply concerned with moral behavior but "the pattern of conduct that flows from belonging to a particular commonwealth, and having allegiance to its ruler."[26]

The word πολιτεύεσθε, without doubt, is drawn from the political life of the Roman *polis* and anticipates the noun πολίτευμα used later in Phil 3:20. However, questions have been raised as to the metaphorical use of citizenship in Phil 1:27, whether it refers to heavenly or earthly citizenship. Gordon Fee argues that the citizenship Paul has in mind is "the heavenly one of course,"[27] by drawing insight from similar language used in Phil 3:17–20. Read in this light, Paul is exhorting the Philippians to "live in the Roman colony of Philippi as worthy citizens of your heavenly homeland."[28] However, Fee further acknowledges that the Philippians should not ignore their earthly responsibilities but show concern for the welfare of "the believing community itself."[29] On the other hand, Raymond

---

25. For example, see 1 Cor 3:3; Gal 5:16; Eph 5:2, 8, 15; Col 2:6; 4:5; 1 Thess 4:1. See also Rom 6:4; 8:4; 13:13; 14:15; 1 Cor 7:17; 2 Cor 4:2; 10:2; Eph 2:2; 2:10; 4:1; 4:17; Phil 3:17–18; Col 1:10; and 1 Thess 4:12.

26. McAuley, *Paul's Covert Use of Scripture*, 91.

27. Fee, *Philippains*, 161. So Fowl, *Philippians*, 61–62.

28. Fee, *Philippians*, 162.

29. Fee, *Philippians*, 162.

Brewer argues that πολιτεύεσθε is a way of speaking about discharging one's obligation as a citizen of the Roman Empire.³⁰ This seems doubtful, as it is uncertain if the large majority of the Philippian Christ-followers were Roman citizens.³¹ Hawthorne provides a better understanding of the word πολιτεύεσθε: "to live as a good citizen of an earthly state, fully discharging one's duties and responsibilities to that state."³² At the same time, being citizens of the heavenly kingdom, the Christ-followers were required to live "as a good citizen of this new state, governing his actions by the laws of this unique πολίτευμα—righteousness, peace, faith, hope, love, mutuality, interdependence, good deeds, service to one another, worship of the living God, and so on."³³ Paul underscores the fact that the way of life of the Gentile Christ-followers must be different from the rest of the pagan citizens in Roman Philippi. While they lived as citizens and sojourners of a Roman colony, they pledged their allegiance to Christ, and not to Caesar. In this respect, Markus Bockmuehl is right to say that "Paul interposes a counter-citizenship whose capital and seat of power are not earthly but heavenly, whose guarantor is not Nero but Christ."³⁴

The manner in which the Philippians were to live out their lives as citizens worthy of the gospel is then spelled out: στήκετε ἐν ἑνὶ πνεύματι (Phil 1:27). The word στήκετε is drawn from a military image portraying soldiers standing in unity by not breaking ranks. This is then followed by the use of two participial clauses, one stated positively (μιᾷ ψυχῇ συναθλοῦντες τῇ πίστει τοῦ εὐαγγελίου) in Phil 1:27 and the other negatively (μὴ πτυρόμενοι ἐν μηδενὶ ὑπὸ τῶν ἀντικειμένων) in Phil 1:28. This exhortation directed at the Philippians clearly shows that they were to stand firm in the face of a formidable foe by being united as a body of Christ.

Who could possibly be the opponents (τῶν ἀντικειμένων) that intimidated and frightened (πτυρόμενοι) the Philippians? It is possible they were the same group described as "enemies of the cross" in Phil 3:18–19, but certainly different from those mentioned in Phil 3:2–3 who were Judaizers or those who believed that circumcision was one of the boundary markers to be imposed on the Gentile Christ-followers. The

---

30. Brewer, "Meaning of *Politeuesthe*."
31. See also Fowl, *Philippians*, 60–61.
32. Hawthorne, *Philippians*, 56.
33. Hawthorne, *Philippians*, 56.
34. Bockmuehl, *Philippians*, 98.

opponents were most likely Roman authorities that caused the Philippians to suffer.³⁵ This suggestion is further strengthened by Phil 1:29–30 where Paul alluded to the fact that the Philippians were suffering for Christ (τὸ ὑπὲρ αὐτοῦ πάσχειν) and that their suffering was described as the same struggle (τὸν αὐτὸν ἀγῶνα ἔχοντες) they witnessed Paul had. Paul mentioned a number of sufferings he went through in Philippi elsewhere in his letters (1 Thess 2:2; 2 Cor 7:5).³⁶ According to Acts 16:11–40, Paul suffered at the hands of the Roman authorities. He also referred to the sufferings of the Macedonian churches in 2 Cor 8:1–2, which could have included the church in Philippi. In addition, Paul alluded to the Philippians as his partners in sharing in his sufferings (Phil 4:14).

What then was the nature of the sufferings experienced by the Philippians? Paul is silent on this. It was not suffering in general but sufferings for the sake of Christ in a world that was openly hostile to the gospel. Pressure was great for a small minority of Christ-followers to conform to the well-established customs, habits, and rituals of the city. They could have refused to participate in the imperial cult or proved unwilling to acknowledge the authority of Caesar, and both of these put them at risk with the Roman authorities.³⁷ Furthermore, Oakes has convincingly argued that refusal to participate in the worship of any Greco-Roman deities could easily result in long term suffering as a consequence of serious economic loss because contacts may have been severed and trade affected.³⁸ In addition, there were social consequences where the Christ-followers may have been excluded from trade guilds and prohibited from participating in networking that was all too important for building social relations. Alienation and harassment from families and other (non-trade-related) social networks could not be discounted either.

In appealing to the cognitive dimension of social identity by pledging allegiance to Christ, Paul's instructions to the Philippians to live out their lives as citizens worthy of the gospel were nothing less than a

---

35. Cousar, *Philippians and Philemon*, 14–15; Fee, *Philippians*, 172. Thompson and Longenecker, *Philippians and Philemon*, 52, suggest that the opponents could also include the local populace who possibly abused Paul.

36. In 2 Cor 7:5, the reference is made to Paul's sufferings in Macedonia, very likely a reference to Philippi.

37. Cf. Fee, *Philippians*, 167. Thompson and Longenecker, *Philippians and Philemon*, 12, suggest that the charges against the Philippians could have included treason for refusing to participate in the imperial cult.

38. Oakes, *Philippians*, 63–70, 89–102. See also his "Economic Situation," 78–81. See also Verhoef, *Philippi*, 23; Fowl, *Philippians*, 64–65.

revolutionary demand—any suggestion of disloyalty to the Roman authorities would inevitably bring them into conflict with the authorities. The residents of the Roman colony would have recognized the importance of living worthily of their citizenship. By using the evaluative dimension, Paul instructed the Philippians to embrace an alternative lifestyle that reflected their allegiance to the gospel of Christ as they made Philippi their earthly residence. The social identity of the Philippians was to be distinct and different from other communities in the Roman colony. This alternative way of life would inevitably bring them persecution by the powerful Roman authorities.[39] Finally, by referring to their rituals and emotional ties with one another, Paul engages the emotive dimension of social identity formation in instructing the Philippians. By refusing to participate in any rituals and customs that stood in contradiction to the gospel of Christ, the Philippian Christ-followers opened themselves to possible hardship and oppression. Their worship should only be directed to Christ, the Lord, and not Caesar. Yet in the midst of sufferings, the Christ-followers were to be united and stand in solidarity with one another.

Phil 2:5–11: The Name, the Lord, that Is Above All Names: A New Lord Is Replacing Caesar

Philippians 2:5–11, commonly known as the *Carmen Christi*, has generated a bibliography that is almost impossible to reproduce here.[40] Much of the work on the *Carmen Christi* has been focused on the christological emphasis as scholars attempt to explain the meaning of words and phrases like μορφῇ θεοῦ, ἁρπαγμόν, εἶναι ἴσα, and ἑαυτὸν ἐκένωσεν amongst others, resulting in the debates on the nature of Christ's incarnation, the ontological Christology, and the structural outline of the hymn. I will not dwell on the debates on these issues. Instead, I will pay attention to Phil 2:9: διὸ καὶ ὁ θεὸς αὐτὸν ὑπερύψωσεν καὶ ἐχαρίσατο αὐτῷ τὸ ὄνομα τὸ ὑπὲρ πᾶν ὄνομα. What is "τὸ ὄνομα τὸ ὑπὲρ πᾶν ὄνομα" given to Christ? Together with most commentators, I take "the name that is above all

---

39. See also Smit, *Paradigms of Being in Christ*, 80–83.

40. For a history of interpretation of *Carmen Christi*, see Martin, *Carmen Christi*. See Nebreda, *Christ Identity*; and Hellerman, *Reconstructing Honor,* for an exhaustive bibliography. See also Fowl, *Story of Christ*, 49–101.

names" bestowed on Christ as the name "Lord", κύριος, and not "Jesus."[41] This name, κύριος, that is above all other names is significant in several ways. Firstly, it signifies that another Lord is exalted and enthroned, and his enthronement is not comparable to the enthronement of the Lord Caesar who rules over a specific territory. The enthronement of this Lord Jesus has universal or cosmic implication—he is the Lord of the entire universe. Christ is superior and more powerful than Caesar, and establishing this truth becomes the cornerstone of the cognitive dimension for social identity formation. Once again, the Philippians were reminded of the true Lord whom they worshipped and served.

Secondly, the "self-lowering-other-regard" ethical pattern as propagated by Horrell[42] seen in the *Carmen Christi* clearly highlights that this κύριος is one who is to be given more honor than Caesar. Christ's disposition and behavior stood in sharp contrast to the prevailing Roman convictions and practices relating to honor, social status, and power. Whereas Caesar, who claimed divine status and utilized and abused this status to further enhance his own glory and honor, Paul presents another Lord who genuinely possessed divine status, yet viewed this status as something not to be taken advantage of but willingly surrendered it for the sake of others. The voluntary relinquishing of power, glory, and status would have struck Caesar as folly and yet it was through this folly that Christ is given the name "Lord" that is above all other names.

Thirdly, since Jesus chose to use his power and status in a manner that constituted a clear rejection of the prevailing social norm, God bestowed upon him the highest honor. This highest honor was found in Phil 2:10–11: "that at the name of Jesus every knee should bow, in heaven and on earth and under the earth, and every tongue acknowledge that Jesus Christ is Lord, to the glory of God the Father." As convincingly argued by Joseph Hellerman, the action by Jesus stood in sharp contrast to the prevailing social conventions of Roman Philippi.[43] Hellerman further argues that Paul portrays Jesus as a *cursus pudorum* (course of ignominies) and by doing so, Paul intentionally frames the *Carmen Christi* to subvert the Roman ideology of *cursus honorum*, the quest of acquiring honor by upward social mobility in a hierarchical society where honor and status seeking was the norm. The honor given by God to Jesus as Lord is

41. See Fowl, *Philippians*, 102–3; Fee, *Philippians*, 221–23; Hansen, *Philippians*, 162–63. See further O'Brien, *Philippians*, 238, for a convincing argument for this view.

42. See Horrell, *Solidarity and Difference*, 204–22.

43. For further discussion, see Hellerman, *Reconstructing Honor*, 129–56.

one that has universal significance, a title of honor that will be publicly acknowledged by all powers and authority, including Caesar.[44] The exalted status of Jesus was not only a challenge to Caesar. In fact, Caesar would eventually bow down to Jesus, the one with greater social status than any other emperor had ever known. This public acknowledgment of Jesus further brought shame and humiliation to Caesar who believed he alone had that honor to be ascribed as Lord. By appealing to the emotive dimension of social identity formation, Paul skillfully navigates his argument in presenting to the Philippians that even Caesar, no matter how powerful he may be perceived in the eyes of the Roman colony, would eventually surrender himself at the feet of Christ. The cosmic worship of Jesus offered by all subjects—both kings and paupers—cemented the distinctiveness of the Christ-followers in Philippi.

Furthermore, Paul structures the hymn in accordance with the language of suffering in which Christ suffered humiliation, weakness, and death on the cross. It is this attitude of humility that Paul wants the Philippian Christ-followers to emulate, as expressed in Phil 2:5: Τοῦτο φρονεῖτε ἐν ὑμῖν ὃ καὶ ἐν Χριστῷ Ἰησοῦ. In this respect, Christ becomes the supreme exemplar for the Christ-followers.[45] Thus Paul not only portrays Jesus as one who suffered, he also redefines the manner in which honor and power were to be utilized by the Christ-followers for the sake of others in order to maintain unity in the midst of opposition (Phil 2:1–4). Here, Paul is appealing to both the cognitive and evaluative dimensions of constructing a social identity of the Christ-followers that was markedly different from any other voluntary associations and religious groups that were found in Roman Philippi.[46] Just as Christ suffered in his humiliation and obedience on the cross, his followers should be prepared to undergo suffering for their faith in Christ.

Phil 3:7–11:
The Fellowship of Christ's Suffering as the Highest Honor

In Phil 3:7–8a, Paul highlights the renunciation of his previous pedigrees in light of his experience in Christ. By employing an accounting

---

44. Hellerman, *Reconstructing Honor*, 148–56.

45. Gorman describes the *Carmen Christi* as Paul's master story of the cross in his narrative thought-world. See Gorman, *Cruciformity*, 88–92.

46. On the nature of voluntary associations in Macedonia and in particular Philippi, see Ascough, *Paul's Macedonian Associations*.

terminology,[47] Paul reverses the plurality of gains (κέρδη) he enumerates in Phil 3:4–6 as a singular loss (ζημίαν), treating it as dung (σκύβαλα) as a result of knowing and gaining Christ. This would have been shocking for the recipients of Paul. Parading one's achievements and displaying one's honor were nothing new in the days of Paul. Hellerman highlights that "(l)isteners steeped in the social world of Roman Philippi could hardly have heard Paul's list of accomplishments without immediately reflecting upon the multitude of inscriptions that confronted them on a daily basis with the honors and achievements of their fellow-colonists."[48]

But Paul does not stop there. In the remaining sentence in Phil 3:8b–11, Paul continues to expound on the privilege of gaining and knowing Christ expressed in the language of suffering and humiliation. My interest is in Phil 3:10:

τοῦ γνῶναι αὐτὸν καὶ τὴν δύναμιν τῆς ἀναστάσεως αὐτοῦ καὶ τὴν κοινωνίαν τῶν παθημάτων αὐτοῦ, συμμορφιζόμενος τῷ θανάτῳ αὐτοῦ.

Most English translations take the objects of γνῶναι as αὐτὸν, τὴν δύναμιν τῆς ἀναστάσεως αὐτοῦ, and τὴν κοινωνίαν τῶν παθημάτων αὐτοῦ, treating the two καί as connecting conjunctions, rendering the meaning that Paul wishes to know: 1) Christ, 2) the power of Christ's resurrection, and 3) the fellowship of Christ's sufferings.[49] However, it is best to take the conjunction καί appearing after τοῦ γνῶναι αὐτὸν as epexegetical as it allows for a better flow of Paul's argument, where the knowledge of Christ is expressed as knowing τὴν δύναμιν τῆς ἀναστάσεως αὐτοῦ and τὴν κοινωνίαν τῶν παθημάτων αὐτοῦ,[50] translating Phil 3:10 as follows: "I want to know him (i.e., Christ), that is, the power of his resurrection and the fellowship of his sufferings." This experience of knowing Christ leads to Paul being conformed to the death of Christ (Phil 3:10b).

Mikael Tellbe suggests that Paul wanted to warn his recipients against the temptation to escape from the present sufferings by compromising on their faith in the gospel of Christ.[51] The presence of Judaizers and the derogatory language Paul uses to describe them in Phil 3:2–3

---

47. See O'Brien, *Philippians*, 382.

48. Hellerman, *Reconstructing Honor*, 123.

49. For example, see KJV, NRSV, NIV, ESV, NASB, and NET, among others.

50. So Koperski, *Knowledge of Christ*, 256–60; Fee, *Philippians*, 328; and Thompson and Longenecker, *Philippians and Philemon*, 110.

51. Tellbe, "Sociological Factors."

("dog," "evil workers," and "mutilators of the flesh") suggest that they were promoting circumcision to the Gentile Christ-followers. This rite was seen as something that was attractive to the Philippians. By being members of Judaism, they would have been recognized as members of a permitted religion and thereby enjoyed some form of protection from Rome. This would have made it easier for them to escape the sufferings imposed by the Roman authorities. Whether Tellbe's reconstruction can be sustained remains to be seen. Even if it were indeed true that the Gentile Christ-followers did find it attractive to be proselytes by performing the rite of circumcision and enjoying some form of protection from Rome as belonging to a recognized religion, it would not have made it any easier for them as they would have suffered some form of economic loss as well since they would have to abandon their worship of pagan deities and abstain from participating in other social activities that were morally or ethically incompatible with Judaism.[52] Suffering would still remain a reality for the Philippians.

For Paul, the notion of suffering and resurrection is closely connected to the *Carmen Christi*.[53] In other words, Paul cannot speak of knowing Christ apart from speaking of sharing in Christ's sufferings. As in Phil 2:6–11, paradoxically, the form of Christ's death is shaped not by the pain of sufferings only, but also by the power of life—the resurrection—leading to vindication. While sufferings remain the hallmark of Christ-followers who lived in tension with those who were in opposition of the gospel, Paul's understanding of suffering remains firmly rooted in the eschatological hope of the resurrection of the body (see Phil 3:21). For Paul, there was no escape from suffering in this present life. But suffering did not have the last word. Sharing in Christ's sufferings is Paul's ultimate hope for sharing in the future power of the resurrection from the dead. As Christ was vindicated by God, so shall Paul and the Philippians be vindicated by God ultimately. This is the highest honor.

Phil 3:20–21: The Citizens of Heaven in a Roman Colony Awaiting the Savior Jesus Christ, not Caesar

While this passage does not deal with suffering directly, it ties together the passages I had earlier considered.[54] In Phil 3:20, Paul declares that

---

52. For further discussion, see Oakes, *Philippians*, 63–70, 89–102.
53. Fowl, *Philippians*, 155; and Smit, *Paradigms of Being in Christ*, 138–44.
54. The connection or close parallels between Phil 3:18–20 to either one or more

"ἡμῶν γὰρ τὸ πολίτευμα ἐν οὐρανοῖς ὑπάρχει." It is interesting to note the emphatic position of ἡμῶν in the beginning of the sentence. This emphasizes the sharp contrast between those who were "enemies of the cross of Christ" (τοὺς ἐχθροὺς τοῦ σταυροῦ τοῦ Χριστοῦ) in Phil 3:18 and those who are citizens of heaven.

The identity of the enemies of the cross has been widely debated, ranging from itinerants who indulged in undisciplined self-indulgence,[55] the same group of Judaizers in Phil 3:2–3,[56] to a deviant local voluntary association.[57] However, it is best to take them as the same group as those who caused suffering to Paul and the Philippians in Phil 1:27–30, in light of similar political language used by Paul in Phil 1:27–30; 3:20–21. I do not think the precise identity of the enemies of the cross would in any way impact the reading of Phil 3:20–21. What is not to be missed here is that Paul seeks to challenge his readers to imitate him (Phil 3:17, note the use of imperative, Συμμιμηταί μου γίνεσθε) by painting a negative picture of the enemies of the cross. These enemies lived their lives by setting their minds on earthly things that led to their ultimate destruction (Phil 3:19). On the other hand, Paul also paints a radiant picture of those who do not belong to the earthly commonwealth but whose citizenship is in heaven. To this group of people, their hope was secure as they eagerly awaited the final triumphant return of a Savior and the transformation of their earthly bodies.

The term πολίτευμα refers to the "place or location in which one has the right to be a citizen"[58] and by extension, also denotes "a colony of foreigners or relocated veterans."[59] It may also refer to the state or commonwealth under the sovereign power of a government. Paul's use of this word reminds the Philippians that their ultimate citizenship was in the heavenly kingdom governed by Christ. At the same time, this colony of citizens was now temporarily relocated in Philippi, a Roman colony.[60] This notion of a colony of heavenly citizens who were now living

---

of the four passages I discussed earlier has been noted by Williams, *Enemies of the Cross*, 236–44; Fee, *Philippians*, 363; Batka, "Paul on Citizenship"; and Silva, *Philippians*, 179–82.

55. Fee, *Philippians*, 375

56. Williams, *Enemies of the Cross*, 247–48.

57. Sergienko, *Our Politeuma Is in Heaven*, 127–82.

58. Louw & Nida, s.v.

59. BDAG, s.v.

60. See Thompson and Longenecker, *Philippians and Philemon*, 49–50.

under the shadow of another sovereign government but whose ultimate loyalty was not to the current government but to Christ is nothing new. Josephus referred to the community of diaspora Jews in Alexandria as a commonwealth (πολίτευμα).[61] Even though this community of diaspora Jews was living in another land, they gathered to hear the instructions of the elders from Jerusalem for the interpretation of the law. They only recognized that the ultimate authority was from Jerusalem and not from Alexandria.

This is significant for the Christ-followers in Philippi. As I have mentioned earlier, Augustus conferred on the city of Philippi the status of a Roman colony. This ensured that the city enjoyed all the rights and privileges of Roman government, and was treated as equal to cities in Italy. With Latin as the official language (as evidenced by the majority of inscriptions excavated), Philippi was very much Roman in its orientation and allegiance. In this respect, the force of Paul's imperial rhetoric cannot be missed. In contrast to the allegiance of the colony of Philippi to her πολίτευμα, the governing powers in Rome, Paul sets forth the opposite claim of Christ-followers that their πολίτευμα, the governing powers, lies elsewhere in heaven.

Paul's use of Roman imperial imagery creates a stark contrast in the next phrase, "we eagerly await a savior from there, the Lord Jesus Christ" (Phil 3:20).[62] Caesar Augustus was bestowed the titles σωτήρ, "Savior", and κύριος, "Lord", because of the *pax Romana* that he placed in order throughout the Empire. The contrast between the self-proclaimed earthly imperial savior of the world and the true savior of the world in the person of Jesus Christ, the Lord, cannot be more pronounced.

By deliberately using imperial language and titles for both the Christ-followers and Christ, Paul explicitly and boldly speaks of both Jesus and his followers in language that subverted the language commonly used by Roman citizens in describing Caesar. By redirecting the attention of the Philippian believers from Caesar, the bogus Savior and Lord, to the true Savior and Lord, Paul not only states that Caesar has been replaced, but also renders him irrelevant. Paul therefore issues the imperative to the Christ-followers to pledge their allegiance to Christ instead of to Caesar. This is because their final hope was not fixed on Caesar but on Christ.

---

61. Josephus, *Antiquities*.12.2.108.
62. NIV.

In the final analysis, Roman citizenship lost its relevance and significance in light of the Christ-followers' citizenship in heaven. In this respect, whatever sufferings the Philippian Christ-followers experienced in this life—be it sufferings caused by the Roman Empire, the pagans, the Judaizers—were at best temporary and only limited to this present life. Paul places the sufferings of the present life in light of the eschatological hope where Christ will eventually triumph over all forces of evil and darkness. The understanding that the Philippians were citizens of heaven awaiting a Savior (Phil 3:20) provides them with a strong cognitive understanding that their sense of belonging to and solidarity with one another in their present sufferings distinguishes them from other groups. In addition, the emotive dimension also serves to remind them that as aliens on earth, they were to offer their worship to the Savior who would return again and not to their current earthly ruler.

Philippians and Social Identity Formation

In examining the five passages related to suffering above, I have highlighted the relationship between suffering and social identity formation. However, in this section, I hope to bring together how a political reading of the passages related to suffering could further help us understand Paul's task of constructing the social identity of the Philippians with respect to the three categories of cognitive, emotional, and evaluative dimensions.

Paul's description of the Philippian believers as citizens of heaven awaiting a Savior (Phil 3:20) provides them with a strong sense of belonging and distinctiveness as compared to other groups. Their citizenship lies elsewhere, not in the citizenship conferred by Caesar. It is important for the Philippians to have this strong conviction of their sense of belonging to Christ as they suffered for his name's sake. This knowledge serves to bond the group together in that, as aliens living in exile, their ultimate allegiance is not to their current earthly ruler but to the Savior who would return again.

In exhorting the Christ-followers to have the mind of Christ (Phil 2:5) by being "like-minded, having the same love, being one in spirit and of one mind . . . (valuing) others above (themselves), not looking to (one's) own interests but . . . to the interests of the others" (Phil 2:2–4),[63] Paul is essentially evoking the emotional dimension to enhance the close

63. This is a modified translation of the NIV.

familial ties in group dynamics to establish a strong sense of solidarity, identity, and belonging to the group. This emotional dimension is further enhanced with the narrative of the humiliation-exhortation of Christ in the *Carmen Christi* (Phil 2:6–11) that leads to the ultimate confession and worship of Jesus Christ as Lord to the glory of the Father. Furthermore, everyone, including Caesar, would one day confess that Jesus is Lord (Phil 2:9–11). The social identity of Christ-followers is reinforced and they are exhorted to stand in solidarity with all those who suffer for the sake of Christ.

By distinguishing the Philippian believers as citizens of heaven from the enemies of the cross of Christ (Phil 3:18–21), Paul provides a very effective evaluative measure for them to rate and compare themselves in relation to others in the Roman Empire. Labelling the out-groups negatively as against the in-group is an effective means of helping the Christ-followers distinguish themselves from others.

Seen from this perspective, Paul's anti-imperial rhetoric is not simply a confrontation or a subversive tool employed to subvert the hegemony, tyranny, or arrogance of imperial powers. It is also a very strong message of encouragement to the Christ-believers that would help them in the formation of their social identity as an alternative assembly called the ἐκκλησία in which Christ is the head. By pledging allegiance to Christ, members of this ἐκκλησία must be distinctive in their identity that sets them apart from the prevailing culture so that they could be responsible sojourners living in a foreign land seeking the welfare of the city while not losing the ultimate hope of the *parousia* of this Savior. This reading, utilizing the *via media* I mentioned earlier, recognizes both the social political reality of the early Christ-movement and yet at the same time pays close attention to the spiritual dimensions of the ἐκκλησία.

Finally, Paul reminds the Philippians that Christ and suffering go hand in hand. It is "suffering *while* believing and suffering *caused* by belief"[64] that underscores the fact that suffering is intrinsic in Paul's call as an apostle to the Gentiles[65] and the cruciform shape of the Christian life. However, this is not a call to search out suffering, and neither should this be used as a reason to justify increased suffering for self. As Christians, our suffering is not a sign of failure or weakness. It is our assurance that we never suffer alone—we suffer in Christ, and with other believers.

---

64. Jervis, *Heart of the Gospel*, 42.
65. See further discussion, see Lim, "Is There a Place for Suffering," 64–78.

It is through Paul's sufferings that we grasp the mystery that God is not absent when we suffer, and we can look forward to our future hope of resurrection.

Reflections and Conclusion

In concluding this essay, I offer some brief remarks on my reading of Philippians in my own context as a minority Christian in a predominantly Islamic context.

Firstly, no amount of intimidation should impede the proclamation of the gospel. Paul's chains and imprisonment, seen as a form of intimidation from the Roman authorities, is not a cause for the early Christ-followers to be fearful of proclaiming the gospel. Likewise, any form of intimidation, persecution, or threat meted out by authorities or individuals should not cause us to be fearful in our task of witnessing to the gospel, particularly for those of us living as a minority within a predominant Islamic context.

Secondly, the embodiment of the humiliation and exaltation of Christ in the *Carmen Christi* serves as a paradigm for our Christian witness and mission. The humiliation and exaltation of Christ reminds us that earthly powers are only temporal. Yet, it does not diminish the possibility of suffering and persecution for those who bear the name of Christ. Those citizens of heaven who wish to follow Jesus must also similarly follow this self-lowering-other-regard pattern as exhibited by Jesus. It also challenges us to stand in solidarity with the poor, the weak, and the marginalized, and those who suffer for the sake of the gospel.

Finally, we are citizens of heaven temporarily living as a colony of sojourners. While we pledge our allegiance to our Savior and Lord Jesus Christ, we are reminded that as Christ-followers living in "exile" in a foreign and strange land, we are to "seek the welfare of the city" where the Lord has sent us into "exile," and "pray to the Lord on its behalf" (Jer 29:7).[66] Citizenship in heaven is not our passport of salvation that merely leads us to heaven. It reminds us of the reality that while living as a colony in a foreign land, we are Christ's ambassadors (cf. 2 Cor 5:20) in wherever God has placed us. As we bear the name of Christ, we are to live as people that would bring honor to the name we bear as Christians.

---

66. NRSV.

Bibliography

Ascough, Richard S. *Paul's Macedonian Associations: The Social Context of Philippians and 1 Thessalonians*. WUNT 2.161. Tübingen: Mohr Siebeck, 2003.

Bakirtzis, Charalambos, and Helmut Koester, eds. *Philippi at the Time of Paul and After His Death*. Harrisburg: Trinity International Press, 1998.

Barentsen, Jack. *Emerging Leadership in Pauline Mission: A Social Identity Perspective on Local Leadership Development in Corinth and Ephesus*. Eugene, OR: Pickwick, 2011.

Batka, Lubomir. "Paul on Citizenship: Pauline Hermeneutics in Philippians 1:27 and 3:20." LWF Studies 3 (2016) 99–109.

Bloomquist, L. Gregory. *The Function of Suffering in Philippians*. JSNTSup 78. Sheffield: JSOT Press, 1993.

Bockmuehl, Markus. *The Epistle to the Philippians*. BNTC. London: A & C Black, 1997.

Brewer, Raymond R. "The Meaning of *Politeuesthe* in Philippians 1.27." *JBL* 73 (1954) 76–83.

Bryan, Christopher. *Render to Caesar: Jesus, the Early Church, and the Roman Superpower*. Oxford: Oxford University Press, 2005.

Cassidy, Richard J. *Paul in Chains: Roman Imprisonment and the Letters of St. Paul*. New York: Crossroad, 2001.

Cousar, Charles B. *Philippians and Philemon: A Commentary*. NTL. Louisville: Westminster John Knox, 2009.

Darko, Daniel K. *No Longer Living as the Gentiles: Differentiation and Shared Ethical Values in Ephesians 4.17–6.9*. London: T & T Clark, 2008.

Deissmann, Adolf. *Light from the Ancient East: The New Testament Illustrated by Recently Discovered Texts of the Graeco-Roman World*. Translated by Lionel R. M. Strachan. New York: Hodder & Stoughton, 1908.

Elliott, Neil. *The Arrogance of Nations: Reading Romans in the Shadow of Empire*. Minneapolis: Fortress, 2008.

———. *Liberating Paul: The Justice of God and the Politics of the Apostle*. Sheffield: Sheffield Academic Press, 1995.

Esler, Philip F. *Conflict and Identity in Romans: The Social Setting of Paul's Letters*. Minneapolis: Fortress, 2003.

Fee, Gordon D. *Paul's Letter to the Philippians*. NICNT. Grand Rapids: Eerdmans, 1995.

Fowl, Stephen E. *Philippians*. THNTC. Grand Rapids: Eerdmans, 2005.

———. *The Story of Christ in the Ethics of Paul: An Analysis of the Function of the Hymnic Materials in the Pauline Corpus*. Sheffield: Sheffield Academic Press, 1990.

Gorman, Michael J. *Cruciformity: Paul's Narrative Spirituality of the Cross*. Grand Rapids: Eerdmans, 2001.

Hansen, G. Walter. *The Letter to the Philippians*. PNTC. Grand Rapids: Eerdmans, 2009.

Hardin, Justin K. *Galatians and the Imperial Cult*. WUNT 2.237. Tübingen: Mohr Siebeck, 2008.

Hawthorne, Gerald F. *Philippians*. WBC. Waco, TX: Word Books, 1983.

Hellerman, Joseph. *Reconstructing Honor in Roman Philippi: Carmen Christi as Cursus Pudorum*. Cambridge: Cambridge University Press, 2005.

Horsley, Richard, ed. *Hidden Transcripts and the Arts of Resistance: Applying the Work of James C. Scott to Jesus and Paul*. Atlanta: SBL, 2004.

———, ed. *Paul and Empire: Religion and Power in Roman Imperial Society*. Harrisburg: Trinity, 1997.

———, ed. *Paul and Politics: Ekklesia, Israel, Imperium, Interpretation*. Harrisburg: Trinity, 2000.

———, ed. *Paul and the Roman Imperial Order*. Harrisburg: Trinity, 2004.

Horsley, Richard, and Neil Asher Silberman. *The Message and the Kingdom: How Jesus and Paul Ignited a Revolution and Transformed the Ancient World*. Minneapolis: Fortress, 2002.

Horrell, David. *Solidarity and Difference: A Contemporary Reading of Paul's Ethics*. London: T & T Clark, 2005.

Jervis, L. Ann. *At the Heart of the Gospel: Suffering in the Earliest Christian Message*. Grand Rapids: Eerdmans, 2007.

Kim, Seyoon. *Christ and Caesar: The Gospel and the Roman Empire in the Writings of Paul and Luke*. Grand Rapids: Eerdmans, 2008.

Koperski, Veronica. *The Knowledge of Christ Jesus My Lord: The High Christology of Philippians 3:7–11*. CBET 16. Kampen: Kok Pharos, 1996.

Lamoreaux, Jason T. *Ritual, Women, and Philippi: Reimagining the Early Philippian Community*. Eugene, OR: Cascade, 2013.

Lim, Kar Yong. "If Anyone Is in Christ, New Creation: The Old has Gone, the New has Come" (2 Cor 5:17): New Creation and Temporal Comparison in Social Identity Formation in 2 Corinthians." In *T & T Clark Handbook to Social Identity and the New Testament*, edited by J. Brian Tucker and Coleman A. Baker, 289–301. London: Bloomsbury, 2014.

———. "Is There a Place for Suffering in Mission? Perspectives from Paul's Sufferings in 2 Corinthians." In *The Soul of Mission: Perspectives on Christian Leadership, Spirituality and Mission in East Asia; Essays in Appreciation of Dr. David Gunaratnam*, edited by Tan Kang San, 64–78. Petaling Jaya: Pustaka Sufes, 2007.

———. *Metaphors and Social Identity Formation in Paul's Letters to the Corinthians*. Eugene, OR: Pickwick, 2017.

———. *"The Sufferings of Christ Are Abundant in Us" (2 Cor 1:5): A Narrative Dynamics Investigation of Paul's Sufferings in 2 Corinthians*. LNTS 399. London: T & T Clark, 2009.

Martin, Ralph P. *Carmen Christi: Philippians 2.5–11 in Recent Interpretation and in the Setting of Early Christian Worship*, Rev. ed. Grand Rapids: Eerdmans, 1983.

May, Alistair Scott. *"The Body for the Lord": Sex and Identity in 1 Corinthians 5–7*. London: T & T Clark, 2004.

McAuley, David. *Paul's Covert Use of Scripture: Intertextuality and Rhetorical Situation in Philippians 2:10–16*. Eugene, OR: Pickwick, 2015.

Marchal, Joseph A., ed. *The People Beside Paul: The Philippian Assembly and History from Below*. Atlanta: SBL, 2015.

Nebreda, Sergio Rosell. *Christ Identity: A Social-Scientific Reading of Philippians 2.5.11*. Göttingen: Vandenhoeck & Ruprecht, 2011.

Neyrey, Jerome H. "Spaces and Places: Whence and Whither." *BTB* 32 (2002) 60–74.

Oakes, Peter. "The Economic Situation of the Philippian Christians." In *The People Beside Paul: The Philippian Assembly and History from Below*, edited by Joseph A. Marchal, 63–82. Atlanta, SBL, 2015.

———. *Philippians: From People to Letter*. Cambridge: Cambridge University Press, 2001.

O'Brien, Peter T. *Epistle to the Philippians*. NIGTC. Grand Rapids: Eerdmans, 1991.
Porter, Stanley E., and Cynthia Long Westfall, eds. *Empire in the New Testament*. Eugene, OR: Pickwick, 2011.
Reasoner, Mark. *Roman Imperial Texts: A Sourcebook*. Minneapolis: Fortress, 2013.
Rock, Ian. *Paul's Letter to the Romans and Roman Imperialism: An Ideological Analysis of the Exordium (Romans 1:1–17)*. Eugene, OR: Pickwick, 2012.
Sack, Robert. *Human Territoriality: Its Theory and History*. Cambridge: Cambridge University Press, 1986.
Schweitzer, Albert. *The Mysticism of Paul the Apostle*. Translated by William Montgomery. New York: H. Holt, 1931.
Sergienko, Gennadi A. *Our Politeuma Is in Heaven: Paul's Polemical Engagement with the "Enemies of the Cross of Christ: In Philippians 3:18–20*. Carlisle: Langham Monographs, 2013.
Silva, Moisés. *Philippians*. 2nd ed. BECNT. Grand Rapids: Baker, 1992, 2005.
Smit, Peter-Ben. *Paradigms of Being in Christ: A Study of the Epistle to the Philippians*. LNTS 476. London: Bloomsbury, 2013.
Standhartinger, Angela. "Letter from Prison as Hidden Transcript: What It Tells Us about the People at Philippi." In *The People Beside Paul: The Philippian Assembly and History from Below*, edited by Joseph A. Marchal, 107–40. Atlanta: SBL, 2015.
Stanley, Christopher D. *The Colonized Apostle: Paul through Postcolonial Eyes*. Minneapolis: Fortress, 2011.
Tajfel, Henri. *Differentiation between Social Groups: Studies in the Social Psychology of Intergroup Relations*. European Monographs in Social Psychology 14. London: Academic Press, 1978.
Tellbe, Mikael. "The Sociological Factors Behind Philippians 3.1–11 and the Conflict at Philippi." *JSNT* 55 (1994) 97–121.
Thompson, James W., and Bruce W. Longenecker. *Philippians and Philemon*. PCNT. Grand Rapids: Baker, 2016.
Tucker, J. Brian. *"Remain in Your Calling": Paul and the Continuation of Social Identities in 1 Corinthians*. Eugene, OR: Pickwick, 2011.
———. *You Belong to Christ: Paul and the Formation of Social Identity in 1 Corinthians 1–4*. Eugene, OR: Pickwick, 2010.
Tucker, J. Brian, and Coleman A. Baker, eds. *T & T Clark Handbook to Social Identity in the New Testament*. New York: Bloomsbury, 2014.
Turner, John C. *Rediscovering the Social Group: Self-Categorization Theory*. New York: Blackwell, 1987.
Verhoef, Eduard. *Philippi: How Christianity Began in Europe, the Epistle to the Philippians and the Excavations at Philippi*. London: T & T Clark, 2013.
Walsh, Brian J., and Sylvia C. Keesmaat. *Colossians Remixed: Subverting the Empire*. Downers Grove, IL: IVP, 2004.
Wansink, Craig S. *Chained in Christ: The Experience and Rhetoric of Paul's Imprisonment*. Sheffield: Sheffield Academic Press, 1996.
Williams, Demetrius. *Enemies of the Cross of Christ: The Terminology of the Cross and Conflict in Philippians*. JSNTSup 223. London: Sheffield Academic Press, 2002.
Winn, Adam, ed. *An Introduction to Empire in the New Testament*. Atlanta: SBL, 2016.
Wright, N. T. *Paul and the Faithfulness of God*. Minneapolis: Fortress, 2013.
———. *Paul: Fresh Perspectives*. London: SPCK, 2005.

9

Semantics of Suffering

Thematic Meaning of the Language of Suffering in Romans and 2 Corinthians

SUNNY CHEN

Introduction

PAUL PORTRAYS SUFFERING VIVIDLY by employing a rich range of terminology in his work, in particular, several so-called "suffering lists" found in Romans and 2 Corinthians (Rom 8:35, 2 Cor 6:4, 2 Cor 11:23–29, and 2 Cor 12:10).[1] Among the various terms on these lists, θλῖψις, στενοχωρία, and their cognates occur significantly more frequently than the other terms in both letters combined.[2] Θλῖψις and its cognates

1. In each of these texts, a list of terms is employed to depict suffering.

2. Besides θλῖψις, στενοχωρία, and their cognates, there are eighteen terms that portray suffering on the above lists, and most of them only occur once or twice in both letters combined. The terms that appear once include ἀκαταστασία, δίψος, ἐπίστασις, μέριμνα, μόχθος, ὕβρις, ῥαβδίζω, λιθάζω, ναυαγέω, and ψῦχος. The terms that occur twice include ἀγρυπνία, γυμνότης, διωγμός, λιμός, μάχαιρα, πληγή, νηστεία, and φυλακή. The only term that appears more than twice is ἀνάγκη (four times). Both ὑπομονή (perseverance) and κίνδυνος (danger) are not considered to be part of the list. Ὑπομονή is found seven times. However, the word denotes virtue instead of suffering. Κίνδυνος occurs ten times, and eight of them are located in 2 Cor 11:26 alone. In that context the word, being employed in a general sense, is combined with different words to portray a specific kind of suffering. Therefore, κίνδυνος is not treated as a specific term depicting suffering. Apart from the "suffering lists," there are also other terms employed to illustrate suffering in 2 Corinthians, which will not be examined

occur seventeen times; and στενοχωρία and its cognates appear seven times.³

This study first reviews the meanings of θλῖψις, στενοχωρία, and their cognates by referring to non-Pauline works: Classical Greek literature, the LXX, and contemporary Koiné Greek literature. It then applies modern linguistic principles to overcome some of the deficiencies in previous scholarship. In particular, it focuses on the thematic meanings of θλῖψις, στενοχωρία, and their cognates in Romans and 2 Corinthians, analyzing the overall pattern in the discourse of each letter. This essay will conclude that Paul's language of suffering emphasizes corporate solidarity and ecclesial relationships.

Modern Linguistics and Thematic Meaning

Before we commence our study, an overview of modern linguistics is needed in order to understand the importance of applying modern linguistic principles in any semantic study. Ferdinand de Saussure, the founder of modern linguistics,⁴ identifies two different dimensions of semantic study. Studying the historical development of a word is defined as the diachronic approach, and studying the meaning of a word by referring to its contemporary literary context is known as the synchronic approach. Saussure suggests that every word "is at the crossroads between the diachronic and the synchronic viewpoint."⁵ Therefore, any semantic studies that adopt either the diachronic or the synchronic approach alone would be inadequate. A more holistic method must involve both the diachronic and the synchronic approaches. In previous scholarship, semantic studies of those Pauline terms of suffering either rely solely on the diachronic approach, or simply adopt the synchronic approach. The diachronic approach involves examining their usage in Hebrew Scriptures, the LXX, and Classical Greek literature; and the synchronic approach involves investigating their occurrences in their immediate context, Pauline corpus, and contemporary Koiné Greek literature. More

---

in this study. They include βάρος and its cognate βαρέω (1:18; 4:17; 5:4), κόπος (6:5; 10:15; 11:23, 27), πληγή (6:5; 11:23), and σκόλοψ (12:7).

3. Θλῖψις and its cognates appear in Rom 2:9; 5:3 (twice); 8:35; 12:12; 2 Cor 1:4 (twice), 6, 8; 2:4; 4:8, 17; 6:4; 7:4, 5; 8:2, 13. Στενοχωρία and its cognates occur in Rom 2:9; 8:35; 2 Cor 4:8; 6:4; 6:12 (twice); 12:10.

4. Ricoeur, *Conflict of Interpretations*, 81.

5. Saussure, *Writing*, 3–4, 6–7, 80, 112–13.

importantly, modern biblical commentators often fail to apply modern linguistic principles.

In conducting synchronic semantic analysis for Paul's terms of suffering, it is imperative to be attentive to modern linguistic principles. In modern linguistics a word is understood as carrying three levels of meanings: lexical meaning, sentence meaning, and thematic meaning.[6]

The lexical meaning of a word refers to the "meaning-potential of a word ... in a system network of lexicogrammatical semantic options."[7] That is, the various potential meanings within an established set of vocabulary as stated in lexica. For a word that is found as part of a sentence or clause, its "fully contextualized meaning" is its sentence meaning.[8] This is ascertained by examining its textual context and identifying one specific connotation out of its different potential meanings. If that word recurs throughout the whole discourse, it may be employed to convey a particular idea, which is known as thematic meaning. Thematic meaning is realized in "a recurrent discourse pattern that is familiar in many texts,"[9] which may or may not align with the lexical or sentence meaning.[10]

To discover the thematic meaning of a word its occurrences must be studied at the discourse level by reviewing its overall pattern throughout the whole discourse.[11] This is achieved by observing and analyzing its clustered occurrences,[12] ascertaining its sentence meaning in all the ap-

---

6. Different linguists use different sets of terms. For Lemke, it is called "lexical meaning, use meaning, thematic meaning" ("Intertextuality," 89); and for Grice, it is "word meaning, sentence meaning, utterer's meaning" ("Utterer's Meaning," 65–76).

7. Lemke, "Intertextuality," 89.

8. Lemke, "Intertextuality," 89. Lemke's "use meaning" is more general, referring to a text, rather than a particular sentence.

9. This resembles Grice's utterer's meaning, which is the intended meaning of an author, and is implicated in the utterance of the author. See Grice, "Utterer's Meaning," 65.

10. The inadequacy of modern commentators' analyses of Paul's terms of suffering is largely due to their sole focus on lexical meaning and sentence meaning.

11. Louw argues that "the structure of a discourse is a vital point in determining its intention. It is the hinge on which the communication turns; it is part and parcel of the semantics of a discourse." Louw, "Discourse Analysis," 104.

12. Grammatical devices can be used to connect different elements together in a discourse, allowing the audience to form "a single overall mental representation" (Dooley and Levinsohn, *Analyzing Discourse*, 23). One of the devices is repetition of a word throughout a discourse (Halliday, *Linguistic Studies*, 8). Furthermore, when two or more occurrences of similar lexical items appearing in close proximity, these lexical items likely belong to the same semantic domain (Halliday, *Linguistic Studies*, 29).

pearances, and, subsequently, identifying the common theme based on the analyses of the clusters and sentence meanings.[13] Having reviewed some key modern linguistic principles, we are in a position to proceed with our analysis.

Θλιψισ and Στενοχωρια in Non-Pauline Works

In the following, θλῖψις, στενοχωρία, and their cognates will be analyzed based on their occurrences in non-Pauline works.

The Meanings of Θλῖψις and Στενοχωρία in Classical Greek Literature and the LXX[14]

In Classical Greek literature, the term θλῖψις means pressure, crushing, oppression, affliction, and tribulation.[15] The connotation usually refers to the distress that is caused "by outward circumstances."[16] The verb form of θλῖψις, θλίβω, means to rub, squeeze, press, compress, and squash in the literal sense; and to afflict and oppress in the figurative sense.[17] Στενοχωρία means "narrowness" in the literal sense; and "distress" and "trouble" in the figurative sense.[18] Στενοχωρία portrays being straitened, confined, and crowded.[19]

In the LXX, θλῖψις appears 229 times. In terms of Paul's quotations of the OT, the Pentateuch, Isaiah, and the Psalms are Paul's most

---

13. For example, οἶκος means house or household (lexical meaning). If the word appears in a sentence, the context would inform whether the word specifically connotes a house or a household (sentence meaning). In Acts, the word repeatedly occurs twenty-five times. An examination of all its appearances has shown that the thematic meaning of οἶκος conveys the idea of the assembly of a faith community as God's family (Chen, *Paul's Anthropological Terms*, 37–38). This thematic meaning certainly transcends its lexical or sentence meaning.

14. The meaning of a word in Classical Greek literature can be ascertained by consulting prominent lexica, such as BDAG, LSJ, and *TDNT*.

15. LSJ, 802; BDAG, 362.

16. BDAG, 362.

17. LSJ, 802; Schlier, "Θλίβω," *TDNT*, vol. 3, 139.

18. BDAG, 766.

19. LSJ, 1639

frequent sources.[20] Therefore, this study only focuses on how θλῖψις and στενοχωρία are employed in the Pentateuch, Psalms, and Isaiah.

In the Pentateuch, θλῖψις occurs nine times,[21] depicting distress due to persecution,[22] oppression,[23] and disobedience to God;[24] and θλίβω, twelve times, seven of which mean to oppress (to be oppressed by the enemy or to oppress the foreigner).[25] Most of the remaining occurrences are found in Deuteronomy 28, connoting to besiege or to constrict.[26] In the Psalms, θλῖψις appears thirty-five times.[27] Based on the textual context,[28] the term denotes distress, in the form of persecution or oppression, caused by the enemy[29] or the wicked.[30] It also connotes oppression, without specifying a cause,[31] or distress due to God's discipline.[32] Θλίβω occurs twenty-five times.[33] Of interest, nearly all of its appearances, except those in Ps 106 (LXX) and Ps 119 (LXX), denote an enemy as the cause of suffering.[34] In Isaiah, θλῖψις occurs sixteen times,[35] a significant

20. According to Harrington, "Paul's Use," 1, Paul's letters, mainly Romans, 1 and 2 Corinthians, and Galatians, contain approximately 100 explicit quotations of the OT, with a large quantity of them being drawn from the Pentateuch (33), Isaiah (25), and the Psalms (19) in the LXX.

21. Gen 35:3; 42:21 (twice); Exod 4:31; Deut 4:29; 28:53, 55, 57; 31:17.

22. Gen 35:3; 42:21.

23. Exod 4:31.

24. Deut 4:29; 28:53, 55, 57; 31:17.

25. Exod 3:9; 22:21; 23:9; Lev 19:33; 25:14, 17; Deut 23:16

26. Deut 28:52, 53, 55, 57.

27. Ps 4:2; 9:10, 22; 19:2; 21:12; 24:17, 22; 31:7; 33:7, 18, 20; 36:39; 43:25; 45:2; 49:15; 53:9; 54:4; 58:17; 59:13; 65:11, 14; 70:20; 76:3; 77:49; 80:8; 85:7; 90:15; 106:39; 107:13; 114:3; 117:5; 118:143; 137:7; 141:3; 142:11 (LXX).

28. In some occurrences, the term connotes trouble or distress without specifying its cause due to limited contextual information. See Ps 19:2; 49:15; 80:8; 85:7; 90:15; 114:3 (LXX).

29. Ps 4:2; 9:10, 22; 21:12; 43:25; 53:9; 54:4; 58:17; 70:20; 107:13; 117:5; 118:143; 137:7; 141:3; 142:11 (LXX).

30. Ps 9:22; 36:39 (LXX).

31. Ps 33:7, 18, 20 (LXX).

32. Ps 24:17, 22; 31:7; 59:13; 65:11, 14; 76:3; 77:49; 106:39 (LXX).

33. Ps 3:2; 12:5; 17:7; 22:5; 26:2, 12; 30:10; 41:11; 43:8; 55:2; 59:14; 68:18, 20; 77:42; 80:15; 101:3; 105:11, 42, 44; 106:6, 13, 19, 28; 119:1; 142:12 (LXX).

34. In Ps 106 (LXX), θλίβω describes suffering due to God's discipline. The suffering in Ps 119 (LXX) is caused by one individual, the person is not clearly identified as an enemy.

35. Isa 8:22; 10:3, 26; 26:16 (twice); 28:10 (twice), 13 (twice); 30:6, 20; 33:2; 37:3;

number of them referring to divine punishment due to the ancient Israelites' disobedience;[36] and θλίβω appears eight times, portraying the act of oppression,[37] being hostile towards (certain people),[38] mocking,[39] or besieging.[40] It is evident that θλῖψις and its cognates frequently connote distress due to oppression or mistreatment. The common notion of an external force causing the distress is obvious.

Στενοχωρία appears thirteen times in the LXX. The term occurs three times in the Pentateuch (Deut 28:53, 55, 57), and all of them denote distress caused by the siege by an enemy. The term and its cognate, στενοχωρέω, are not found in the Psalms. But it appears three times in Isaiah, and all of them depict the distress due to divine punishment (Isa 8:22; 9:1; 30:6).[41] In light of this, στενοχωρία connotes the distress that is caused by external influence. Στενοχωρέω only occurs twice in Isaiah (none in the Pentateuch), connoting narrow or small in a literal sense (49:19) or metaphorical sense (28:20). Narrowness, siege, and distress due to divine punishment are the common meanings of στενοχωρία and its cognates in the LXX.

The Meanings of Θλῖψις and Στενοχωρία in First-Century Koiné Greek Literature

In terms of Paul's contemporary authors, despite the vast quantity of Koiné Greek literature in the first century, this study only examines the work of Philo, Epictetus, and Plutarch due to the following reasons.[42] First, all of them contributed a significant volume of work. Second, they shared a similar background as thinkers in the first century Greco-Roman world: Paul was a Hellenistic Jewish theologian; Philo was a Hellenistic Jewish philosopher; Epictetus was a Hellenistic Stoic philosopher; and Plutarch was a Hellenistic Platonic philosopher. Third, recent scholarship has

---

57:13; 63:9; 65:16.

36. Isa 8:22; 26:16; 30:6, 20 33:2; 63:9; 65:16
37. Isa 19:20; 49:26; 51:13
38. Isa 11:13
39. Isa 28:14
40. Isa 29:7
41. In 8:22, the word is used in conjunction with θλῖψις.
42. Philo's corpus dates back to the first half of the first century, and the corpus of both Epictetus and Plutarch dates back to the second half of the first century.

identified that there is a meaningful connection between Paul's theology and Stoicism.⁴³

In Philo's corpus, θλῖψις occurs once and its cognates appear three times.⁴⁴ The term θλῖψις is used in conjunction with θυμός and ὀργή to depict the affliction caused by God's punishment.⁴⁵ Concerning its cognates, ἐκθλῖψις denotes affliction due to divine punishment of the wicked,⁴⁶ ἀποθλίβω and ἐκθλίβω are used to portray the process of pressing fruit (for wine making⁴⁷ and grape juice⁴⁸ respectively), and ἐναποθλίβω means to infuse (thieves infusing their souls with what they have stolen).⁴⁹

In Epictetus' corpus, θλῖψις is not found but its cognate θλίβω occurs sixteen times. The verb connotes to oppress,⁵⁰ to incommode,⁵¹ to constrain (by custom),⁵² to afflict (due to fever),⁵³ to pressure (due to negative events),⁵⁴ to embarrass,⁵⁵ to hurt (due to suffering in life),⁵⁶ or to distress (due to humiliation).⁵⁷ There is a common notion connecting all of the above meanings: an external force causing affliction.⁵⁸

---

43. For example, Lee, *Paul, the Stoics*, 23–26; Engberg-Pedersen, *Paul and the Stoics*, 33–79.

44. All the reviewed Greek literature in this study is directly cited from Thesaurus Linguae Graecae® Digital Library, the digital version of *TLG*.

45. *De gigantibus* 17. Quoting Ps 78:49 (77:49, LXX), Philo comments on good and evil angels as an illustration.

46. *De praemiis et poenis et De exsecrationibus* 151.

47. *De agricultura* 157.

48. *De somniis* 2.159.

49. *De congressu eruditionis gratia* 150.

50. *Dissertationes ab Arriano digestae* 1.2.

51. *Dissertationes ab Arriano digestae* 1.25. This passage discusses the potential distress when one sits where the senators are, a desire that is considered as tormenting and incommoding oneself. On three occasions, θλῖψις or its cognate appears in conjunction with στενοχωρία or its cognate: ὅτι σὺ σαυτῷ στενοχωρίαν παρέχεις, σὺ σαυτὸν θλίβεις; ὅτι ἑαυτοὺς θλίβομεν, ἑαυτοὺς στενοχωροῦμεν; τὰ δόγματα ἡμᾶς θλίβει καὶ στενοχωρεῖ.

52. *Dissertationes ab Arriano digestae* 1.27.

53. *Dissertationes ab Arriano digestae* 3.10.

54. *Dissertationes ab Arriano digestae* 3.13.

55. *Dissertationes ab Arriano digestae* 4.1.

56. *Enchiridion digestae* 16.

57. *Enchiridion digestae* 24.

58. On three occasions, θλίβω appears in conjunction with στενοχωρία or στενοχωρέω.

In Plutarch's corpus, θλῖψις appears once, and its cognates, ἐκθλῖψις and θλίβω, twice and eighteen times respectively.[59] Θλῖψις depicts the compression of atoms in a discussion of how wine heats up the human body.[60] Ἐκθλῖψις connotes privation (in hunger),[61] or upward force (causing light pebbles to float in a jar of oil).[62] Θλίβω means to straiten,[63] to pinch,[64] to impose pressure,[65] to crush (using weight),[66] to distress (due to strait or physical burden),[67] to endanger,[68] to hard-press,[69] to be afflicted (by poverty),[70] to be bent down (by weight),[71] and to rub.[72] As above, the common notion of external force or pressure is present in their meanings.

To sum up, θλῖψις and its cognates may or may not depict affliction in the works of Philo, Epictetus, and Plutarch; nonetheless, there is a common notion of external force or pressure being applied.

Concerning στενοχωρία, only its cognate στενοχωρέω occurs in Philo's corpus (once). The verb appears together with θλίβω to depict a fool being straitened.[73] Στενοχωρία and στενοχωρέω occur once and four times, respectively, in the corpus of Epictetus. On three occasions στενοχωρία (or στενοχωρέω) is found in close proximity with θλῖψις (or θλίβω). The three couplets describe the distress when someone becomes a senator.[74] In the remaining occurrences, στενοχωρέω means to crowd in.[75] In Plutarch's corpus, στενοχωρία occurs six times, and its cognate

59. The verb θλίβω occurs eighteen times. The cognates of θλίβω, such as ἀποθλίβω and συνθλίβω, appear thirty-five times. This study only focuses on θλίβω instead of the cognates of θλίβω.
60. *Adversus Colotem* 6.
61. *Quaestiones Convivales* 6.3.
62. *De sollertia animalium* 10.
63. *Alcibiades* 25.1.
64. *Aemilius Paulus* 5.4; *Conjugalia Praecepta* 22.
65. *Aemilius Paulus* 14.2.
66. *Pyrrhus* 33.7; *Quaestiones Convivales* 5.6; 6.9.
67. *Nicias* 21.4; *Alexander* 39.3.
68. *Agesilaus* 34.6.
69. *Pompeius* 25.1.
70. *Regum et imperatorum apophthegmata* 26.
71. *Quaestiones Convivales* 8.4.
72. *Amatorius* 765c (Stephanus page).
73. *Quaestiones in Genesim* 4.33a.
74. *Dissertationes ab Arriano digestae* 1.25.
75. *Dissertationes ab Arriano digestae* 1.6; 4.1.

συστενοχωρέω, once. Στενοχωρία means narrowness (of space under siege),[76] narrow quarter (that Demetrius lodged),[77] confinement,[78] and inadequate space (for diners).[79] Συστενοχωρέω connotes to confine (geographically).[80]

In conclusion, στενοχωρία and its cognates may or may not denote distress in the works of Philo, Epictetus, and Plutarch; nevertheless, there is a common notion of narrowness in depicting a physical or emotional constraint.

Based on the literature reviewed above, θλῖψις, στενοχωρία, and their cognates share a similar semantic domain: external force, pressure, or narrowness causing distress, pressure, or confinement, either in literal or metaphorical sense.

Θλιψισ and Στενοχωρια in Romans and 2 Corinthians

In Romans and 2 Corinthians, θλῖψις and its cognates occur seventeen times, and στενοχωρία and its cognates, seven times. In the following, Paul's usage of θλῖψις and στενοχωρία will be examined.

The Thematic Meaning of Θλῖψις and Στενοχωρία in Romans

The verbs θλίβω and στενοχωρέω are not found in Romans. The nouns, θλῖψις and στενοχωρία, appear five times and twice respectively.[81] Since the two occurrences of στενοχωρία appear in conjunction with θλῖψις, the two words are examined together below.

To ascertain the thematic meaning of a particular word, the overall context and pattern of how the word appears throughout the whole discourse, in this case the whole letter, must be examined. The following analysis first reviews the structure and thematic division of Romans, and then examines the pattern of the appearances of θλῖψις and στενοχωρία

---

76. *Eumenes* 11.4.
77. *Demetrius* 23.6; *Regum et imperatorum apophthegmata* 29.
78. *De exilio* 7.
79. *Quaestiones Convivales* 5.6.
80. *De exilio* 6.
81. The occurrences of θλῖψις: Rom 2:9; 5:3 (twice); 8:35; 12:12. The occurrences of στενοχωρία: Rom 2:9; 8:35.

in the whole letter, as well as their individual occurrences in their immediate textual context.

Table 1 shows the division of Romans as identified by some major modern commentators;[82] and based on that division Table 2 shows where the occurrences of θλῖψις and στενοχωρία are located in the letter. It shows that there are three major clusters in terms of the appearances of θλῖψις and στενοχωρία.

Table 1. The Division of Romans

Letter Division		1:8–17	1:18–3:20	3:21–4:25	5–8	9–11	12:1–15:13	15:14–33	16:1–23
Commentators' View		Byrne	Deibler	Hultgren	Barrett	Barrett	Byrne	Byrne	Byrne
		Cranfield	Fitzmyer	Käsemann	Byrne	Byrne	Deibler	Deibler	Dunn
		Stuhlmacher	Longenecker	Longenecker	Fitzmyer	Deibler	Dunn	Dunn	Fitzmyer
			Schreiner	Schreiner	Hultgren	Dunn	Fitzmyer	Fitzmyer	Moo
			Stuhlmacher	Fitzmyer	Jewett	Hultgren	Jewett	Moo	Schlatter
					Longenecker	Jewett	Longenecker	Schlatter	Schlatter
					Moo	Longenecker	Moo	Schreiner	
		Dunn, Fitzmyer,			Schreiner	Moo	Schlatter	Jewett, Stuhlmacher	
		Hultgren, Stuhlmacher				Schlatter	Schreiner		
				Byrne, Jewett, Moo		Schreiner	Stuhlmacher		
						Stuhlmacher			

82. This table is an update of that found in Chen, *Paul's Anthropological Terms*, 140. This table only focuses on the work contributed by commentators during the last thirty years. Both the letter-opening and the letter-closing are excluded in this table. See Barrett, *Romans*, 14–15; Byrne, *Romans*, 27–28; Deibler, *Romans*, 23–34; Dunn, *Romans 1–8*, vii–xi; Fitzmyer, *Romans*, viii–xii; Hultgren, *Romans*, v–viii; Longenecker, *Romans*, v–viii; Moo, *Romans*, 33–35; Schlatter, *Romans*, v–vi; Stuhlmacher, *Romans*, 14–16; Jewett, *Romans*, vii–ix; Schreiner, *Romans*, 25–27. Note that there are some minor differences in terms of individual commentator's view on the divisions of Romans. For example, Byrne, *Romans*, 27–28, regards 1:1–7 and 1:8–17 as two sub-segments of 1:1–17.

162   SUFFERING IN PAUL

Table 2. Occurrence of Θλῖψις and Στενοχωρία in Romans

Letter Division	I 1:8–17	II 1:18–3:20	III 3:21–4:25	IV 5–8	V 9–11	VI 12:1–15:13	VII 15:14–33	VIII 16:1–23
Occurrence of θλῖψις & στενοχωρία		(*^)		(** *)		*		

*: a single occurrence of θλῖψις; ^: a single occurrence of στενοχωρία

◯: cluster

The first cluster occurs in Romans 2, inside segment II (1:18–3:20). The wider context of this segment centers on the argument that both the Greeks and the Jews are in need of God's salvation from God's divine judgement, which is illustrated by the repeated phrase, the Jew first and also the Greek (2:9, 10; 3:9). The future divine judgement is clearly portrayed in the clause, ἐν ἡμέρᾳ ὅτε κρίνει ὁ θεὸς τὰ κρυπτὰ τῶν ἀνθρώπων (2:16). This judgment is further highlighted in the concluding remark in this segment: ὑπόδικος γένηται πᾶς ὁ κόσμος τῷ θεῷ (3:19). The first cluster of θλῖψις and στενοχωρία (2:9) is employed to depict the future calamity faced by those who follow unrighteousness and disobey the truth (2:8). The future aspect of θλῖψις and στενοχωρία is illustrated by the future tense of ἀποδώσει (2:6) in the previous clause, which indicates the impending calamity as the future judgment.[83] Appearing together with ὀργή and θυμός (2:8), the combination of θλῖψις and στενοχωρία highlights divine punishment, a usage that is found in both the LXX[84] and Philo's work.[85] Not only do both terms signify an external force causing the affliction, στενοχωρία also highlights divine chastisement as in the case of the LXX.

83. Byrne suggests that θλῖψις and στενοχωρία "designate punishment following the eschatological judgment." Byrne, *Romans*, 280.

84. Longenecker explains that the combination of these terms should be understood as "distress and anguish," describing God's attitude toward "wicked people in Isa 8:22 and 30:6, and it parallels in synonymous fashion with the couplet ὀργὴ καὶ θυμός ("wrath and anger") at the end of Rom 2:8." Longenecker, *Romans*, 258,

85. As previously mentioned, Philo also employs θλῖψις in conjunction with θυμός and ὀργή to depict divine punishment.

In the wider context of segment II, the polemical relationship between the Jews and the Gentiles underpins Paul's argument.[86] A list of sins is depicted in Rom 1:21–32 in which the use of third person plural personal pronouns and third person plural verbs alludes to the Gentiles as the culprit.[87] This focus on the Gentiles becomes evident when Paul immediately shifts from 1:32 to 2:1, stating Διὸ ἀναπολόγητος εἶ.[88] The use of second person singular verbs and second person singular personal pronouns in 2:1–29 indicates the shift from the Gentiles to the Jews.[89] The singular number does not describe a single person in 2:17, Εἰ δὲ σὺ Ἰουδαῖος ἐπονομάζῃ, it is clear that Paul employs the singular number to refer to the Jewish people in a corporate sense.[90]

In light of these points, the suffering depicted by θλῖψις and στενοχωρία in this first cluster does not concern *individual* suffering caused by divine punishment. Rather, Paul's argument centers on the corporate dimension of the two groups, the Jews and the Gentiles.

Both the second cluster and the third cluster appear in segment IV (5–8). The wider context of this segment focuses on issues relating to a faith community, which is marked by the repeated use of ἀδελφοί (7:1, 4; 8:12, 29).

In the second cluster θλῖψις occurs twice in Rom 5:3: ἀλλὰ καὶ καυχώμεθα ἐν ταῖς θλίψεσιν, εἰδότες ὅτι ἡ θλῖψις ὑπομονὴν κατεργάζεται. The first person plural καυχώμεθα denotes believers, as indicated by the ἔχομεν in 5:1. The term is then used to portray *current* suffering endured by believers, which could lead to perseverance (θλῖψις ὑπομονὴν κατεργάζεται).

---

86. Kruse contends that "Paul's unflattering depiction of the Gentile world of the first century is based on traditional Jewish polemic against Gentiles." Kruse, *Romans*, 115.

87. There are twelve third person personal pronouns and fourteen third person plural verbs in 1:21–32. There is no second-person personal pronouns or second person verbs in this segment.

88. Kruse suggests that "Paul proceeds to show that those who take the high moral ground, in particular the Jewish people, are also culpable, and have no special immunity when it comes to the judgment of God." Kruse, *Romans*, 117.

89. There are twenty-two second person singular verbs and seven second person personal pronouns in 2:1–29.

90. The use of second singular pronoun to depict the nation of Israel as a corporate entity should be a familiar to Paul. For example, in the well-known *Shema* in Deut 6:5, a second person singular pronoun, in the form of the suffix ך, is used to portray Israel as a singular entity. Accordingly, the LXX also has the singular pronoun σου.

In the third cluster, θλῖψις appears as the first word on the suffering list (8:35). Of interest, the term is placed next to στενοχωρία on this list which is considered "the first of seven types of peristalsis catalogues," depicting human hardship.[91] Jewett details how this kind of suffering list was commonly employed in the work of the Greco-Roman philosophers and religious teachers to "demonstrate 'divine power' to overcome adversity and thus confirm the legitimacy of a philosopher or apostle."[92] The list is also considered neither exhaustive nor random in portraying hardship.[93]

There are two different understandings in interpreting the list.

First, the suffering list depicts future events,[94] with θλῖψις referring to the "eschatological tribulation"[95] and θλῖψις and στενοχωρία together denoting the "fearsome tribulation of the end time."[96] This is supported by the use of future tense verbs in the immediate context, ἐγκαλέσει (8:33), κατακρινῶν (8:34), and χωρίσει (8:35).

Second, the list depicts a current situation. The argument in 8:31–35 illustrates the previous clause that is written as a first class condition in 8:31,[97] simply setting forth an argument instead of articulating an actual future event.[98] The suffering list, as Fitzmyer has argued, details the sufferings mentioned in 8:18.[99] In other words, the list concerns a real contemporary situation, with θλῖψις reflecting the "on-going and nearly ever-present reality of [Paul's] life . . . [and] his converts,"[100] as the apostle

---

91. Jewett, *Romans*, 544.

92. Jewett, *Romans*, 544–46. By analyzing various tribulation lists in the first century literature, Hodgson proposes that "Paul subsume[s] such diverse tribulation traditions as the Stoic, apocalyptic, Jewish historiographic and prophetic, and gnostic into his own unified vision of apostleship and gospel." Hodgson, "Paul the Apostle," 80.

93. Wu, *Suffering in Romans*, 189.

94. Wallace, *Greek*, 570.

95. Käsemann, *Romans*, 249.

96. Dunn, *Romans 1–8*, 504.

97. Despite the absence of any verbs in this conditional clause marked by εἰ, it is certain that both the second class condition, which requires the presence of ἄν in the apodosis, and the third class condition, which require the use of ἐάν in the protasis, can be ruled out. For the discussion of conditional sentences, see Wallace, *Greek*, 689.

98. Wallace, *Greek*, 690.

99. Fitzmyer, *Romans*, 534.

100. Kruse, *Romans*, 362. Moo, Byrne, and Wu hold a similar view, arguing that the list of words show "some of those hazards [Paul] himself has encountered in his apostolic labors" (Moo, *Romans*, 543) and "the perils and hardships of his own life as

is enumerating the trials that he has experienced.[101] The term θλῖψις, therefore, should be viewed as describing "suffering in a generic manner... [meaning] affliction or suffering."[102] Jewett further conjectures that the combination of θλῖψις and στενοχωρία can be traced back to its occurrence in 2 Corinthians, in which the conflict between the "strong" and the "weak" is depicted as a dominant contemporary struggle among the Corinthians.[103] The apostle, as a result, reflects in Romans "a rhetorical situation in which voices were being raised in Rome against the "weak" who consisted predominately of Jewish Christians whose leaders had been expelled from Rome by the Edict of Claudius."[104] Regardless of whether Jewett's conjecture is accurate, the word θλῖψις means affliction. Suffering is the reality that both believers and the apostle share.

Based on our previous diachronic study, θλῖψις and its cognates frequently connote distress due to oppression or mistreatment in the LXX. It is possible that Paul draws on this connotation from the LXX, alluding to oppression or mistreatment suffered by believers. Furthermore, the word στενοχωρία also carries the essence of external force or pressure as noted in Paul's contemporary literature. Therefore, the combination of θλῖψις and στενοχωρία is best viewed as the suffering that is caused by *external force*: persecution or oppression. However, the letter is silent on the possible causes of this kind of oppression, mistreatment and persecution. Based on the silence, the two different understandings are not necessarily mutually exclusive: the terms can be employed to highlight current suffering endured by believers, whilst alluding to the future tribulation at the end of the ages.

When taking all three clusters into consideration, the cluster in Romans 2 depicts the suffering in future divine judgment, the two clusters in Romans 5 and Romans 8 refer to believers' current suffering, possibly alluding to the future tribulation. At first glance, the future aspect seems to be a recurring theme on two occasions. Nonetheless, there is one common pattern that underlies all three clusters. The language of suffering

---

apostle ... [and] the earthly trials of the elect in the period leading up to it," (Byrne, *Romans*, 280), and the "socioeconomic hardships" suffered by the audience (Wu, *Suffering in Romans*, 190).

101. Cranfield, *Romans*, 440; Hultgren, *Romans*, 340.

102. Wu, *Suffering in Romans*, 190.

103. Both the "strong" and the "weak" are collective categories, referring to groups, not individual, in the Corinthian community. See Jewett, *Romans*, 545.

104. Jewett, *Romans*, 546.

is not employed to denote *individual* suffering. Instead, the language highlights the corporate dimension of suffering. In segment IV, both clusters denote suffering endured by believers (and Paul), emphasizing the solidarity within the Christian community regardless of whether the suffering is contemporary or eschatological. Furthermore, divine punishment is in view in the cluster located in segment II, as the suffering will be faced by those who disobey the truth. Nonetheless, as explained above, Paul does not focus on individual suffering,[105] as the apostle centers his argument on the corporate dimension of the two groups, the Jews and the Gentiles: Ἰουδαίου τε πρῶτον καὶ Ἕλληνος (2:9).

The last occurrence of θλῖψις does not appear in clustered form, it appears alone in Rom 12:12 (τῇ ἐλπίδι χαίροντες, τῇ θλίψει ὑπομένοντες, τῇ προσευχῇ προσκαρτεροῦντες). If θλῖψις refers to persecution or oppression, then this understanding would form a coherent argument with its immediate context. In 12:14, the Romans are given an imperative: εὐλογεῖτε τοὺς διώκοντας [ὑμᾶς]. The phrase τοὺς διώκοντας forms a perfect match with the previous clause: endure persecution (v.12) . . . bless those who persecute you (v.14). More importantly, θλῖψις occurs in segment VI, a segment that is commonly considered as Paul's concern for the faith community,[106] which is illustrated by the repeated call from the apostle, urging members of the faith community in Rome to love one another (12:9; 13:8; 13:10; 14:15).[107]

To sum up, by examining the three clustered appearances of θλῖψις and στενοχωρία, investigating the sentence meaning of each of those occurrences, the overall pattern informs us that the thematic meaning of θλῖψις and στενοχωρία in Romans points to corporate solidarity, whilst alluding to the eschatological dimension. The language of suffering in

---

105. The number of the two nouns θλῖψις and στενοχωρία being singular does not indicate *individual* suffering. In Paul's authentic letters, the majority of the occurrences of θλῖψις and στενοχωρία appear in singular (θλῖψις appears seventeen times as singular but only three times in plural). For example, the singular θλῖψις in the phrase ὑμῖν θλῖψις (2 Cor 8:13) is clearly employed to depict the suffering of the Corinthian community, as indicated by the combination of the plural pronoun and the singular noun.

106. This is a common view among commentators. Byrne, *Romans*, 361–62; Dunn, *Romans 9–16*, 705; Fitzmyer, *Romans*, 637; Jewett, *Romans*, 738; Moo, *Romans*, 746–47; Schlatter, *Romans*, 227; Schreiner, *Romans*, 49; Stuhlmacher, *Romans*, 185. Moxnes, "Quest for Honor," 217–19, further explains the passage in 12:3–16 is Paul's exhortation to the Romans, encouraging the community to have unity.

107. Kim, "Reading Paul," 318, contends that the love urged by Paul in Rom 12–15 is the element that can foster unity between the Jews and the Gentiles in the faith community in Rome.

Romans, exemplified by the use of θλῖψις and στενοχωρία, does not concern the affliction faced by an individual. Rather, it highlights the affliction in corporate and communal solidarity.

The Thematic Meaning of Θλῖψις and Στενοχωρία in 2 Corinthians

In 2 Corinthians, θλῖψις and its cognates appear twelve times; and στενοχωρία and its cognates appear five times.[108]

There are two issues that require brief delineation before conducting semantic analysis: the unity of 2 Corinthians; and the frequent use of first person plural pronouns and verbs.

First, in NT scholarship the view on the unity of 2 Corinthians is divided.[109] Some consider the letter as a conglomerate of multi-letters;[110] others regard it as one single epistle.[111] Despite differences in view, it is reasonable to treat 2 Cor 1–9 as a single discourse for this analysis for the following reasons. Scholars who hold the multi-letter theory usually agree that 2 Cor 1–9 is a single letter.[112] Those who advocate the single-letter theory agree that the themes covered in 1–9 are vastly different from those in 10–13.[113] Of all the appearances of θλῖψις, στενοχωρία, and their cognates, there is only one occurrence located beyond 2 Corinthians 9 (στενοχωρία in 12:10). Therefore, this study will focus on 2 Corinthians 1–9, treating it as one single discourse for our semantic analysis.

---

108. The occurrences of θλῖψις and its cognates: 2 Cor 1:4 (twice), 6, 8; 2:4; 4:8, 17; 6:4; 7:4, 5; 8:2, 13. The occurrences of στενοχωρία and its cognates: 2 Cor 4:8; 6:4, 12 (twice); 12:10. Of interest, Θλῖψις and its cognate, θλίβω, occur four times in the first chapter.

109. For a detailed discussion of this issue, see Thrall, *2 Corinthians 1–7*, 3–49; Harris, *Corinthians*, 8–51.

110. Furnish, *II Corinthians*, 35–54; Barrett, *Second Corinthians*, 23–24; Thrall, *2 Corinthians 1–7*, 3–49; Betz, *2 Corinthians 8 and 9*, 3–36; Roetzel, *2 Corinthians*, 24–35.

111. Martin, *2 Corinthians*, xxxix–xl; Barnett, *Corinthians*, 24–25; McCant, *2 Corinthians*, 23; Witherington, *Corinthians*, 328, 333–36; Keener, *Corinthians*, 151; Watson, *Second Corinthians*, 96. See also Amador, "Revisiting 2 Corinthians," 92–111; DeSilva, "Measuring Penultimate," 41–70.

112. For example, Furnish, *II Corinthians*, xi, considers 2 Cor 1–9 as Letter D.

113. For example, McCant, *2 Corinthians*, 7, holds that 2 Corinthians should be divided into three parts: 1–7; 8–9; 10–13.

The second issue concerns the frequent use of first personal plural pronouns and verbs throughout the whole letter.[114] Does Paul use these plural to depict both his colleague and himself, or epistolary plural to denote only the apostle himself?[115] Many commentators commonly consider that Paul uses epistolary plural in a number of passages in 2 Corinthians to describe his own experiences.[116] The main reason is that Paul spends a significant portion of the letter to explain and defend his apostolic ministry amongst the Corinthians. Hence, the first person plural is best understood as epistolary plural.

Table 3 shows the division of 2 Corinthians 1–9 as identified by some major modern commentators;[117] and based on that division, Table 4 shows where the occurrences of θλῖψις and στενοχωρία are located in the letter. It shows that there are three major clusters in the whole letter.

---

114. There are 108 first person plural personal pronouns and ninety-four first person plural verbs in 2 Corinthians. These numbers are strikingly large when compared with another Pauline letter, 1 Corinthians. Although 1 Corinthians is more than 2,000 words longer than 2 Corinthians, it only has fifty-four first person plural personal pronouns and seventy-one first person plural verbs.

115. Kijne and Verhoef provide a detailed discussion on this topic. See Kijne, "We, Us and Our," 171–79; Verhoef, "Senders of the Letters," 417–25.

116. The phrase ἡ καρδία ἡμῶν in 6:11 serves as a good example. Many commentators consider the phrase refers to Paul himself despite the use of a plural personal pronoun ἡμῶν. The pronoun is well explained by the use of epistolary plural. For detailed discussion, see Chen, "Distributive Singular," 118, 126–27.

117. This table is an update of that found in Chen, *Paul's Anthropological Terms*, 166. This table only focuses on the work contributed by commentators during the last thirty years. The letter-opening is excluded in this table. See Barrett, *Second Corinthians*, 51–2; DeSilva, *2 Corinthians*, vii; Guthrie, *2 Corinthians*, vii; Harris, *Second Corinthians*, ix–xi; Lambrecht, *Second Corinthians*, v–vi; Matera, *II Corinthians*, vii–viii; McCant, *2 Corinthians*, 7; Oropeza, *Second Corinthians*, vii–ix; Thrall, *2 Corinthians 1–7*, xiii–xiv; Thrall, *2 Corinthians 9–13*, ix–x; Watson, *Second Corinthians*, vii–viii; Witherington, *Corinthians*, viii–ix. Note that there are some minor differences in terms of individual commentator's understanding of division. For example, the beginning of a new segment is marked by 7:2 (Witherington) or 7:3 (DeSilva) instead of 7:5.

Table 3. The Division of 2 Corinthians 1–9

Letter Division	1:3–2:13	2:14–7:4	7:5–16	8:1–9:15
Commentators' View	Barnett	Barnett	DeSilva	Guthrie
	Barrett	Barrett	Guthrie	Harris
	Lambrecht	Guthrie	Harris	Lambrecht
	Matera	Harris	Keener	Matera
	Thrall	Lambrecht	Lambrecht	McCant
	Witherington	Matera	Matera	Oropeza
		Roetzel	Thrall	Thrall
		Thrall	Witherington	Watson
				Witherington

Table 4. Occurrences of Θλῖψις and Στενοχωρία in 2 Cor 1–9

Letter Division		I 1:3–2:13	II 2:14–7:4	III 7:5–16	IV 8:1–9:15
Occurrence of	θλῖψις & στενοχωρία	(*** * *)	*** *	(* *)	* *

*: a single occurrence of θλῖψις or its cognate;

^: a single occurrence of στενοχωρία or its cognate;

⊂⊃: cluster

The first cluster appears in segment I. In this segment, Paul centers on his relationship with the Corinthians by informing them his clear conscience, his sincerity, and his pure motive: τῆς συνειδήσεως ἡμῶν, ὅτι ἐν ἁπλότητι καὶ εἰλικρινείᾳ τοῦ θεοῦ (1:12). In 1:4, the noun appears twice (πάσῃ τῇ θλίψει ἡμῶν and ἐν πάσῃ θλίψει); and in 1:6 the verb θλίβω occurs once (εἴτε δὲ θλιβόμεθα). The meaning of θλῖψις and θλίβω in the passage becomes clear, as Paul specifies the nature of this affliction: τῆς θλίψεως ἡμῶν τῆς γενομένης ἐν τῇ Ἀσίᾳ (1:8). Therefore, the four occurrences of θλῖψις and its cognate refer to the apostle's own affliction in his ministry.[118] Referring to his experience in Asia the word describes a real situation instead of a hypothetical event, although Paul does not specify the details of his suffering.[119] Regardless of what θλῖψις illustrates, the incident likely takes place in the form of pressure or persecution.[120]

The second cluster occurs in segment II. Paul defends his apostolic ministry in this segment, pronouncing that his ministry to the Corinthians is ordained by God who gives the apostle the ministry of reconciliation (5:18-20). He then provides different arguments to prove that he is an authentic apostle. In the middle of his defense, the term θλῖψις appears together with στενοχωρία and its cognate in 2 Corinthians 6. In 6:4, Paul first mentions his suffering due to his apostolic ministry: ἐν θλίψεσιν (6:4) ἐν στενοχωρίαις (6:4). Subsequently, he expresses his affection towards his audience: Τὸ στόμα ἡμῶν ἀνέῳγεν πρὸς ὑμᾶς, Κορίνθιοι, ἡ καρδία ἡμῶν πεπλάτυνται· οὐ στενοχωρεῖσθε ἐν ἡμῖν, στενοχωρεῖσθε δὲ ἐν τοῖς σπλάγχνοις ὑμῶν (6:11-12). As previously mentioned, most commentators consider the phrase ἡ καρδία ἡμῶν as describing the apostle's own experience. Thus, the suffering (θλῖψις) and the persecution/pressure (στενοχωρία) are what Paul endures as an apostle.

The third cluster is located in 7:4-5, transitioning from segment II to segment III. Paul continues to make known his experience as an apostle. The θλῖψις in 7:4 serves as the conclusion of the segment II, articulating the apostle's suffering as discussed above. Then, the substantival participle, θλιβόμενοι depicts his experience when he arrives in Macedonia: Καὶ γὰρ ἐλθόντων ἡμῶν εἰς Μακεδονίαν οὐδεμίαν ἔσχηκεν ἄνεσιν ἡ σὰρξ ἡμῶν ἀλλ᾽ ἐν παντὶ θλιβόμενοι (7:5). Some argue that this part resumes the apostle's earlier discussion of his suffering in 2:13.[121] Follow-

118. The use of plural pronoun ἡμῶν and first person plural verb θλιβόμεθα can well be considered as epistolary plural, a view adopted by a number of modern interpreters.

119. See the discussion of Oropeza, *Second Corinthians*, 84-86; and Thrall, *2 Corinthians 1-7*, 115-17. For example, according to Oropeza, *Second Corinthians*, 407, the suffering mentioned in 2 Cor 1 may refer to the beating and imprisonment in Philippi and the riot in Ephesus experienced by Paul, which is described by Luke's account in Acts 16:16-24; 19:24-41.

120. Seifrid, *Second Corinthians*, 116.

121. For example, Lambrecht, *Second Corinthians*, 129.

ing the argument above, the term θλῖψις, despite the presence of a plural pronoun, depicts Paul's own suffering relating to his apostolic ministry.

Considering all three clusters, the use of θλῖψις, στενοχωρία, and their cognates are employed by Paul to either articulate or defend his apostolic ministry. The language of suffering portrays Paul's own suffering, serving as a proof that he is indeed an authentic apostle, being sent by God to fulfill the ministry of reconciliation among the Corinthians.

For the remaining individual occurrences of those terms of suffering, most of them are again used to depict the apostle's personal experience due to his apostolic ministry, except the one in 8:2. In expressing his own anguish concerning a letter previously written to the Corinthians, Paul conveys to them that ἐκ γὰρ πολλῆς θλίψεως καὶ συνοχῆς καρδίας ἔγραψα ὑμῖν διὰ πολλῶν δακρύων (2:4). The term describes the apostle's own suffering caused by a particular incident that is mentioned in 2:5–7, dealing with a problematic person. Θλίβω also appears in 4:8, within segment II in which Paul defends his apostolic ministry. The verb appears in conjunction with στενοχωρέω in ἐν παντὶ θλιβόμενοι ἀλλ' οὐ στενοχωρούμενοι (4:8). The occurrence of στενοχωρέω further explicates the persecution or pressure that the apostle faces. Paul continues to describe his experience in 4:9–18. The clause, τὸ γὰρ παραυτίκα ἐλαφρὸν τῆς θλίψεως ἡμῶν (4:17), reveals how the apostle reflects on his own suffering. Again, the plural pronoun ἡμῶν and the first person plural verbs should be treated as epistolary plural, as Paul describes his own suffering in his apostolic ministry. Στενοχωρία last appears in 12:10, the context concerns the apostle's boasting. Paul boasts about his weakness, expressing his own contentment ἐν διωγμοῖς καὶ στενοχωρίαις. Given the notion of external pressure or force underlying the connotation of στενοχωρία, the phrase διωγμοῖς καὶ στενοχωρίαις can be considered as referring to the same situation instead of two different occasions. In other words, στενοχωρία portrays the persecution faced by Paul because of his apostolic ministry. As mentioned, the only exception where the terms of suffering do not illustrate the apostle's own experience is located in 8:2. In that context the term θλῖψις denotes the suffering of the Macedonians, and the suffering may well be defined as their deep poverty: ἡ κατὰ βάθους πτωχεία (8:2). In the proceeding context, Paul discusses offering monetary support. Paul mentions suffering in a statement: οὐ γὰρ ἵνα ἄλλοις ἄνεσις, ὑμῖν θλῖψις, ἀλλ' ἐξ ἰσότητος (8:13). The context, which is aligned with the argument in 8:1–2, likely concerns the lack of material resources or money.

The three clustered appearances, together with the majority of individual occurrences of the terms of suffering, are employed to illustrate Paul's experience in his apostolic ministry. Seemingly, the key pattern of their appearances signifies an *individual* suffering, Paul's suffering in particular. Nonetheless, in defending his apostolic ministry Paul's suffering must not be understood as a mere individual experience. Rather, the utterance of his suffering is a means for Paul to invite his audience, a faith community, to reflect on their relationship with the apostle. In other words, the coherent pattern of the occurrences of the language of suffering points to a deep ecclesial aspect in light of the following considerations.

First, Paul begins 2 Corinthians by stating the impact of his suffering on the Corinthians: εἴτε δὲ θλιβόμεθα, ὑπὲρ τῆς ὑμῶν παρακλήσεως καὶ σωτηρίας· εἴτε παρακαλούμεθα, ὑπὲρ τῆς ὑμῶν παρακλήσεως τῆς ἐνεργουμένης ἐν ὑπομονῇ τῶν αὐτῶν παθημάτων ὧν καὶ ἡμεῖς πάσχομεν (1:6). This statement at the beginning of this epistle reveals that there is a close connection between the apostle's suffering and the Corinthian community.[122]

Second, when Paul describes his own suffering in the letter content, he also makes explicit reference to his relationship with the community. For example, as previously mentioned, Paul declares that his heart has been opened wide to the Corinthians (6:11) after mentioning his suffering in 6:4 (ἐν θλίψεσιν, ἐν στενοχωρίαις).[123] Guthrie succinctly sums up Paul's declaration in 2 Corinthians 6: it demonstrates that in this "ministry partnership, one of intimacy and integrity, seems to be Paul's longing."[124] As well illustrated by Seifrid, by mentioning his own suffering Paul "invites the Corinthians to . . . share in his experience of distress and deliverance . . . [and] to enter into the fellowship . . . of suffering and comfort."[125] The language of suffering employed by Paul in 2 Corinthians may well be fulfilling the purpose of demonstrating Paul's "congruence with the suffering Christ."[126] However, in light of the above evidence, at

---

122. Lambrecht argues that Paul's suffering "is certainly also linked with that of the (Corinthian) Christians." Lambrecht, *Second Corinthians*, 115.

123. Martin suggests that 6:1–13 "closes with a heartfelt appeal to the Corinthians. . . . Paul has opened his heart to them . . . he looks for a reciprocal response." Martin, *2 Corinthians*, 325.

124. Guthrie, *2 Corinthians*, 348.

125. Seifrid, *2 Corinthians*, 35, explains the suffering depicted in 2 Cor 1.

126. Jewett, *Romans*, 545.

the discourse level the overall pattern of the language of suffering reveals a significant ecclesial dimension.

Therefore, the thematic meaning of θλῖψις, στενοχωρία, and their cognates highlights the ecclesial relationship between a faith community and the apostle who is called by Christ to be their minister.

Conclusion

This study has ascertained the meanings of θλῖψις, στενοχωρία, and their cognates, by adopting both diachronic and synchronic approaches. More importantly, this study has applied modern linguistic principles by ascertaining the thematic meanings of those terms in Romans and 2 Corinthians. Through observing their clustered appearances at the discourse level, examining the sentence meanings in each of the occurrences, the overall pattern has reviewed the thematic meanings of both terms: they carry a strong eschatological and corporate dimension. Paul's language of suffering, as illustrated by these terms in these two epistles, does not largely center on *individual* suffering. Rather, the language emphasizes corporate solidarity and ecclesial relationships, as the faith community anticipates the advent of the eschaton. Reflecting on the connotations shared by these terms, suffering due to external force, and communal implications in the face of suffering, Paul's language of suffering reminds believers to see the suffering that they have little control over as something that can and should be faced in corporate solidarity and communal relationship here and now, in light of the coming eschaton.

Bibliography

Amador, J. D. H. "Revisiting 2 Corinthians: Rhetoric and the Case for Unity." *NTS* 46 (2000) 92–111.

Barnett, Paul. *A Commentary on the Second Epistle to the Corinthians*. BNTC. London: A & C Black, 1973.

———. *The Second Epistle to the Corinthians*. NICNT. Grand Rapids, MI: Eerdmans, 1997.

Barrett, C. K. *The Epistle to the Romans*. BNTC. London: A & C Black, 1991.

Betz, Hans Dieter. *2 Corinthians 8 and 9: A Commentary on Two Administrative Letters of the Apostle Paul*. Hermeneia: A Critical and Historical Commentary on the Bible. Philadelphia: Fortress, 1985.

Byrne, Brendan. *Romans*. SP 6. Collegeville, MN: Liturgical, 1996.

Chen, Sunny. "The Distributive Singular in Paul: The Adequacy of a Grammatical Category." *JGRChJ* 11 (2015) 104–30.

———. *Paul's Anthropological Terms in the Light of Discourse Analysis.* Publications in Translation and Textlinguistics. Dallas, TX: SIL International, 2019.

Cranfield, C. E. B. *A Critical and Exegetical Commentary on the Epistle to the Romans: Introduction and Commentary on Romans I–VIII.* ICC 28. Edinburgh: T & T Clark, 1975–1979.

Deibler, Ellis W. *A Semantic and Structural Analysis of Romans.* Edited by John Banker. Dallas: SIL, 1998.

deSilva, David A. *The Credential of an Apostle: Paul's Gospel in 2 Corinthians 1–7.* Bibal Monograph Series 4. N. Richland Hills, TX: Bibal, 1998.

———. "Measuring Penultimate against Ultimate Reality: An Investigation of the Integrity and Argumentation of 2 Corinthians." *JSNT* 52 (1993) 41–70.

Dooley, Robert A., and Stephen H. Levinsohn. *Analyzing Discourse: A Manual of Basic Concepts.* Edited by Bonnie Brown. Dallas: SIL International, 2001.

Dunn, James D. G. *Romans 1–8.* WBC 38A. Waco, TX: Word, 1983.

Engberg-Pedersen, Troels. *Paul and the Stoics.* Louisville, KY: Westminster John Knox, 2000.

Fitzmyer, Joseph A. *Romans: A New Translation with Introduction and Commentary.* AB 33. New York: Doubleday, 1993.

Furnish, Victor Paul. *II Corinthians: A New Translation with Introduction and Commentary.* AB. New York: Doubleday & Company, 1984.

Grice, H. P. "Utterer's Meaning, Sentence-Meaning, and Word-Meaning." In *Pragmatics: A Reader*, edited by Steven Davis. New York: Oxford University Press, 1991.

Guthrie, George H. *2 Corinthians.* BECNT. Grand Rapids, MI: Baker Academic, 2015.

Halliday, M. A. K. *Linguistic Studies of Text and Discourse.* Edited by Jonathan Webster. London: Continuum, 2002.

Harrington, Daniel J. "Paul's Use of the Old Testament in Romans." Paper presented at the Conference *Paul of Tarsus: The Apostle to the Gentiles in His Jewish Context* at Boston College, Boston, MA, March 15, 2009.

Harris, Murray J. *The Second Epistle to the Corinthians: A Commentary on the Greek Text.* NIGTC. Grand Rapids, MI: Eerdmans, 2005.

Hodgson, Robert. "Paul the Apostle and First Century Tribulation Lists." *ZNW* 74 (1983) 59–80.

Hughes, Philip Edgcumbe. *Paul's Second Epistle to the Corinthians.* NICNT. Grand Rapids, MI: Eerdmans, 1967.

Hultgren, Arland J. *Paul's Letter to the Romans: A Commentary.* Grand Rapids, MI: Eerdmans, 2011.

Jewett, Robert. *Romans: A Commentary.* Hermeneia: A Critical and Historical Commentary on the Bible. Minneapolis: Fortress, 2007,

Käsemann, Ernst. *Commentary on Romans.* Edited and translated by Geoffrey W. Bromiley. Grand Rapids, MI: Eerdmans, 1980.

Keener, Craig S. *1–2 Corinthians.* NCBC. New York: Cambridge University Press, 2005.

Kijne, J. J. "We, Us and Our in I and II Corinthians." *NovT* 8 (1966) 171–79.

Kim, Dongsu. "Reading Paul's καὶ οὕτως πᾶς Ἰσραὴλ σωθήσεται (Rom. 11:26a) in the Context of Romans." *Calvin Theological Journal* 45 (2010) 317–34.

Kruse, Colin G. *Paul's Letter to the Romans.* PNTC. Grand Rapids, MI: Eerdmans, 2012.

Lambrecht, Jan. *Second Corinthians.* SP 8. Collegeville, MN: Liturgical, 1999.

Lee, Michelle V. *Paul, the Stoics, and the Body of Christ.* New York: Cambridge University Press, 2006

Lemke, Jay L. "Intertextuality and Text Semantics." In *Discourse in Society: Systemic Functional Perspectives, Meaning and Choice in Language: Studies for Michael Halliday*, edited by Peter H. Fries et al. Vol. L in Advances in Discourse Processes. Norwood: Ablex, 1995.

Liddell, Henry George, Robert Scott, and Henry Stuart Jones. *A Greek-English Lexicon*. 9th ed. Oxford: Clarendon, 1996.

Longenecker, Richard N. *The Epistle to the Romans*. NTGTC. Grand Rapids, MI: Eerdmans, 2016.

Louw, Johannes P. "Discourse Analysis and the Greek New Testament." *BT* 24 (1973) 101–118.

Martin, Ralph P. *2 Corinthians*. WBC 40. Waco, TX: Word, 1986.

Matera, Frank J. *II Corinthians*. NTL. Louisville, KY: Westminster John Knox, 2003.

McCant, Jerry W. *2 Corinthians*. Readings: A New Biblical Commentary. Sheffield: Sheffield Academic, 1999.

Moo, Douglas. *The Epistle to the Romans*. NICNT. Grand Rapids, MI: Eerdmans, 1996.

Moxnes, Halvor. "The Quest for Honor and Unity of the Community in Romans 12 and in the Orations of Dio Chrysostom." In *Paul in His Hellenistic Context: Studies of the New Testament and Its World*, edited by Troels Engberg-Pedersen. Edinburgh: T & T Clark, 1994.

Oropeza, B. J. *Exploring Second Corinthians: Death and Life, Hardship and Rivalry*. Rhetoric of Religious Antiquity 3. Atlanta: SBL, 2016.

Plummer, Alfred. *A Critical and Exegetical Commentary on the Second Epistle to the Corinthians*. ICC. Edinburgh: T & T Clark, 1925.

Ricoeur, Paul. *The Conflict of Interpretations: Essays in Hermeneutics*, edited by Don Ihde. Evanston: Northwestern University Press, 1974.

Roetzel, Calvin J. *2 Corinthians*. ANTC. Nashville: Abingdon, 2007.

Saussure, Ferdinand de. *Writing in General Linguistics*. Translated by Carol Sanders and Matthew Pires. New York: Oxford University Press, 2006.

Schlatter, Adolf. *Romans: The Righteousness of God*. Translated by Siegfried S. Schatzmann. Peabody, MA: Hendrickson, 1995.

Schlier, Heinrich. "Θλίβω." In *TDNT* 3:139–48.

Schreiner, Thomas R. *Romans*. BECNT. Grand Rapids, MI: Baker Academic, 1998.

Seifrid, Mark A. *The Second Letter to the Corinthians*. PNTC. Grand Rapids, MI: Eerdmans, 2014.

Stuhlmacher, Peter. *Paul's Letter to the Romans: A Commentary*. Edinburgh: T & T Clark, 1994.

Thrall, Margaret E. *2 Corinthians 1–7*. Vol. 1 of *A Critical and Exegetical Commentary on the Second Epistle to the Corinthians*. ICC. Edinburgh: T & T Clark, 1994.

———. *2 Corinthians 9–13*. Vol. 2 of *A Critical and Exegetical Commentary on the Second Epistle to the Corinthians*. ICC. Edinburgh: T & T Clark, 1994.

Thesaurus Linguae Graecae Digital Library. Edited by Maria C. Pantelia. University of California, Irvine. http://www.tlg.uci.edu.

Verhoef, Eduard. "The Senders of the Letters to the Corinthians and the Use of 'I' and 'We.'" In *The Corinthian Correspondence*, edited by R. Bieringer. Bibliotheca Ephemeridum Theologicarum Lovaniensium 125. Leuven: Leuven University Press, 1996.

Wallace, Daniel B. *Greek Grammar Beyond the Basics: An Exegetical Syntax of the New Testament*. Grand Rapids, MI: Zondervan, 1996.

Walter, Bauer, Frederick W. Danker, W. F. Arndt, and F. W. Gingrich. *Greek-English Lexicon of the New Testament and Other Early Christian Literature.* 3rd ed. Chicago: University of Chicago Press, 2000.

Watson, Nigel. *The Second Epistle to the Corinthians.* Epworth Commentaries. London: Epworth, 1993.

Witherington, Ben, III. *Conflict and Community in Corinth: A Socio-Rhetorical Commentary on 1 and 2 Corinthians.* Grand Rapids, MI: Eerdmans, 1995.

Wu, Siu Fung. *Suffering in Romans.* Eugene, OR: Pickwick, 2015.

PART 2: RESPONSES

10

Making Sense of Christian Suffering

Contextual Implications for Christians Today

Sanyu Iralu

Introduction

Human suffering is a common feature of earthly existence. It is a universal experience that makes no distinction between the rich and the poor, the righteous and the wicked, the young and the old—across all genders and races. And yes, suffering is as old as human history: when Adam and Eve disobeyed God and sinned, they suffered the penalty (Gen 3:16–19). Thus, the sin-suffering connection is clear in the Old Testament. However, there are instances in the Old Testament where suffering is not associated with sin; such is the suffering of Job and the righteous in the Psalter.

A similar sin-suffering connection is found in the New Testament, where specific sins (Matt 25:41–43; Acts 5:1–11) are interpreted as the immediate cause of human suffering. Yet tangential to this understanding we find believers who suffer for their faith in Christ (Phil 1:13). This new idea speaks of a suffering that is common only to those who believe in Jesus Christ. This suffering is expected rather than dreaded. Christians may suffer individually or corporately, but it is a suffering in which they willingly participate (cf. 1 Pet 4:12–13).

The Rationale for Christian Suffering

How can Christians willingly participate in suffering? Mere human logic fails to accommodate volitional suffering. What, then, is the rationale that allows Christians to accept suffering? Certainly, powerful motives must lie behind a believer's willingness to suffer for one's faith. Foremost, among other reasons, is that Christ has already willingly suffered in advance, and has become the example *par excellence* for Christians to emulate (cf. 1 Pet 2:21).[1] Alongside this understanding is the notion of a fuller life that flows out of suffering, exemplified by Jesus' suffering and his resurrection from the dead. The idea is that prior to experiencing resurrection life on earth, one has to suffer as Christ suffered.

Having understood the above, Paul has no hesitation in wanting to experience the power of Christ's resurrection and share in the fellowship of his sufferings (Phil 3:10). In other words, participation becomes an alluring motif such that believers consider it the highest honor to suffer for Christ. Kar Yong Lim has this to say:

> For Paul, there was no escape from suffering in this present life. But suffering did not have the last word. Sharing in Christ's sufferings is Paul's ultimate hope for sharing in the future power of the resurrection from the dead. As Christ was vindicated by God, so shall Paul and the Philippians be vindicated by God ultimately. This is the highest honor. (143)

Consequent to his Damascus conversion experience, Paul has clearly weighed the consequences of following Christ. He considers his privileged lot in Judaism (Phil 3:4–6b) "dung" (σκύβαλα; 3:8). Using "accounting terminology,"[2] Paul shows how former apparent assets (κέρδη; 3:7) have proven to be unprofitable investments (ζημίαν; 3:7). Thus, Paul boldly declares his new-found values in light of the surpassing greatness of the knowledge of the righteousness that comes through faith in Christ, apart from the law (3:9). By contrasting his former state with the new status he has received from God, Paul expresses his willingness to suffer for Christ—if need be.

---

1. Thus, Sean Winter speaks of Paul's christological framing of his suffering in that "Paul cannot talk about his own sufferings without relating his experience to his participation in the sufferings of Christ." (65)

2. O'Brien, *Epistle to the Philippians*, 382.

The Due Rewards in Christian Suffering

To suffer for Christ means that a believer can respond to suffering in the knowledge of a due reward in the afterlife.[3] Indeed, it holds a heavenly dimension and purpose. Paul's discourse on suffering in Romans 8, especially in vv. 16–17, centers on this idea. Here, Paul talks about how the Spirit testifies that believers are the children of God, who are, in turn, the co-heirs of God with Christ. Those heirs who co-suffer with Christ will share in Christ's glorification. Thus, Roy Ciampa observes: "So believers are 'joint heirs with Christ' with an important rider: 'if, in fact, we suffer with him so that we may also be glorified with him.' Suffering with Christ must precede glorification with him" (21). The implication is clear "that we who are joint-heirs must participate in what Christ, as heir of God, has experienced before we too can participate in his glory."[4] This is an amazing formula, indeed, a huge incentive for believers to get on the bandwagon of suffering.

As we can see, there are abundant reasons for Christians to accept suffering for Christ. It is no wonder Paul is not averse, but rather willing to suffer; likeminded Christians follow suit. So, Siu Fung Wu says:

> [S]uffering can be seen as a shared experience between Paul and his audience. Suffering is where their life-stories intersect. And suffering is for the sake of, and on behalf of, Christ. Indeed, it seems that Paul sees suffering as participation in Christ, for the whole existence of the believing community (as individuals and corporately) has everything to do with Christ's death and life. (85)

This motivation prompts believers to abandon other religions and risk their lives without regard for the suffering that may come their way. If one decides to embrace the Christian faith in a context where all others adhere to a non-Christian faith, in that moment one's life situation changes drastically. There are many ways to intimidate and exert pressure to recant, or to make life miserable for any who remain resolute in the new-found faith. Thus, Bindulata Barik pertinently observes:

---

3. As Lim notes: "The understanding that the Philippians were citizens of heaven awaiting a Savior (Phil 3:20) provides them with a strong cognitive understanding that their sense of belonging to and solidarity with one another in their present sufferings distinguishes them from other groups." (146)

4. Iralu, "Theme of Christian Suffering," 15.

> Indian Christians suffer for their Christian faith in the twenty-first century. They undergo physical and mental torture, financial deprivation, and social humiliation. Christian believers, pastors, priests, evangelists and workers, whether men or women, children or elderly, have been beaten, mocked, thrown out of the house or church, and forced into exile. They have been imprisoned through false accusations.[5]

Truly, suffering for one's faith and belief is a reality for Christians in the Indian sub-continent where I am from. India is a multi-religious nation composed of ethnically diverse peoples that, ironically, espouses secularism. But because the majority follow a particular religion, oftentimes, the majority's clout overrules sanity. In the process, small minority communities that practice a different religion are easily ostracized and oppressed. Speaking of similar persecutions in the early church, Lim says:

> [R]efusal to participate in the worship of any Greco-Roman deities could easily result in long term suffering as a consequence of serious economic loss where contacts may have been severed and trade affected. In addition, there were social consequences where the Christ-followers may have been excluded from trade guilds and prohibited from participating in networking that was all too important for building social relations. Alienation and harassment from families and (non-trade-related) social networks could not be discounted either. (138)

Likewise, Barik laments for Indian Christians: "Christians are accused of breaking social peace. Imprisonment has caused humiliation and harassment, and often reduced families to poverty, with families of martyrs becoming destitute and losing their security and social ties."[6] Such are the lot of Christians in India who suffer because they choose to follow Christ. But they plod on because they are motivated by their desire to follow Jesus. At the same time, they eagerly await their future reward.

Suffering for Christ has other rewards. By suffering in solidarity in a common participation in Christ's suffering, Christians share together in a common consolation that comes through the consolation accorded by God.[7] Yes, Christians, including Paul, suffer greatly—psychologically, emotionally, even economically. They are physically battered, humiliated,

---

5. Barik, *Persecution and Hope*, 118.
6. Barik, *Persecution and Hope*, 119.
7. Winter concurs: "[T]here is solidarity in suffering by virtue of the common participation of Paul and the Corinthians in the suffering and vindication of Christ." (77)

and deprived of their identity (cf. 2 Cor 6:4–10). Yet, Paul confidently asserts that his suffering promotes the cause of the gospel, even benefitting others, instead of limiting it (Phil 1:12–14). So, Lim says:

> While Paul may have been placed under arrest, this imprisonment further reinforced his social identity as an apostle, the bearer of the good news. He could take comfort that instead of silencing him, his imprisonment and sufferings served to advance the gospel, and freed others from being fearful of proclaiming the gospel. In the final analysis, the effects of his imprisonment were quite the opposite of what was expected. (135)

Truly, Christians suffer vicariously to bless others; far more, to reward others through their sufferings.

Contextual Implications in Christian Suffering

The Nagas from Nagaland in the North East of India heard the gospel in the latter part of the nineteenth century.[8] Back in those days, when our forefathers were animists, they resisted the gospel. The few who gradually accepted Jesus were quickly driven from the village; they could no longer remain in the village because many feared they would anger the spirits that the villagers worshipped. V. Leno Peseyie-Maase observes the harsh treatment meted out to one Angami Christian convert from animism (Angami is a Naga tribe):

> Whenever the animists observed the *genna* days, he was forced to observe them too. If he refused to observe, he was threatened to have to live outside of the village. He was treated like an outcaste. [sic][9]

The village was the hub of life in those days; they still are, even today. There was a strong sense of community, security, and camaraderie; to be banished from such environs was very costly. Nonetheless, the new converts in Nagaland were willing to suffer ostracism, the loss of family property, and to endure loneliness and extreme hunger—in order to suffer for the sake of knowing Jesus Christ. Frederick S. Downs recounts another convert's experience:

---

8. I belong to the Angami Naga tribe among whom the American Baptists brought the gospel in the latter part of the nineteenth century.

9. Peseyie-Maase, *From Headhunter to Soul Winner*, 63.

> A young man of a village about 20 miles from Impur was converted in 1904 and began to preach to his neighbours. The warriors became so angry with him that they took their spears and chased him from the village like a wild animal. . . . Despite this hostile reaction the young man returned again and again to preach. He was badly treated at first but he eventually won the respect of the village—and a few converts. By 1913 there was a church of 351 members in this village and it had distinguished itself in giving and evangelistic activity.[10]

Likewise, there are myriad cases in the Indian sub-continent, where, from among the majority Hindu, Muslim, or Buddhist communities, many decide to become followers of Jesus Christ. Such people are persecuted and driven from their homes. Many suffer silently. But they cannot be cowed into silence; instead, they grow bolder and become martyrs for the faith and the kingdom. Such is the resilient nature of the converts and their die-hard attitudes, and the extraordinary transformation of their lives, that soon, others will join their band. Gradually, but slowly, many others accept the gospel of Jesus.[11]

Christian Suffering Makes Sense

All over the world, many people, Christians and non-Christians alike, have heard how Graham Staines and his two young sons (Philip and Timothy) were burnt to death in a most gruesome way on January 23, 1999 in Manoharpur, Orissa, India.[12] This was a heinous crime against humanity. A dedicated Australian doctor treating ostracized lepers was murdered along with his young sons.

The most touching dimension of this tragedy was that Gladys, Graham Staines' wife, and her daughter Esther declared that they had forgiven the perpetrators of the inhuman crime. In the words of Gladys: "I truly pray, Father forgive them, for they know not what they are doing."[13] Esther, their daughter declared: "I'm thankful that God allowed them

---

10. Downs, *Mighty Works of God*, 119.

11. This is what has happened in Nagaland. Despite much suffering, converts from the animistic faith have stood firm. Today, the majority of the Nagas have embraced the gospel of Jesus Christ.

12. Barik, *Persecution and Hope*, 115.

13. The Voice of the Martyrs, *Hearts of Fire*, 253.

to suffer for his sake."[14] There was no bitterness, revenge, or retaliation under unimaginable suffering. Instead, the undergirding strength stems from the fact that Christ suffered under similar circumstances. Such is the sense of participation in Christ's suffering that overshadows the obvious pain experienced in being battered without good reason. Sean Winter rightly sums it up: "Suffering is a form of missional solidarity." (77) The sacrifice of the Staines family also highlights another concept of Christian suffering. Paul asserts that his suffering brings comfort to others through the comfort that he receives from Christ (2 Cor 1:3–7). Such is the endearing, beckoning hope that is further enriched through suffering. Paul suffers at the merciless hands of senseless people who barrage him with untold, inexplicable evil and violence. And yet, Paul is sure that his suffering leads to the betterment of others.

Likewise, Gladys Staines' heart-warming declaration of forgiveness for her husband and sons' murderers has comforted and drawn many to be more merciful and gracious. This is hard to comprehend from a human perspective, but it is exactly what Paul similarly postulates concerning his own suffering. Speaking on the essence of Christian forgiveness graciously shown by Gladys Staines, Vijay Martis, and M. B. Desai observe:

> The massacre of Graham Staines and his two little sons in Manoharpur has justly pricked the conscience of the nation. Very few events in recent history have evoked such strong, spontaneous and universal indignation as this inhuman deed has. The reason for this lies in the way Mrs. Staines and her daughter have coped with this unspeakable tragedy. It is important that this inspiring aspect of what is otherwise a gloomy event should not be lost on us.[15]

Such is the catalytic impact that believers bequeath to those who belittle and afflict them unjustly for their faith in Christ. In the end, those who suffer for Christ are emboldened with greater hope. At the same time, God turns evil into good: the inhuman murder of the Staines family galvanized a whole nation to examine the essence of the Christian faith, which beckons its adherents to endure suffering because they are following in the footsteps of their master:

---

14. The Voice of the Martyrs, *Hearts of Fire*, 253.
15. Martis and Desai, *Burnt Alive*, 107.

So it is not surprising that people all over the country, cutting across barriers, recognized this as the finest moment of true spirituality. To the Staines family, this spirituality was exemplified in the life and crucifixion of Jesus Christ.[16]

In the final analysis, Christian suffering makes very good sense; in no way does it befuddle the Christian.

Conclusion

It is difficult to explain general human suffering. Even within the ambit of Christian experience, suffering remains baffling and humanly very difficult to embrace. Yet Christians suffer willingly, knowing that the prior example has been set by God himself in the person of Jesus Christ, who suffered willingly and vicariously for us. In him, through him, and for him, we are motivated to suffer likewise. This amazing idea is the banner that Christians all over the world take up as they suffer for God and the work of Christ's kingdom on earth. It is a suffering worth embracing. To suffer for Christ is to know the utmost satisfaction, comfort, joy, and future glory that anyone could wish for.

Bibliography

Barik, Bindulata. *Persecution and Hope: Exploring Suffering in the Book of Revelation*. Bangalore: SAIACS, 2015.

Downs, Frederick S. *The Mighty Works of God—A Brief History of the Council of Baptist Churches in North East India: The Mission Period 1836–1950*. Panbazar, Gauhati: Christian Literature Centre, 1971.

Iralu, Sanyu. "The Theme of Christian Suffering in the Writings of Peter and Paul: Compared and Contrasted." ThM Thesis, Regent College, Vancouver, 2000.

Martis, Vijay, and M. B. Desai. *Burnt Alive*. Mumbai, India: GLS, 1999.

O'Brien, Peter T. *The Epistle to the Philippians: A Commentary on the Greek Text*. Grand Rapids: Eerdmans, 1991.

Peseyie-Maase, V. Leno. *From Headhunter to Soul Winner*. Covina, CA: Kandid Litho, 2005.

The Voice of the Martyrs. *Hearts of Fire: Eight Women in the Underground Church and Their Stories of Costly Faith*. Nashville: Thomas Nelson, 2003.

---

16. Martis and Desai, *Burnt Alive*, 109.

11

Hopeful and Unsettled

Reckoning with Suffering

Timothy G. Gombis

I am grateful for the opportunity to engage with these essays on suffering in Paul. I must confess that I read the essays with a mixture of hope and discomfort. I found myself feeling hopeful as I read them for I have found that the pervasive theme of suffering in Paul has helped me make sense of the world. I was raised in a wonderful Christian environment that had a kind of hopefulness about it, but found that this was mainly characterized by a shallow sentimentality that was fed by an American triumphalist version of Christianity. Over the years of coming to grips with the world as it is and not as we wanted it to be, I was forced to read Scripture more carefully. I discovered that the sort of romantic sentimentality that I was raised with was not found in Scripture, but that Paul's letters were actually animated by a recognition that this world was not the world that God created it to be. I discovered through my studies that Paul, and the rest of the biblical writers, had a very clear conception of the Christian life as one of suffering in solidarity with Christ and the suffering church. This vision of suffering made sense of my experience of enduring painful loss and also explained the condition of the world. For this reason, I resonated with these essays and found myself once again fired with hope that suffering drives perseverance, leads to exaltation with Christ (or, is itself co-exaltation) in the end, and is the normal pattern of Christian existence in a not-yet-redeemed world.

At the same time, I found myself growing increasingly uncomfortable. I occupy a highly privileged position as a professional biblical scholar in a comfortable cultural location in North America. I have received tenure in a secure and well-established institution in the heart of "Christian" America (Grand Rapids, Michigan) and in the last year achieved the status of full professor. I am part of a church that is located in one of the wealthiest parts of a prosperous city that is experiencing robust economic growth that is displacing the poor and ruining already marginalized communities. To once again face up to the characterization of Christian identity as participation in a suffering community is to confront the reality that there is a great distance between being Christian as Paul conceived it and my life as a confessing Christian. I take some comfort in our church's active engagement in a program that relieves the suffering of homeless families by helping them find sustainable housing, but I cannot be involved in exposing the idolatries that pervade my culture without recognizing that I am a product of that culture and still participating in it. So, while I am grateful to the editor for the invitation to respond to these essays, I must register my twin reactions of hope and discomfort.

Xiaxia Xue's excellent essay on Paul's vicarious intercession and prophetic identity was perhaps for me most unsettling. I found it an excellent exposition of Paul's inhabitation of a prophetic posture toward his people and especially his identity as a sufferer on behalf of his kinsmen according to the flesh. Indeed, in many of Paul's autobiographical passages, Paul constructs his identity as the sort of life that his audience should imitate in some way. While Xue did not draw out this implication, I found myself wondering how my vocation as a biblical scholar should be inhabited in light of Paul's example. I am not certain that I need to be an evangelist, necessarily, to my culture in the same way that Paul hoped in the salvation of his people. But perhaps biblical scholars in comfortable environments ought to consider how they might play the role of biblical prophet in identifying idolatries that have infected the church cultures they inhabit and bring to bear a vision of God's justice that ought to shape the imaginations of their churches. At the very least, Pauline scholars cannot imagine the object of their study as a comfortable theologian working away in an office far removed from conditions of suffering. Engaging with Xue renewed my concern to set before my students and to represent in my work—in addition to my life—a vision of the apostle who was concerned that his churches become increasingly just communities that seek out opportunities of solidarity with the suffering and marginalized.

Haley Goranson Jacob's persuasive essay did little to relieve my sense of unease. She argued that in the well-known passage regarding Christ's humiliation and exaltation in Philippians 2:5-11, exaltation did not follow humiliation, but that the humiliation was itself exaltation. Her argument resonated with Paul's ambition in the beginning of the letter that Christ would be exalted in his body, whether in life or in death (Phil. 1:20). It seems that Paul viewed his own body as a script for Christ's exaltation and that his suffering was itself a depiction of Christ in his exaltation, with the implication that the Philippians, as they faced their own situation of persecution, as Jacob notes, might see Christ exalted even in the midst of their suffering. It is not that they ought to endure suffering, knowing that exaltation was on its way, but that their very experience of suffering was itself an advertisement of co-exaltation.

Jacob reveals the same unease I have expressed over Christians in comfortable situations claiming a Christian identity and seeing various minor stresses in their lives as instances of suffering. While these should not be dismissed, Christians in situations of relative ease should give careful consideration to the sorts of extreme suffering faced by their sisters and brothers in other parts of the world, if not other parts of our cities. Greater awareness of the suffering in our world should shape our praying and also our efforts. The configuration of Christian identity as co-suffering might also determine strategies of helping. While those who have means often think first of giving money to send others to help, Christian identity as sharing in the sufferings of others might shape our imaginations so that we consider ways to be involved ourselves to bring relief. This would, in turn, affect the ways we pray and also further work to shape our conception of Christian action in the world.

Kar Yong Lim's political reading of Philippians resonated strongly with my own work in Paul whereby he constructs the church as an alternative *polis*, distinct from any other political entity on earth. God's people are a "holy people," new, distinct and different from any nation or political interest group. Lim argues, using social identity theory, that Paul constructed the Philippians' identity over against the imperial Roman order. In Phil 1:27 he uses the unique exhortation πολιτεύεσθε rather than the usual περιπατεῖτε to exhort the Philippians to conduct themselves as citizens of a heavenly political order. Such a configuration of the church as the embodiment of an alternative political entity would be salutary in any situation, not least in my own North American context in which Christian identity is often wrapped up with identity as "American." This idolatrous confusion of identities has caused no end of trouble and I do not envision any easy resolution to this situation as its root lies deep in our national past.

I enjoyed Roy Ciampa's chapter on Romans, not least because of his self-conscious recognition of hermeneutical factors that have focused the history of interpretation on that letter away from a context of suffering. The "history of American and Western European scholarship" (14) is mostly carried out by people who operate in privileged and elite social situations, removed from suffering and pain. I would add that this interpretive tradition is largely concerned with individual guilt and the status of individuals before God, which determines many of the questions interpreters ask and therefore shapes how Paul's theological vision is delivered to churches. Indeed I would agree with Ciampa's hint that traditional hermeneutical lenses tend to filter out issues of real-world suffering in favor of an abstract theological vision.

Ciampa notes that many of the texts Paul cites from Israel's Scripture come from passages of complaint to God on the part of those who are suffering. In discussing Paul's paradigmatic citation of Hab 2:4, he makes the following comment:

> While, arguably, Paul uses this text primarily to introduce and underwrite his understanding of the relationship between faith and righteousness (the meaning of each of these terms being disputable), it seems relevant to remind ourselves that Hab 2:4 fits within a larger context that is not concerned with the question of how God can find it possible to forgive and be reconciled with sinful people, but with the question of what God will do to intervene when violence and injustice are thriving even among the people of God. (8)

Further, the prophet cries out against "violence, wrongdoing, trouble and destruction," which "remind us that Habakkuk's concern was not focused on the problem of guilt as it was on the problem of suffering perpetrated on some people by others." (8–9)

This is instructive, as it indicates that perhaps the received wisdom of the Western Protestant interpretive tradition does not account fully for the shape of Paul's argument. He goes on to note that the catena of scriptural texts in Rom 3:10–18, which are largely regarded as being marshaled by Paul to make his case for universal sinfulness, are taken from biblical passages that complain about unjust treatment at the hands of others. Ciampa notes that this raises the question as to whether Paul had no concern for their original contexts and whether he simply co-opted them in service of his project of establishing universal sinfulness.

I found Ciampa's discussion, and his drawing upon the work of Ochsenmeier, highly suggestive and wondered if perhaps it might be brought into fruitful conversation with a recent proposal about the situation among the Roman Christians. A number of scholars have questioned the traditional reconstruction of the Roman audience as being composed of Jewish and non-Jewish Christians.[1] Building on the work of Runar Thorsteinsson, they have argued that the audience was composed entirely of gentiles, some of whom have become convinced that in order to enjoy the salvation of the God of Israel in Jesus Christ, they are compelled to convert to Judaism, taking on Jewish practices.[2] Others among the Roman Christians are not so convinced, and this has led to a situation of community conflict. Paul addresses this situation of conflict with a range of arguments, aimed at bringing about a unified community and establishing them as a church (a term he does not use in the letter).

Whether or not this argument carries the day with regard to the specific contours of the audience of the letter, the historical occasion remains one of community conflict, which provides an excellent situation in which Paul's citations make good sense. The group that is looking to the Scriptures of Israel in order to endorse their claim of superiority over the other is actually mistreating them. They are acting unjustly and are in fact the cause of the community breakdown. They regard themselves as acting with faithfulness toward Scripture, looking to it to endorse their claims of moral superiority. Because of their constructed identity, they imagine that they have separated themselves from the long history of gentile sinfulness (1:18–32), while the other group remains mired in ungodliness, tainted by human idolatry and rebellion against God. Paul argues in 2:1—3:20 that no one has an inside track with God and therefore no one stands outside of human sinfulness and rebellion. They are all united under condemnation, but they are all united in their status as justified before God.

---

1. See the essays in Rodriguez and Thiessen, *So-Called Jew*.
2. Thorsteinsson, *Paul's Interlocutor in Romans 2*.

This is all to say that, whether the audience is one of mixed ethnicity or not, Paul marshals the texts from Israel's Scriptures in the catena (3:10–18) to inveigh against the group boasting in its identity as morally superior (cf. 3:27). Not only does this body of Scripture establish that all those who boast in a Jewish identity are sinners like the gentiles, but, taking up Ciampa's insights, they are also a people who are provoking complaints to God about being treated unjustly and suffering abuse. Such a reconfiguration of the nature of Paul's quotations, along with a clarifying of hermeneutical vision regarding Paul's argument in Romans, might offer a renewed word of rebuke to a contemporary church that is divided along ethnic, racial, and national lines, if not others. To the extent that the Western church has been consumed with questions arising from a theological vision of the individual standing before God, it has certainly disregarded what Romans might have to say regarding a whole host of ethical issues about the ways Christians treat one another, and others.

I found David Starling's chapter on the "weapons of righteousness" especially instructive for a context very much like my own, one in which Christians feel besieged on all sides by a culture that feels that it is spinning out of control. In such a situation, Christians face the constant temptation to, as Starling indicates, make common cause with political movements that offer stability. Rhetoric in Paul's letters having to do with weaponry and spiritual warfare seem to offer an endorsement of the adoption of postures of political conflict and agitation. But this only results in constructing suspicious "others" whom we fear and vilify, behaving in ways that situate us squarely within a worldly political position on a map configured by the present evil age.

"Weapons of righteousness" refers to Christians engaging in postures of humility and an embrace of suffering and hardship. Christians become such "weapons" only when they surrender the fight for culture and submit themselves as slaves to righteousness—full participants in the ongoing transformation of the Christian community by the power of God. Starling's chapter struck a strong chord as I read it within a politicized culture that has co-opted the church as the participant in a worldly battle. Much of the evangelical church in North America has succumbed to triumphalism, which is simply idolatry and a departure from the one true gospel for another gospel that is no gospel at all. For the cause of the gospel is not the advancement of a triumphalist "Christian culture," but the transformation of Christian communities into the image of Christ, the one who suffered for the life of the world.

I must close this response as I opened it. I read a few of these essays on a plane ride to take my son to university on which I also read an essay about the pitifully poor state of the first Christians and their lives of suffering. In a context of immense privilege in which I can take my child to a university several thousand miles away that costs large sums, it was jarring to consider my life and the life of the community inaugurated by a suffering Messiah and explicated by a suffering apostle. I am grateful for the clarifying experience.

Bibliography

Rodriguez Rafael, and Matthew Thiessen, eds. *The So-Called Jew in Paul's Letter to the Romans*. Minneapolis: Fortress, 2016.

Thorsteinsson, Runar M. *Paul's Interlocutor in Romans 2: Function and Identity in the Context of Ancient Epistolography*. Stockholm: Almqvist & Wiksell, 2003.

12

Power in Weakness
Conclusion and Reflection

Siu Fung Wu

Introduction

I WOULD LIKE TO express my sincere gratitude to the authors of this book for their contributions. I greatly enjoyed reading their essays. In this chapter I will highlight some key findings in the essays that I find particularly useful, which will set the stage for my reflection on suffering in Paul as an Asian-Australian.[1]

Since different migrants have different perspectives, depending on their experiences, social locations, and countries of origin, I will write briefly about my own cultural and social background.[2] I lived in a low socioeconomic area in East Asia from the 1960s to the 1980s, where Christianity was a minority religion. Most of us worked very long hours in order to make ends meet. Christians in my part of the world were very much aware of the cost of following Jesus. They did not worship traditional gods and they believed that Christ was their Lord.[3] Rejection by

---

1. I am very grateful to Dr. David Fenn, Dr. Armen Gakavian, and Professor Timothy Gombis for their helpful comments on the early versions of this essay.

2. I am aware that even those with very similar backgrounds have different perspectives of life. But nonetheless I should inform readers of what may have potentially influenced my view of suffering.

3. They did not, however, totally abandon their cultural practices and traditional

family and friends was not uncommon because of their commitment to follow Christ. I remember that most Sunday sermons referred to suffering and what it meant to follow Jesus wholeheartedly. This is not surprising, given our social location and religious background. We knew very well that suffering was part and parcel of our faith in Christ.

I migrated to Australia nearly thirty years ago. I have since found that life is dramatically different here. Australia is an affluent country and Christianity is not a minority religion.[4] Suffering and cross-bearing are not favorite topics among Christians. Of course, the church does recognize that these are important. After all, no one is exempt from suffering, and commitment to Christ is a biblical concept. But I think it is fair to say that these topics are mentioned less frequently than in the church in my country of origin. Obviously, even in Australia there are people living on the margins of society. In my own church, there are low-income earners, people living with a long-term mental illness, and refugees who have fled from persecution in their home countries. For them, life is no bed of roses.

Suffering, Community, and Participation in Christ

I now turn to the essays of this book. I am, in broad terms, in agreement with the authors, and for the sake of space I will avoid discussion of minor differences here.[5] In the following I will list some key findings in the essays that I find particularly relevant to me, both as a scholar and as someone from the social-cultural background mentioned above. After that, I will discuss the implications of the findings for Christians in the world today.

Kar Yong Lim skillfully explores how suffering may be understood in light of the social realities faced by the Philippians as a minority group in the Roman Empire. Lim argues that the Philippians, as citizens of heaven whose allegiance is ultimately to Christ and not to Caesar, have a strong sense of identity. This identity is reinforced by their confession of the lordship of Christ. In my view, reading Paul against the backdrop

---

values. In fact, they kept many of them.

4. Although Christianity is declining in Australia, the 2016 census showed that 52 percent of the population were Christian. See Australian Bureau of Statistics, "2016 Census Data."

5. As such, this chapter functions as a reflection on and conclusion to the book.

of the Empire enhances our understanding of his view of suffering. This is vital when interpreting Philippians, as Lim demonstrates. But it is also important for interpreting Paul's other letters.[6] The apostle lived and ministered in the Roman Empire, and he was imprisoned in Roman jails. All his audiences were residents of the Empire. For Paul, Christ was the cosmic Lord of all, and the believing community's confession of the lordship of Christ set them on a collision course with the Roman authorities and the prevailing value system that existed under Caesar's rule and the imperial cult.

Lim also notes that Paul encourages the Philippians to stand in solidarity with those who suffer for Christ. Likewise, in his lucid analysis of 2 Cor 1:3–11, Sean Winter says that "the Corinthians are 'partners' in Paul's apostolic suffering and consolation. Partnership with Paul is the main focus of their solidarity with him in the sufferings and consolation that apostle and congregation experience together in and through Christ" (76). In addition, in his meticulous study of the terms θλῖψις and στενοχωρία, Sunny Chen concludes that these words emphasize corporate solidarity and communal relationship. For Paul, mutual support and commitment to one another within a suffering community are crucial.

But Paul's view of suffering has to be understood in terms of the death and resurrection of Christ. As Winter perceptively points out, "Paul wants to place past, present, and future hardship into a theological framework that directs his readers back to the centrality of the Christ-event and forward to the hope of eschatological consummation" (78). And, as noted in my chapter, participation in Christ's suffering and glorification is an integral and essential part of Christian existence. The fact that suffering and glory take place at the same time is paradoxical. As Haley Goranson Jacob remarks in her insightful essay, "Christians are called . . . to lead lives worthy of the gospel of Christ—lives characterized by glorious suffering, paradoxical though it is" (120). Associated with the notion of glory is triumph. Just as suffering and glory are interconnected, so are suffering and triumph. As David Starling argues in his judicious study, suffering is inseparable from the triumph and transformation that God has accomplished through Paul's ministry and his "crucicentric message" (60). For Starling, the use of the "weapons" in 2 Cor 6:7 cannot be disconnected from "the vulnerability and integrity" of believers (62)

---

6. By this I do not mean that we have to read Paul's letters as political anti-imperial documents (cf. Rom 13:1–7), but that the context of the empire is one important matter we should always bear in mind.

One cannot fully grasp Paul's theology without studying Romans. I am, therefore, particularly encouraged by the fact that two authors write about suffering in Romans.[7] In his intriguing and perceptive study of the intertexts in Romans 1–8, Roy Ciampa argues, among other things, that the complaints of Habakkuk (linked to Paul's letter via Rom 1:16–17) and of the original speakers of the catena (in Rom 3:10–18) are not addressed until Romans 5–8. For Ciampa, it is in Rom 5:1–9 and 8:19–39 that "Paul explains both why people cause suffering in the world and what God has done, is doing, and will do to bring about the end of such suffering and the universal establishment of righteousness throughout creation. According to Paul, through Adam's sin he unleashed a reign of sin and death upon the world, one that God is undoing through Christ (Rom 5:12–14, 17, 21; 6:9, 12)" (19). Here, Ciampa rightly brings into view God's purpose for the entire creation.

To this I would add:

> [The] υἱοί of God are to suffer with the υἱός of God. Just as God's Son suffered and died for humanity, his children suffer with the Son. And just as the Son was glorified at his resurrection and exaltation, God's children will also be glorified with the Son at the renewal of the entire creation. Indeed . . . the glorification of the children of God has a present dimension, for their suffering is a visible display of Christ's glory. (98)

Also,

> [The believing community's] *vocation of suffering with Christ is an integral part of conformity to the Son's image, and hence of displaying God's glory as his image-bearers.* (100)[8]

How does this image-bearing and display of God's glory take place? I have argued in my chapter that conformity to Christ's image takes place in the transformed communal life of believers, which Paul speaks of in Romans 12. But Xiaxia Xue's essay provides further food for thought.

Xue's analysis of Paul's use of Scripture in several key passages in Romans 9–11 (Rom 9:1–5; 9:30—10:21; 11:1–36) is an exegetical feast.

---

7. Since my book, *Suffering in Romans*, focuses on Rom 5–8, I am grateful that Xiaxia Xue's study is on Rom 9–11, and that Roy Ciampa examines, among other matters, the use of Hab 2:4 in Rom 1:16–17, the scriptural catena in Rom 3:10–18, as well as Abraham and Sarah in Rom 4:16–21.

8. Emphasis in original. The statement is largely based on, among other things, Rom 8:17, 29.

Xue argues that Paul sees himself as a prophet of the new aeon of Christ, and mirrors himself to Moses, Elijah, and Isaiah. All of these prophets "share the effects and characteristics of the ministry in the Mosaic tradition. They all long for the salvation of Israel and experienced oppression or persecution because of Israel's disobedience. Like Moses, Paul would suffer and sacrifice himself for the sake of his kindred" (46). Given the fact that Romans 9–11 immediately follows Paul's extended discussion of suffering in 8:17–39, I suggest that we may consider Paul's identification with the suffering prophets and Moses to be an example of how one may, through suffering and the Spirit's empowerment, participate in Christ and reflect God's glory.

Power in Weakness

With the above findings in mind, I will offer my reflection on suffering in Paul based on my own experience—as a migrant who has seen suffering in a relatively poor Asian city, as well as the prosperous and more stable life in Australia. Through a scholarship and divine providence, I was able to study at university, a rare privilege among my peers in East Asia. After graduation, I joined a warm and welcoming church of about one hundred members, and it was in this church that I married my wife. The vast majority of the congregation came from relatively low socio-economic backgrounds, and I was one of the few who had the benefit of post-secondary education. People in this church were familiar with suffering. I remember that a young lady shared with us that her mother was sick and required regular dialysis. We knew very well that life was going to be tough for them, not only because of the physical sickness but also the financial hardship they had to endure as a result.

We enjoyed the lively worship in the church. The drummer in the band, if I remember correctly, was a partially vision-impaired man. His disability made it difficult for him to find employment. But he managed to find work as a "garbage remover," which meant that he collected rubbish from house to house and cleaned the streets early in the morning every day. In our shame-based culture, this type of work was despised, and was one of the lowest paying jobs in society. But I doubt that anyone in the church would look down on him, for people tended to treat one another as sister and brother in Christ and they knew what it meant to live at the lower end of the social hierarchy.

I believe that most people in that congregation were unashamed to call Jesus their Lord and Savior. Just as many of the earliest Christians turned from emperor worship to Christ, many of them had turned away from idol worship and traditional religions. They no longer relied on the traditional gods in their suffering, whether it was sickness, poverty, or religious oppression. Their identity was found in Christ. They knew that their lives were to be oriented towards and shaped by his cruciform death and resurrection. Standing in solidarity with one another was vital when they faced trials. The sharing of financial resources was not so much about the rich giving to the poor, but rather the slightly better resourced embodying the self-giving pattern of Christ by providing for the material needs of others. In this way, the members of this church sought to display the glory of God in a love-filled community.[9] In my view, this was how the members of this church might share in Christ's suffering and glory, in anticipation of the future renewal of God's creation. Of course, this church was not perfect. We had many flaws. The fact is, suffering can potentially draw us away from God and from one another. But in our struggles, we learn to rely on God and love each other.

Now that I have lived in the West for nearly three decades, I realize that the ample choices available to me in an affluent country create obstacles that hinder me from living according to Christ's self-sacrificial pattern. There is little to discourage Christians from choosing a self-centered, individualistic life orientation, and embracing the materialistic value system. But these choices mean succumbing to the enslaving power of sin and death. Paul's teaching on solidarity in community, however, urges believers to resist the allure of sin, and choose to share their lives (as individuals and as church communities) with those who suffer from broken relationships, depression, severe physical disability, mental illness, domestic violence, child abuse, racial discrimination, and financial hardship. It invites Christians to resist the temptation to concern themselves only with personal holiness. It urges them to stand in solidarity with those who are persecuted for the sake of Christ. It calls them to stand with the disadvantaged and marginalized, such as Indigenous peoples who are living with the effects of dispossession and colonization, the victims of human trafficking, and those who suffer from the effects of climate change.

---

9. Trebilco is right to say, "Perhaps we tend to think of urban ministry as ministry to the poor in the inner city. When it comes to NT Christians, we should think of ministry *by the poor* to the poor." Trebilco, "Early Christian Communities," 33.

In the 1980s I loved singing a song entitled "Give Thanks with a Grateful Heart," which had a line that said, "let the weak say I am strong." When I came to Australia, I attended a meeting in which the speaker, Dr. Athol Gill, said that we should rather sing, "let the strong say I am weak." At the time, I could not understand what he meant by that. But recently my son explained that it was because most in the West are not weak, economically or socially. Now I realize that worshipping God from a position of weakness differs greatly from worshipping from a place of power and privilege. When the apostle Paul lamented over Israel in Rom 9:1–5, he assumed a position of weakness and identified himself with the Israel that was under Rome's oppressive rule. In worshipping God with songs of praise back in my church in East Asia, I identified with the weaknesses of a community that was familiar with pain and sorrow. For the members of this church, the references in those songs to the power and the glory of God had nothing to do with triumphalism, for they knew very well that suffering and glory were inseparable.

I am humbled by Sanyu Iralu's and Tim Gombis's essays. Iralu speaks of the persecution experienced by South Asian Christians and their resolute commitment to following Christ, and Gombis humbly shares his discomfort as a Christ-follower in North America reading the essays in this volume. Their interactions with the other contributors in this book invite us to evaluate our own lives in light of Paul's teaching. I believe that intentional East-West conversations—that is, conversations with the Majority World, Indigenous Christians, and migrant Christians—may offer a greater appreciation of Paul's thoughts on suffering, and hence a better understanding of God's purpose in the world.[10] Likewise, listening to the voices and experiences of the poor and oppressed Jesus-communities in the non-Western world presents affluent Christians in the West with an opportunity to better understand suffering.[11]

Of course, I do not mean that non-Western Christians are superior to their Western counterparts. Neither are those living in poverty superior to the wealthy. I know many faithful Christians in the West and in the non-Western world. I appreciate my friends in Australia, who dedicate their time, energy, and professional expertise to serve the poor. I am grateful for the biblical scholars around me, who teach their students to

---

10. Graham Hill provides succinct definitions for the terms "Majority World," "Indigenous Christians," and "diaspora/immigrant Christians" in Hill, "GlobalChurch."

11. I do not mean that Christians in the West do not know suffering, but that the experiences of others are invaluable resources.

seek justice for the oppressed. At the same time, I admire the Christians in many parts of the non-Western world, whose resilience, tenacity, and resourcefulness in the midst of poverty and persecution are so inspiring.

Finally, it grieves me to see the widening gap between the rich and the poor in many Asian cities today—a phenomenon also found in ancient cities like Rome.[12] Unfortunately, the disparity between rich and poor is growing everywhere in the world.[13] Often, the urban poor are "hidden" because magnificent commercial high-rise buildings, splendid shopping malls, and entertainment centers give people the illusion that poverty does not exist.[14] Sadly, in many parts of the world the poor often suffer from both poverty and persecution because of their faith in Jesus. Unfortunately, we do not hear their voices enough, even though it is precisely they who can teach us most about suffering. I believe we will learn a lot if we seek their wisdom, for I think they are well positioned to comprehend what Paul says in 2 Cor 12:9–10:

> But he said to me, "My grace is sufficient for you, for power is made perfect in weakness." Therefore, *I will boast all the more gladly of my weaknesses*, in order that the power of Christ may dwell in me. For this reason, I am content with weaknesses, insults, hardships, persecutions, and calamities for the sake of Christ—*for whenever I am weak*, then I am powerful.[15]

Bibliography

Australian Bureau of Statistics. "2016 Census Data Reveals 'No Religion' Is Rising Fast." June 27, 2017. http://www.abs.gov.au/AUSSTATS/abs@.nsf/mediareleasesbyReleaseDate/7E65A144540551D7CA258148000E2B85?OpenDocument.

Christian, Jayakumar. "Rise of the Urban Poor." *William Carey International Development Journal* 3.3 (2014) 34–42.

Goheen, Michael W. *Introducing Mission Today*. Downer Grove, IL: IVP, 2014.

---

12. A recent report showed that 19.9 percent of the population in Hong Kong, an affluent city, lived below the poverty line, and more than one third of them were elderly. Source: Lam, "Poverty in Hong Kong." See Wu, *Suffering in Romans*, 25–30, regarding the economic situation of the poor in ancient Rome.

13. In a wealthy country like Australia, one in 200 people are homeless on any given night. Source: Homelessness Australia, "Homelessness in Australia."

14. The issues and causes of urban poverty are common topics of discussion in recent years. See Goheen, *Introducing Mission Today*, 374–78; Smith, *Seeking a City*, 34–39; Christian, "Rise of the Urban Poor," 34–42.

15. My translation. Emphasis added to highlight the importance of weakness.

Hill, Graham. "GlobalChurch: Learning from Majority World, Indigenous and Diaspora Christians." The Global Church Project, December 29, 2015. https://theglobalchurchproject.com/post-1/.

Homelessness Australia. "Homelessness in Australia." January 2016. https://www.homelessnessaustralia.org.au/sites/homelessnessaus/files/2017-07/Homelessness%20in%20Australiav2.pdf.

Lam, Jeffie. "Poverty in Hong Kong Hits Record High, with 1 in 5 People Considered Poor." *South China Morning Post*, November 17, 2017. https://www.scmp.com/news/hong-kong/community/article/2120366/poverty-hong-kong-hits-7-year-high-one-five-people.

Smith, David W. *Seeking a City with Foundations: Theology for an Urban World*. Nottingham: IVP, 2011.

Trebilco, Paul. "Early Christian Communities in the Greco-Roman City." *Ex Auditu* 29 (2013) 25–48.

Wu, Siu Fung. *Suffering in Romans*. Eugene, OR: Pickwick, 2015.

Author Index

Abasciano, Brian J., 34n31, 34n32, 34n33
Adewuya, J. Ayodeji, 29n1, 30n8, 30n9, 32n18
Aernie, Jeffrey W., 41n64, 42n68
Amador, J. D. H., 167n111
Arzt-Grabner, Peter, and Ruth Elisabeth Kritzer, 58n22
Ascough, Richard S., 141n46
Bakirtzis, Charalambos, and Helmut Koester, 133n17
Barentsen, Jack, 132n15
Barik, Bindulata, 182n5, 182n6, 184n12
Barnett, Paul, 58n20, 167n111
Barrett, C. K., 54n8, 58n21, 161n82, 167n111, 168n117,
Barth, Karl, 111n18, 116, 116n35, 116n36, 116n38, 117, 117n41,
Batka, Lubomir, 144n54
Bauckham, Richard, 117, 117n40,
Beale, Greg K., 72, 72n26, 92n49
Beker, J. Christiaan, 1, 1n3, 15, 19n28, 20n33
Berge, Loïc P. M., 74n33
Betz, Hans Dieter, 167n110
Bieringer, Reimund, 71n22,
Blackwell, Ben C., 91, 91n42, 91n45, 93n53, 102, 102n90
Bloomquist, L. Gregory, 130, 130n10
Bockmuehl, Markus, 88n30, 111n18, 113n21, 114, 114n24, 137, 137n34
Bolton, David, 65n5

Bryan, Christopher, 129n8
Byrne, Brendan, 97n69, 98n75, 99n76, 161n82, 162n83, 164n100, 165n100, 166n106
Byrskog, Samuel, 75n36
Campbell, Constantine R., 82, 82n2, 83, 83n5, 99, 99n78, 99n79
Campbell, Douglas A., 67n11
Campbell, William S., 43n72
Capes, David B., Rodney Reeves, and E. Randolph Richards, 41n61
Cassidy, Richard J., 84n7, 134n22
Chen, Sunny, 3, 3n8, 155n13, 161n82, 168n116, 168n117
Ciampa, Roy E., 3, 19n29, 19n29
Childs, Brevard, 32n17, 39, 39n53, 39n54, 39n55, 39n56, 39n57, 41n65, 42n66,
Christian, Jayakumar, 201n14
Clark, Bruce T., 2n6
Clements, Ronald E., 38n50
Cohick, Lynn H., 88n32, 109n11, 110, 110n14, 113, 113n20, 113n21, 118, 118n45, 120n52
Collins, Raymond F., 95n62
Cousar, Charles B., 138n35
Cranfield, C. E. B., 31, 31n12
Crisler, Channing L., 2n6, 22n39
Crossan, John Dominic, 108n10
Darko, Daniel K., 132n15
Davey, Wesley Thomas, 2n6, 83n4, 83n5, 87n24, 89n34, 97n68, 100n83, 100n86, 102n89

AUTHOR INDEX

Deibler, Ellis W., 161n82
Deissmann, Adolf, 127, 128, 128n3, 128n4, 131
deSilva, David A., 167n111, 168n117
Dodd, C. H., 13n18, 30n10, 196n1
Dooley, Robert A., and Stephen H. Levinsohn, 154n12
Downs, Frederick S., 183, 184n10
Dunn, James D. G., 23, 23n42, 30n10, 32n19, 32n20, 33n25, 34n27, 34n28, 34n30, 35, 25n36, 37, 37n42, 97n68, 97n69, 100n84, 161n82, 164n96, 166n106,
Dunne, John Anthony, 2n6
Eastman, Susan, 86, 86n15, 86n16, 86n17, 86n18, 86n19, 86n20, 102n88
Elliott, Neil, 128n5
Esler, Philip F., 132n15
Evans, C. A., 41n63,
Fee, Gordon D., 1, 1n2, 85n11, 87n25, 87n26, 88n27, 88n28, 88n32, 90n37, 90n38, 90n39, 90n40, 91n44, 92n51, 99, 99n76, 99n78, 99n79, 108n8, 109n11, 110n15, 113n22, 114, 114n26, 114n27, 114n28, 134n20, 136, 136n27, 136n28, 136n29, 138n35, 138n37, 140n41, 142n50, 144n54, 144n55
Fitzgerald, John T., 64n2
Fitzmyer, Joseph, 161n82, 164, 164n99, 166n106
Flemming, Dean, 87n26, 88n27, 88n32, 88n33, 108n9, 114n25, 115n31, 121, 121n53
Flett, John G., 79, 79n45
Fowl, Stephen E., 84n7, 136n27, 137n31, 138n38, 139n40, 140n41, 143n53,
Fredrickson, David E. 15n20, 18, 18n26, 18n27, 19n28
Free, Marian, 2n6, 103n91
Friesen, Ivan, 39n53, 39n57

Fung, Ronald Y. K., 97n68
Furnish, Victor Paul, 68n12, 75n36, 78n44, 167n110
Getty, Mary Ann, 44n75
Gieniusz, Andrzej, 16n20, 17, 17n24, 21n36, 98n75
Gignilliat, Mark S., 55, 55n11, 55n12, 65, 65n7, 72n26
Goheen, Michael W., 201n14
Goldingay, John, 99n82, 115n33, 117, 117n42, 117n 43
Gorman, Michael J., 82, 82n1, 82n3, 83, 83n5, 86n14, 87, 87n22, 87n23, 102, 103n91, 115n33, 141n45
Green, William Scott, 12, 12n14
Grice, H. P., 154n6, 154n9
Guthrie, George H., 57n18, 59n26, 78n44, 90n37, 90n39, 90n40, 93n53, 94n54, 94n57, 168n117, 172, 172n124
Hafemann, Scott, 1, 1n1, 29n1, 30n8
Halliday, M. A. K., 154n12
Hansen, G. Walter, 134n18, 135, 135n23, 135n24, 140n41
Harrington, Daniel J., 156n20
Harris, Murray J., 25n47, 56n16, 56n17, 58n19, 58n22, 58n23, 59n26, 60n28, 68n14, 74, 74n34, 77n43, 167n109, 168n117
Hays, Richard B., 9n7, 12, 30n11
Hellerman, Joseph H., 85n11, 87n25, 88n27, 88n28, 88n30, 88n32, 109n13, 111n18, 115n33, 133n17, 139n40, 140, 140n43, 141n44, 142n48
Hill, Graham, 200n10
Hill, Wesley, 87n21
Hodgson, Robert, 164n92
Hofius, Otfried, 70, 71n21
Holloway, Paul A., 70n17
Horrell, David, 140, 140n42
Horsley, Richard, 128, 128n5
Horsley, Richard, and Neil Asher Silberman, 128n5
Huang, Caleb K., 97n68, 99n76

AUTHOR INDEX   205

Hughes, Philip Edgcumbe, 174
Hultgren, Arland J., 161n82,
    165n101
Hunter, James Davison, 52n4
Iralu, Sanyu, 181n4
Jacob, Haley Goranson, 109n12
Jervis, L. Ann, 1, 2n4, 2n5, 20,
    20n32, 20n33, 83n5, 147n64
Jewett, Robert, 18n26, 22, 22n40,
    23n41, 42n69, 42n71,
    99n76, 161n82, 164, 164n91,
    164n92, 165, 165n103,
    165n104, 166n106, 172n126
Käsemann, Ernst, 164n95
Keener, Craig S., 167n111
Keesmaat, Sylvia C., 11n12, 24n43,
    24n45
Kijne, J. J., 168n115
Kilner, John F., 92n50
Kim, Dongsu, 166n107
Kim, Seyoon, 45n79, 129n8
Kincaid, John A., and Michael
    Patrick Barber, 99n77
Kleinknecht, Karl Theodor, 68n13
Koch, Dietrich-Alex, 10n10
Koperski, Veronica, 142n50
Kreitzer, Larry J., 112n19
Kruse, Colin G., 163n86, 163n88,
    163n89, 164n100
Kujanpää, Katja, 9n7
Lam, Jeffie, 201n12
Lamoreaux, Jason T., 133n17
Lee, Michelle V., 158n174
Lemke, Jay L., 165n6, 165n7, 165n8
Levenson, Jon D., 92n49
Lim, Kar Yong, 29n1, 65n3, 66n8,
    66n10, 130n12, 132n15,
    147n65
Long, Fredrick J., 90n40, 91n46,
    94n57
Longenecker, Richard N., 12n15,
    16n21, 20n34, 161n82,
    162n84
Macaskill, Grant, 92n48
Martin, Ralph P., 106n1, 116n38,
    139n40, 167n111, 172n123
Martin, Ralph P., and Brian J. Dodd,
    106n1

Martis, Vijay, and M. B. Desai, 185,
    185n15
Matera, Frank J., 94n55, 95n61,
    168n117
May, Alistair Scott, 132n15
McAuley, David, 136n26
Middleton, J. Richard, 92n49,
    99n80, 99n81
Moo, Douglas J., 20n34, 20n34,
    34n33, 37n46, 43n71,
    44n74, 44n75, 97n68, 97n69,
    161n82, 164n100, 166n106
Moxnes, Halvor, 166n106
Moyise, Steve, 13n18, 14n18
Munck, Johannes, 43, 44n73
Nebreda, Sergio Rosell, 133n17,
    139n40
Nee, Watchman, 47n88,
Neyrey, Jerome H., 134n21
O'Brien, Peter T., 88n27, 111n18,
    114n24, 114n25 116n38,
    119, 119n47, 140n41,
    142n47, 180n2
O'Kane, Martin, 32n17, 46n86
Oakes, Peter, 83n6, 84n8, 108n9,
    133n17, 138, 138n38,
    143n52
Ochsenmeier, Erwin, 8n4, 9n5, 9n6,
    10, 10n11, 12, 13, 16n21, 18,
    18n25, 19, 19n30, 20n31
Oropeza, B. J., 168n117, 170n119,
Pate, C. M., 29n1, 29n2
Peseyie-Maase, V. Leno, 183, 183n9
Pietersma, Albert, and Benjamin G.
    Wright, 71n23
Pobee, John S., 29n1, 30n6
Porter, Stanley E., 127n2
Rabens, Volker, 93n54
Reasoner, Mark, 10n9, 133n17
Ricoeur, Paul, 153n4
Rock, Ian, 128, 128n5
Rodriguez Rafael, and Matthew
    Thiessen, 191n1
Roetzel, Calvin J., 167n110
Sack, Robert, 134n21
Sandnes, Karl Olav, 44n75, 44n78,
    45n79
Saussure, Ferdinand de, 153, 153n5

Schlatter, Adolf, 161n82, 166n106
Schlier, Heinrich, 155n17
Schmeller, Thomas, 64n1
Schreiner, Thomas R., 97n69, 161n82, 166n106
Seeley, David, 30n7
Seifrid, Mark A., 10n11, 51n2, 58n20, 59n24, 59n25, 59n26, 59n27, 172, 172n125
Sergienko, Gennadi A., 144n57
Shen, Paul, 97n68
Shum, Shiu-Lun, 10n11
Silva, Moisés, 108n9, 144n54,
Smit, Peter-Ben, 139n39, 143n53, 201n14
Smith, Barry D., 29n1, 29n2, 29n3, 30n4, 31n14
Smith, David W., 201n14
Standhartinger, Angela, 134n20
Stanley, Christopher D., 10n10, 13n17, 128, 128n7
Starling, David, 2n6, 3, 3n8, 16n20, 21n35, 51, 51n1, 51n2, 53n5, 53n6, 54n9, 55n10, 61n29
Stewart, Tyler, 21n35
Still, Todd D., 16n20, 17n23, 22n38, 25, 26n49
Strack, Herman Leberecht, and Paul Billerbeck, 73n29
Stuhlmacher, Peter, 161n82, 166n106
Tajfel, Henri, 132, 132n14
Tang, Samuel Y. C., 29n1, 38n51, 38n52, 47n87
Tannehill, Robert C., 76, 76n38
Tellbe, Mikael, 142n51
Thielman, Frank, 115n29, 115n31, 116n38
Thompson, James W., and Bruce W. Longenecker, 87n26, 138n35, 142n51, 144n60
Thorsteinsson, Runar M., 191, 191n2
Thrall, Margaret E., 25n47, 56n17, 58n19, 58n21, 66, 66n10, 68n15, 75n37, 77, 77n41, 90n37, 90n38, 90n39, 91n44,
93n52, 93n53, 167n109, 167n110, 168n117, 170n119
Tillar, Elizabeth K., 32n15, 32n16
Trebilco, Paul, 199n9
Tucker, J. Brian, 132n15, 132n16
Turner, John C., 132, 132n15
VanGemeren, Willem A., 42n68, 45, 45n80, 45n81, 45n82, 45n83, 46n84, 46n85
Vanlaningham, Michael G., 32n17, 41n60
Vegge, Ivar, 54n10, 55, 64n1
Verhoef, Eduard, 133n17, 138n38, 168n115
Voice of the Martyrs, 185n14
Wagner, J. Ross, 37, 37n44, 38n49, 42n69, 73n27
Wakefield, Andrew H., 30n10, 31n11
Wallace, James Buchanan, 65n6, 98n70
Wallace, Daniel B., 98n70, 164n94, 164n97, 164n98
Walsh, Brian J., and Sylvia C. Keesmaat, 128n5
Walsh, Jerome T., 41, 41n64, 41n65
Walton, John H., 92n49
Wansink, Craig S., 84n7, 134n22
Watts, Rikk E., 92n49
Webb, William J., 72n26
Welborn, L. L., 65n4
Whybray, R. N., 39n56
Widmer, Michael, 35n35
Wiles, Gordon P., 31n13
Williams, Demetrius, 144n54, 144n56
Windisch, Hans, 69n16
Winn, Adam, 127n2, 183n9
Witherington, Ben, III, 85n13, 88n31, 167n111, 168n117
Wright, N. T., 30n11, 71n23, 123n57, 128, 128n6
Wu, Siu Fung, 2n6, 15n20, 16n22, 17n23, 18n25, 20n34, 21n36, 22n37, 22n38, 24, 24n44, 24n46, 29n1, 30n5, 77n42, 92n49, 96n63, 96n64, 96n65, 96n66, 96n67, 97n68, 97n69,

98n71, 98n72, 98n73,
98n74, 98n75, 99n76, 99n77,
100n85, 100n86, 164n93,
164n100, 165n100, 165n102,
201n12

Xue, Xiaxia E., 32n21, 33n23,
33n25, 33n26, 34n29, 35n37,
36n38, 36n39, 37n41, 37n43,
37n45, 37n47, 38n48, 40n58,
40n59, 41n62, 42n69, 43n72,
44n75, 44n76, 44n77, 45n79

Index of Ancient Sources

OLD TESTAMENT

Genesis

1	109, 123
1–3	96, 98
1:3	91n47
1:26–27	91, 93, 100
3	96
3:16–19	179
15–18	15
15:6	13
21	15
35:3	156n21, 156n23
42:21	156n21, 156n22

Exodus

3:9	156n25
4:22	99
4:23	99
4:31	156n21, 156n23
13:22	38
14:19	38
17:2–4	42n67
17:4	42n67
19:9	32n17, 41
20:18–19	41
22:21	156n25
23:9	156n25
32–24	34
32:10	35
32:11–14	35
32:30–32	32, 33
32:30–33	34
32:32	34, 35
33:3	34
33:5	34
33:22	41
34	41
34:9	34
34:28	41
34:29–35	91
34:34	90

Leviticus

18:5	13
19:33	156n25
25:14	156n25
25:17	156n25

Numbers

20:2–5	42n67

Deuteronomy

4:9–10	41
4:29	156n21, 156n24
5:24–25	41
6:5	163n90
18:15	38
18:18	38
23:16	156n25
28:52	156n26
28:53	156n21, 156n24, 156n26, 157

28:55	156n21, 156n24, 156n26, 157	21:12	156n29
		22:4 LXX	70n19
28:57	156n21, 156n24, 156n26, 157	22:5 LXX	70n19
		23:4	70n19
31:17	156n21, 156n24	23:5	70n19
31–32	32n17	24:17	156n32
31–34	46	24:22	156n32
32:1	38	31:2 LXX	13
		31:7	156n32
1 Samuel		33:7	156n31
7:5–11	37	33:18	156n31
		33:20 LXX	156n31
2 Samuel		36	11
7:10–15	99	36:1	11
		36:10	11
		36:10–12	11
1 Kings		36:39 LXX	156n30
18–19	42n67	38:3	14n19
19:1–2	40	43:25	156n29
19:1–18	32n17, 40	44	22, 23, 24, 24n43
19:3–18	40	44:5	23
19:8	41	44:13	23
19:10	40	44:14	23
19:11	41	44:15–16	23
19:11–13	41	44:17–18	24
19:14	40	44:22	7, 21, 21n35, 22, 23, 24
19:18	40	44:26	24
		49:15	156n28
2 Kings		53:9	156n29
17–21	46	54:4	156n29
17:7–23	32n17	58:17	156n29
21:1–15	32n17	59:13	156n32
		65:11	156n32
		65:14	156n32
Psalms		70:20	156n29
4:2	156n27, 156n29	70:21	70n19
5:1–4	11	71:21 LXX	70n19
5:5–7	11	76:3	70n19, 156n32
8	109, 123	77:2 LXX	70n19
8:5–6	109	77:49	156n32
9:10	156n29	77:49 LXX	158
9:22	156n29, 156n30	78:49	158
10:2	11	80:8	156n28
10:8–9	11	85:7 LXX	70n19, 156n28
14:1	11	85:17 LXX	70
19 LXX	156n20	86:7	70n19
19:2	156n28	86:17	70

Psalms (continued)

88:27–28	99
89	99
89:6–10	99
89:11–12	99
89:13 LXX	70n19
89:14	99
89:20	99
89:26–27	99, 99n82
90:13	70n19
90:15	156n28
93:19 LXX	70n19
94:19	70n19
106 LXX	156, 156n34
106:39 LXX	156n32
107:13	156n29
110	115
110:1	24n45
114:3 LXX	156n28
117:5	156n29
118:6	24n45
118:50 LXX	70n19
118:52 LXX	70
118:143	156n29
119	156
119 LXX	156n34
119:76	70n19
119:82	70n19
125:1 LXX	70n19
134:14 LXX	70n19
135:14	70n19
137:7	156n29
140	11
140:1–2	11
140:4	11
141:3	156n29
142:11 LXX	156n29

Proverbs

14:30	14n19

Ecclesiastes

7:15–17 LXX	11n13
7:20 LXX	11n13

Isaiah

6:11	45, 45n79
8:22	156n35, 157, 157n36, 162n84
9:1	157
10:3	156n35
10:26	156n35
11:13	157n38
19:20	157n37
25 LXX	156n20
26:16	156n35, 157n36
28:10	156n35
28:13	156n35
28:14	157n39
28:20	157
29:7	157n40
29:10	42
30:6	156n35, 157, 157n36, 162n84
30:20	156n35, 157n36
33:2	156n35, 157n36
35:10	33
37:3	156n35
40–55	71, 72, 115n33
40:1–2	71
40:11	71
41:27	72
43:6	72
45	116n34
45:23	115
49:8	55, 72
49:13	72, 72n25, 73n32
49:13 LXX	72
49:19	157
49:26	157n37
51:3	71, 72n25
51:11	33
51:12 LXX	71
51:12–13	72
51:13	157n37
51:19 LXX	71
52:1–12	38
52:1—53:12	38
52:6	117
52:7	38, 117
52:9	72n24, 72n25

52:9 LXX	72
52:10	117
52:11	38, 72
52:11–12	38
52:13	117
52:13—53:12	38
53	39, 117
53:1	38
53:1–12	38
53:2–3	39
53:4–10	39
53:5	39
53:8	39
54:10	55n12
54:11	71, 73
54:11 LXX	72n25
55:10	72
57:13	157n36
57:18	71
59	11
59:3	11
59:7	9
59:9–11	11
63:9	157n35, 157n36
65:1–2	38
65:2	35
65:16	157n35, 157n36
66:3	71

Jeremiah

4:19	33
4:19–21	33
14:17	33
15:17	39
19–22	37
20:7	39
20:10	39
29:7	148
31:31–34	91
31:33	93
42:2–4	37

Ezekiel

36:25–27	91
36:26–27	93

Daniel

9:26	45n79
12:1–2	34
12:3	119n50

Hosea

6:2	73n32

Habakkuk

1:2	9
1:2–3	8
1:3	9
2:4	7, 8, 8n4, 13, 190, 197n7

∾

NEW TESTAMENT

Matthew

22:44	115n32
25:41–43	179

Mark

12:36	115n32

Luke

2:25	73
20:42	115n32

John

3:14	117
8:28	117
12:32–34	117
20:22	90n41

Acts

2:36	115n32
5:1–11	179
7:17–44	32
16:11–40	138
16:15	119n49

Acts (*continued*)

16:16–24	170n119
16:18	90n41
16:33	119n49
19:24–41	170n119
21:27–36	43n71
21:27—22:21	41
22:3	41
23:1	136

Romans

1–3	8n4, 9n6
1–4	7, 14, 15, 20
1–8	7, 30, 31, 197
1:1–7	161n82
1:1–15	31
1:3–4	99
1:4	8
1:8	67
1:8–17	161, 161n82, 162
1:16	8, 9
1:16–17	7, 197, 197n7
1:17	8
1:18–32	191
1:18—3:20	52, 161, 162
1:21–32	163, 163n87
1:32–2:1	163
2:1–29	163, 163n89
2:1—3:20	191
2:6	162
2:8	162
2:9	7n1, 153n3, 160n81, 162, 166
2:10	162
2:16	162
2:17	163
3	9, 17, 19
3–4	31
3:5f	13n18
3:9	13n18, 162
3:9–10	9
3:10–12	12n15
3:10	9, 11n13
3:10–18	7, 9, 12, 13n18, 19, 24, 26, 192, 197, 197n7
3:12	14
3:12–18	13
3:12–17	25
3:13	14
3:13–18	12n15
3:14	14
3:15–16	14
3:16	9
3:17–18	14
3:18	12n15
3:19	10, 13n18, 162
3:21—4:25	52, 161, 162
3:23	13n18
3:24	19, 34
3:27	192
3:31	13n18
4	7, 13, 15, 17, 25
4:10	95n60
4:11	95n60
4:16–21	7, 14, 197n7
4:17	18
4:17–19	15
4:18	17, 17n23
4:19	17
4:19–21	15
4:20	17
4:24	18
4:25	94
5	16, 16n22, 17n23, 165
5–8	7, 15, 16, 19, 20, 24, 26, 95, 96, 98, 161, 162, 163, 197, 197n7
5:1	163
5:1–9	19, 197
5:1–11	29n2
5:2	18
5:3	153n3, 160n81, 163
5:3–5	17
5:5	18, 96
5:9	52
5:9–11	18
5:10–11	96
5:12–14	19, 197
5:12–21	96, 100
5:17	19, 197
5:21	19, 52, 197

6:1	13n18	8:22–23	21
6:1–11	29n2, 97	8:23	18, 96
6:3–11	67n10, 119n49	8:23–27	18
6:4	52, 136n25	8:25	77
6:6	19	8:26	31
6:7	52	8:28–30	100
6:9	19, 197	8:29	88, 95, 96, 100, 101
6:11	34		
6:12	19, 197	8:28–39	21
6:13	13n18, 52, 53, 58	8:29	19, 22, 88n30, 95, 98, 99, 100, 100n86, 163, 197n8
6:22	52		
6:23	34		
7:1	163		
7:4	163		
7:5	7n1	8:29a	99
8	16n22, 17n23, 18, 24n43, 31, 53, 77n42, 165, 181	8:30	98
		8:31	164
		8:31–35	164
		8:31–39	96n64, 97
8:1	34	8:32	21, 94
8:2	19, 34, 97	8:33	164
8:3	96	8:33–34	52
8:4	20, 52, 136n25	8:34	22, 24n45, 31, 90, 164
8:9	90n41		
8:12	163	8:35	7n1, 22, 23, 97, 152, 153n3, 160n81, 164
8:14	90n41, 96		
8:14–17	18		
8:15	96	8:35–39	20, 22, 31
8:15–17	21	8:36	7, 21, 21n35, 22
8:15–39	21	8:37	22, 24
8:16–17	181	8:38–39	34
8:16–18	31	8:39	22, 34
8:17	7n1, 30, 82, 83n4, 95, 96, 97, 98, 99, 100, 197n8	9–11	30, 31, 32, 35, 45, 161, 162, 197, 197n7, 198
8:17–39	21, 29n2, 95, 97, 100, 100n86, 101n87, 198	9–16	25n4
		9:1	33
		9:1–2	33, 33n23
8:18	21, 164	9:1–3	33, 37, 40
8:18–23	96	9:1–5	31, 33, 37, 197
8:18–25	53	9:1–29	32, 33
8:18–30	100	9:2–3	33
8:18–39	19, 26, 9	9:3	31, 34
8:19	18, 21, 47, 77	9:4–5	35
8:19–23	100	9:30	35
8:19–39	197	9:30–31	42, 42n69, 43
8:21	18, 21, 96	9:30–33	36
8:21–25	77	9:30—10:4	31, 36
8:22	21	9:30—10:21	32, 35, 197

Romans (*continued*)

10	37
10:1	31, 32, 36, 39, 40
10:2–3	37
10:2–4	36, 37
10:4	36
10:9	36
10:14–17	39
10:14–21	35, 37
10:15	31, 38
10:16	38
10:18–21	37
10:19–21	37
10:20–21	38
10:21	35, 39
11	42, 44
11:1	39, 41
11:1–2	32, 39, 40
11:1–10	43
11:1–36	32, 39, 197
11:2–4	40
11:3	40
11:3–4	40
11:5–7	42, 43
11:5–10	42
11:7	42, 43
11:8	42
11:11–15	44
11:13	31
11:13–14	31, 44
11:14	40
11:16–24	44
11:23–27	97
11:25	44
11:25–26	31
11:25–32	44
11:25–36	44
12	101, 160n81
12–13	53
12–16	31
12:1—15:13	161, 162
12:2	95, 101
12:9	166
12:12	7n1, 101, 153n3, 166
12:12–14	101n87
12:13	101
12:14	101, 166
12:14–21	53
12:16	101
12:16–17	101n87
12:17	101
12:21	101
13:1–7	197
13:1–9	53
13:8	166
13:8–10	20
13:9	20
13:10	20, 166
13:12	53
13:13	136n25
14:1—15:6	31
14:15	136n25, 166
15:5	68n15
15:7–13	100
15:14–33	161, 162
15:30–31	43
15:31	43
16:1–23	161, 162

1 Corinthians

1:6	67
1:18	1
2:8	122
3:3	136n25
4:11	29n2
7:17	136n25
15:21–28	109
15:35–58	29n2, 89

2 Corinthians

1	74
1–5	60
1–7	60, 66, 75
1–9	167, 167n112, 168, 169
1–13	64
1:2–3	75
1:3	66, 67, 68, 70, 71, 72, 75, 76
1:3–7	66, 68, 74, 75, 77
	95
1:3–11	64, 66n10, 78, 196

INDEX OF ANCIENT SOURCES

1:3–14	60	4	59
1:3—2:13	169	4:1	93
1:4	70, 71, 74n34 75, 76, 77, 153n3, 167n108, 169	4:2	136n25
		4:4	91n47, 92, 93, 95, 100
1:4–5	75	4:4–10	65
1:4–7	74, 75	4:5	55, 93
1:4a	75, 76	4:6	91n47, 93
1:4b	75, 76	4:7	94n55
1:4c	75	4:7—5:10	94n55
1:5	30, 66, 67, 69, 74, 75	4:7–9	94
		4:7–12	67
1:6	68, 70, 74, 75, 169, 76n39, 153n3, 167n108, 172	4:8	64, 153n3, 167n108, 171
		4:8–9	64
1:6–7	71, 76	4:9–18	171
1:7	77, 88, 167n113	4:10	30, 90, 92, 94
1:8	70, 71, 153n3, 170	4:10–12	92, 93
		4:10–14	65n7
1:8–9	68, 167n113	4:11	94
1:8–11	75, 77	4:11–12	90, 93, 94
1:11	76, 78	4:17	64, 153n2, 153n3, 167n108, 171
1:11b	78		
1:12	60, 60n28	5–7	72
1:12–13	75	5:4	153n2
1:14	60	5:11	55n10
1:15—2:13	54, 56	5:12	60
1:15—5:21	54, 56	5:14–21	55
1:18	153n2	5:14—6:10	62
2:4	65, 153n3, 171	5:17	119n49
2:5–7	171	5:18–20	170
2:6–8	89	5:20	148
2:11	89	6	170
2:12–13	75	6–7	55n10
2:13	170	6:1	55n10, 56n14
2:14–5:21	54, 56	6:1–2	56
2:14—7:4	169	6:1–10	29n2
3:1–16	91	6:1–13	172n123
3:1–18	91	6:1—7:16	54
3:6	93	6:2	55, 72
3:8	93	6:3–4	56n14
3:9	53, 53n7, 54n7, 93	6:3–9	60
3:16	90	6:3–10	55n13, 56n15, 59, 61
3:17	90, 92		
3:17–18	90	6:4	55, 64, 152, 153n3, 167n108, 170, 172
3:18	90, 91, 91n43, 91n46, 92, 93, 93n54, 101		
		6:4–7b	59

1 Corinthians (*continued*)

6:4b–5	56n17, 58
6:4b–7a	56, 57
6:4–10	64, 65, 65n7, 183
6:5	153n2
6:6–7	56n13
6:6–7a	57, 58
6:7	61
6:7b	57, 59
6:7b–8a	57, 59
6:4b–10	56
6:6–7	56
6:8–9	65
6:8a	59
6:8b–10	56, 57, 59
6:9	65n7
6:10	65n7
6:11	172
6:11–12	170
6:11–13	56
6:12	153n3, 167n108
6:14	60n29
6:14—7:1	60
6:16–18	72
7:2	168n117
7:3	168n117
7:4	69, 76, 153n3, 167n108, 170
7:4–5	65, 170
7:5	138, 138n36, 153n3, 167n108, 168n117, 170
7:5–6	75
7:5–16	169
7:7	69
7:13	69
8–10	56
8:1–2	138, 171
8:1—9:15	169
8:2	153n3, 167n108, 171
8:9	65n7
8:13	153n3, 166n105, 167n108, 171
8:23	77n40
8:24	60
9	167
9:2–4	60
9:10	72
10:2	136n25
10:4	62
10:4–5	61
10–13	59, 66, 167, 167n113
10:15	153n2
11:2–3	60
11:15	53
11:23	78, 153n2
11:23–27	23, 64, 65
11:23–29	29, 29n2, 152
11:24–26	64
11:25	25n47
11:25–26	64
11:26	64, 152
11:27	153n2
11:28	64
11:30–33	66
11:31	66, 68n14
12–15	166n107
12:1–10	59n26
12:3–16	166n106
12:7	65, 153n2
12:9	66
12:9–10	201
12:10	64, 66, 152, 153n3, 167, 167n108, 171
12:19–21	54
12:20–21	60
13:4–10	60
13:9–10	60
13:10	60

Galatians

2:20	94, 102n88
3	13
3:26–29	29n2
4:8—6:10	131n13
4:19	102n88
4:26	29n2
5:16	136n25
6:12–18	29n2
6:15	119n49

INDEX OF ANCIENT SOURCES 217

Ephesians

1:15–23	29n2
1:17	68n14
2:2	136n25
2:10	136n25
3:13	29n2
4:1	136n25
4:1—6:9	131n13
4:17	136n25
5:2	136n25
5:8	136n25
5:15	136n25

Philippians

1:1	113
1:5	107
1:6	67, 121
1:7	83, 108n6
1:12–13	84
1:12–14	108n6, 135, 183, 185
1:12–18	129, 130, 131, 133
1:12–30	83
1:13	83, 133, 134, 179
1:14	83, 134
1:15–17	108n7
1:15–18	135
1:15–18a	83, 84
1:17	83, 134
1:18–19	84
1:19–21	108n6
1:20	84, 85, 189
1:20b–21	84
1:21	84
1:22–26	84
1:23–26	84
1:24–30	84
1:26	113
1:27	85, 109, 110, 112, 119n48, 136, 137, 189
1:27–28	108, 108n8
1:27–30	29, 29n2, 107, 112, 113, 129, 131, 131n13, 136, 144
1:28	85, 110, 110n5, 121
1:28–29	121
1:28–30	110
1:29	84, 85
1:29–30	108, 137
1:30	84, 85
2:1	113
2:1–4	141
2:1–5	87
2:2	112, 119n48
2:2–4	146
2:3	111
2:3–4	111, 112
2:4	111, 112
2:5	111, 112, 113, 119, 119n48, 141, 146
2:5–11	29n2, 85, 106n1, 131, 139, 189
2:6	85n14
2:6–7	88
2:6–8	106, 110, 111, 116, 121
2:6–11	88, 111, 117, 119, 120, 121, 129, 130, 143, 147
2:7	93
2:7–8	86
2:7a	85
2:7b	86
2:8	110
2:9	114, 115, 139
2:9–11	87, 110, 112n19, 116, 119, 121, 147
2:10	115
2:11	87, 93, 116n34
2:12–15	113
2:15	119n50
2:17	107, 113
2:19–30	129
2:21	108n8
3:2–3	108n8, 108n9, 110, 137, 142, 144
3:3	113
3:4–6	142
3:4–6b	180
3:7	180
3:7–8a	141

Philippians (*continued*)

3:7–11	141
3:8	87, 118, 180
3:8b–11	142
3:8–16	118
3:9	118, 180
3:9–10	113, 117
3:10	30, 67n10, 88n33, 98, 118, 127, 129, 139, 143, 145, 147, 149, 180
3:10a	89n35
3:10b	142
3:10–11	87, 121
3:10–18	131
3:10–21	29n2
3:12	119
3:12–13	118
3:14	113, 118
3:15	119n48
3:15–21	131n13
3:16	119, 119n48
3:17	144
3:17–18	136n25
3:17–20	136
3:18	144
3:18–19	108n8, 110, 110n5, 121, 137
3:18–20	130, 143
3:18–21	109, 110, 118, 120, 121, 147
3:19	109n13, 110, 119n48, 120, 144
3:20	110, 112, 119, 120, 136, 143, 145, 146, 181
3:20–21	110, 117, 121, 123n57, 131, 143, 144
3:21	87, 88n30, 89, 89n35, 98, 109n13, 110, 120, 121, 143
4:4	129
4:4–7	108n7
4:7	113
4:10–13	48
4:10–14	129
4:14	138
4:21	113
4:22	134, 135

Colossians

1:10	136n25
1:15–29	29n2
2:6	136n25
3:1—4:6	131n13
3:1–11	29n2
3:5	100
4:5	136n25

1 Thessalonians

1:3	67
1:6	29
2:2	138
3:11	68n14
4:1	136n25
4:12	136n25

2 Thessalonians

2:1–12	29n2

1 Timothy

2:1–15	29n2

2 Timothy

2:8–13	29n2

Hebrews

1:13	115n32

1 Peter

2:21	180
4:12–13	179
4:13	88n33

Revelation

1:19	44n78
5:6	116

… INDEX OF ANCIENT SOURCES 219

11QMelch (11Q13)   73n31

APOCRYPHA AND SEPTUAGINT

Sirach (Sir)
48:24   73
49:10   73

OLD TESTAMENT PSEUDEPIGRAPHA

Psalms of Solomon (Pss. Sol.)
13   73

Second Baruch (2 Bar)
44:6   73

Testament of Joseph (T. Jos)
1:6   73n28
2:6   73n28

DEAD SEA SCROLLS

Hymns of Thanksgiving (1QH)
17:13   70n19
19:32   70n19

4QBarki Napshi (4Q436)   73n31

1QLitPr (1Q34)   73n31

11QMelch (11Q13)   73n31

MISHNAH, TALMUD, AND RELATED LITERATURE

Targumic Texts
b. Makk.
5b   73n29

b. Hag.
16b   73n29

b. Ketub.
67a   73n29

b. Pesah.
54b   73n29

b. Sanh.
37b   73n29

b. Sebu.
34a   73n29

b. Taan.
11a   73n29

CLASSICAL AND ANCIENT CHRISTIAN WRITINGS

Adversus Colotem
6   159

Aemilius Paulus
5.4   159n64
14.2   159n65

220 INDEX OF ANCIENT SOURCES

Agesilaus
34.6 — 159n68

Alcibiades
25.1 — 159n63

Alexander
39.3 — 159n67

Amatorius
765c — 159n72

Conjugalia Praecepta
22 — 159n64

De agricultura
157 — 158n47

De congressu eruditionis gratia — 150

De gigantibus
17 — 158n45

De praemiis et poenis et De exsecrationibus
151 — 158n46

De sollertia animalium
10 — 159n62

De somniis
2.159 — 158n48

De exilio
6 — 160n80
7 — 160n78

Demetrius
23.6 — 160n77

Dissertationes ab Arriano digestae
1.2 — 158n50
1.25 — 159n74
1.27 — 158n52
1.6 — 159n75
3.10 — 158n53
3.13 — 158n54
4.1 — 158n55, 159n75

Enchiridion digestae
16 — 158n56
24 — 158n57

Eumenes
11.4 — 160n76

Nicias
21.4 — 159n67

Pompeius
25.1 — 159n69

Pyrrhus
33.7 — 159n66

Quaestiones Convivales
5.6 — 159n66
6.3 — 159n61
6.9 — 159n66
8.4 — 159n71

Quaestiones in Genesim
4.33a — 159n73

Regum et imperatorum apophthegmata
26 — 159n70
29 — 160n77

www.ingramcontent.com/pod-product-compliance
Lightning Source LLC
Chambersburg PA
CBHW051638230426
43669CB00013B/2359